COLLABORATIVE CONSULTATION

COLLABORATIVE CONSULTATION

SECOND EDITION

Lorna Idol, PhD
Institute for Learning and Development
Austin, Texas

Ann Nevin, PhD
Arizona State University West

Phyllis Paolucci-Whitcomb, EdD
University of Vermont

pro·ed
8700 Shoal Creek Boulevard
Austin, Texas 78757-6897

pro·ed

© 1987, 1994 by PRO-ED, Inc.
8700 Shoal Creek Boulevard
Austin, Texas 78757-6897

Library of Congress Cataloging-in-Publication Data

Idol, Lorna.
    Collaborative consultation / Lorna Idol, Ann Nevin, Phyllis
Paolucci-Whitcomb. — 2nd ed.
        p.   cm.
    Includes bibliographical references and index.
    ISBN 0-89079-583-5
        1. Handicapped—Education—United States.   2. Teachers of
handicapped children—United States.   3. Teaching teams—United
States.   4. Educational consultants—United States.
5. Mainstreaming in education—United States.   I. Nevin, Ann.
II. Paolucci-Whitcomb, Phyllis.   III. Title.
LC4019.I35   1993
371.9—dc20   92-42907
                                                         CIP

This book is designed in $11\frac{1}{2}/13$ Weiss (text).

Production Manager: Alan Grimes
Production Coordinator: Adrienne Booth
Art Director: Lori Kopp
Reprints Buyer: Alicia Woods
Editor: Marilyn Novell
Editorial Assistant: Claudette Landry

Printed in the United States of America

2   3   4   5   6   7   8   9   10   98   97   96   95   94

Contents

Acknowledgments

THE AUTHORS EXTEND SINCERE APPRECIATION to their students, colleagues, mentors, friends, and spouses who have supported the concepts and practices of Collaborative Consultation.

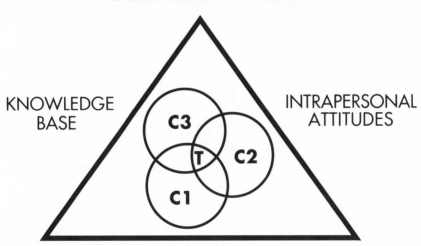

ix

Preface

THE PURPOSE OF THIS BOOK (both first and second editions) is to facilitate the effective education of all learners through implementation of the Collaborative Consultation Model in school settings that include learners with diverse learning needs. Collaborative Consultation is an interactive process that enables teams of people with diverse expertise to generate creative solutions to mutually defined problems. The process creates synergy, with different outcomes that are better than the original solutions that any team member would produce independently. This book is intended to stimulate and encourage collaboration among classroom, special education, and remedial education teachers and other support staff and administrators who are jointly responsible for the education of learners enrolled in general education classes. We refer to these classes as *inclusive classes*, as they include learners who have special needs and those who are at risk for school failure.

Throughout this book we refer to *learners with special needs.* We use this term in a noncategorical sense, and we use it to include learners enrolled in special education programs, as well as learners who are at risk for school failure. Further, we believe that the use of the Collaborative Consultation Model will enable teachers to be more effective with those learners considered to be average, as well as those who have special gifts and talents. Due to the generic potential of this model, we have purposefully *not* focused on any one class of handicapping condition. The Collaborative Consultation Model is broad enough to be applied to any category of exceptionality or any type of learning or behavior problem a learner might be experiencing. When writing about learners enrolled in special education, we are referring to two types of special education learners: (a) those who are sent to a special education support program but who spend most of their school day in the general education program and (b) those who spend most of their school day in a special education class and who attend selected mainstreamed classes. We refer to general educators as *classroom teachers.* We refer to all members of the collaborative team as *collaborators.*

The essence of the book is the Collaborative Consultation Model. This model includes a six-stage problem-solving process, supported by generic principles of Collaborative Consultation and principles and techniques that support each of the six stages in problem solving. It is this model that has been used to educate and include successfully many learners with special needs in general classroom programs, using either a consulting teacher or a collaborative team approach for supporting the classroom teacher.

In this book we also refer, at times, to a *collaborative consultation process*. As implied by the above definition of Collaborative Consultation, this is the interactive process of problem solving, an integral part of the model. However, in many different contexts where groups of adults, sometimes including learners, are required to make collective decisions, we have found the collaborative process and generic principles of collaboration to be useful in facilitating the team process. We find that such groups use the collaborative problem-solving process to solve a myriad of problems, not just as a model of service delivery for learners with special needs.

It is within the Collaborative Consultation Model itself that we expect to see positive changes in learners or targeted problems in the inclusive classroom and school. Certainly, any collaborator wants to see positive changes in targeted learners and their problems. In this book collaborators are encouraged to improve their problem-identification skills and to use accurate and simple methods of tracking student progress and changes in other types of student-related problems.

However, it is within the collaborative consultation process itself that we find two other types of very important changes that can occur as adults become better collaborators. These include (a) changes in the collaborators themselves and (b) changes in the organizational system.

First, we can anticipate that collaborators will increase their individual knowledge bases by learning from each other. Second, it is also expected that such collaborators will improve their interpersonal skills (communication, group interaction, and problem solving). Third, it is likely that collaborators will make cognitive and emotional shifts in their own intrapersonal attitudes toward how to be more effective team members and toward what the learning possibilities might be for learners who have special needs or who are currently experiencing school failure.

In essence, the collaborative process results in collaborators building a common language, establishing norms for collaborative behavior, and developing a common set of goals and ideas that evolve into a collective vision. This vision can result in effective, and sometimes even dramatic, implementation of the Collaborative Consultation Model, serving learners with special needs and including them in the most educationally enhancing environment possible.

At the systems level collaborators will find that their collective vision begins to impact on policies and procedures and patterns of human behavior within the organization itself. Changes may occur in such important areas as making shared decisions, sharing authority, communicating frequently, sharing resources, developing high interpersonal trust, encouraging risk-taking behavior, and confronting conflict by negotiation. Fewer learners may be referred to special education programs, how problems are assessed and reconciled may change, teachers may make more modifications and adaptations in instruction and materials, and how educators evaluate their own professional growth and development may change. Thus, we hope this book provides readers with an opportunity to explore the multifaceted implications of what it means to be a collaborator and that the process will not only enrich their own lives but ultimately will result in improved education for all learners.

CHAPTER 1
The Collaborative Consultation Model

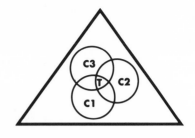

PRIMARILY, COLLABORATIVE CONSULTATION IS an interactive process that enables groups of people with diverse expertise to generate creative solutions to mutually defined problems. The outcome is enhanced and altered from original solutions that group members would produce independently. Collaborative Consultation can be characterized by the following basic elements (Nevin, Thousand, Paolucci-Whitcomb, & Villa, 1990): (a) Group members agree to view all members, including learners, as possessing unique and needed expertise; (b) they engage in frequent face-to-face interactions; (c) they distribute leadership responsibilities and hold each other accountable for agreed-on commitments; (d) they understand the importance of reciprocity and emphasize task or relationship actions based on such variables as the extent to which other members support or have the skill to promote the group goal; and (e) they agree to consciously practice and increase their social interaction and/or task achievement skills through the process of consensus building.

Collaborative Consultation is a process that can be applied to various configurations such as multidisciplinary or child study teams, service delivery options such as teaching teams, and school-based management practices such as staff development and curriculum teams (Idol & West, 1991). The application of collaborative consultation processes can improve the functioning of school-based programs such as teacher assistance teams (e.g., Chalfant & Pysh, 1989), consulting teacher programs (e.g., Idol, 1993; Paolucci-Whitcomb & Nevin, 1985), and teaching teams (Thousand & Villa, 1990). Idol and West (1991), in suggesting how collaborative processes are helpful in school reform activities, noted that consultation is not an end unto itself:

> It is a catalytic process used in interactive relationships among individuals working toward a mutually defined, concrete vision or outcome (e.g., students who become well-adjusted and productive citizens. . . . [It] may be used as a team process for effective planning, decision making, as well as problem solving; thus, it can be an effective tool for proactive strategic planning or reactive, but efficient problem solving in any organizational structure in the school environment. (pp. 4–5)

As shown in Figure 1.1, the collaborative consultation process involves multiple collaborators who bring their unique knowledge, skills, and attitudes

1

FIGURE 1.1.   Collaborative Consultation: An interactive teaming process for improving school-based practices.

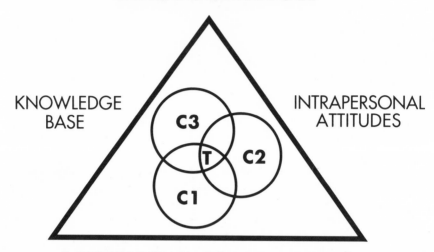

COLLABORATIVE CONSULTATION

KNOWLEDGE BASE

INTRAPERSONAL ATTITUDES

C3

T   C2

C1

INTERPERSONAL COMMUNICATIVE, INTERACTIVE PROBLEM-SOLVING SKILLS

C1, C2, C3 = Various members of a collaborative school-based team.
   T = Targeted collaborative activities (e.g., co-teaching, co-planning for an Individualized Education Program, co-tutoring, monitoring tutors, co-conducting parent conferences, collaboratively adapting curriculum materials for assessment and instruction, etc.) designed to ameliorate a specified problem or address an identified issue.

to the process. Their own intrapersonal and interpersonal growth and development influences their level or ability to practice both the science and the art of consultation. To use the collaborative consultation process effectively, group members should have expertise in the following three areas: (a) an appropriate underlying knowledge base; (b) interpersonal communicative, interactive, problem-solving skills; and (c) intrapersonal attitudes. More specifically, the *underlying knowledge base* for the collaborative consultation process is what Idol (1990) defined as the scientific base of consultation. A modified version of her original definition follows:

The scientific base is the content or knowledge base the collaborator brings to the collaborative problem solving process. This knowledge is comprised of a wide span of content pertaining to the technical aspects of program implementation and includes techniques in assessment, instructional interventions, curricular and materials modifications and adaptations, as well as classroom and student management.

A general description of the underlying knowledge base is introduced in Chapter 2 with a history provided in Chapter 3. Throughout Chapters 4 through 8 (representing the various stages of the problem-solving process), the reader will find more detailed descriptions of the relevant knowledge base and specific techniques that apply to each stage.

The second area of expertise, *interpersonal communicative, interactive, and problem-solving skills,* represents the kinds of behaviors that collaborators may use to enhance and facilitate the group problem-solving process. Idol (1990) described this second area of expertise as "the artful base of consultation" (p. 5). Her original definition modified for generality follows:

The artful base is basically the way in which collaborators work with one another to solve problems. This base consists of group process skills. It is a demonstrable knowledge of how to bring about effective decision making, how to solve problems with others, and how to interact and communicate effectively with others. (p. 5)

In Chapter 2 we describe several generic principles of Collaborative Consultation that are essential to all phases of the problem-solving process. In addition, in Chapters 4 through 9, the reader will find more detailed descriptions of the relevant interpersonal skills and specific techniques that apply to each chapter.

The third area of expertise, *intrapersonal attitudes,* reflects the personal attitudes and related behaviors that each collaborator brings to the group process. These beliefs, values, and experiences are unique to each individual, yet impact greatly on the group process. In Chapter 2, we offer elaborations of specific statements to serve as a guide to each collaborator in the development of a personal set of self-preservation and survival attitudes.

We recommend that anyone interested in using a collaborative consultation process consider the development of all of these three areas of expertise. Collaborators are invited to conduct self-assessments in each of these areas to determine which, if any, need improvement. Needs assessment instruments and additional training materials can be found in West, Idol, and Cannon (1989) for the interpersonal communicative, interactive, and problem-solving skills and for some of the intrapersonal attitudes and in Idol and West (1993) for the underlying knowledge base. As described above, Collaborative Consultation is a specific type of interactive process that can be applied systematically to any group decision-making task. Collaborators who use this process are expected to bring to the process an appropriate knowledge base for the type of problem being solved; interpersonal communication, interaction, and problem-solving skills; and relevant intrapersonal attitudes.

PROBLEM-SOLVING STAGES IN THE COLLABORATIVE CONSULTATION PROCESS

The collaborative consultation process is described as a series of decision-making steps, exemplified by the use of six stages. These stages are similar to those commonly accepted in the consultation literature. In the early 1980s the authors adapted the accepted stages so as to deliver special education and general education programs via the Collaborative Consultation Model. Specifically, the stages reflect the organizational framework for the majority of the chapters in this book, a convenient way to organize and elaborate the knowledge bases and interpersonal skills needed for each stage.

Stage 1. Gaining Entry and Establishing Team Goals (also known as the Entry/Goal stage; described in Chapter 4)

Stage 2. Problem Identification (includes both Assessment and Goal Setting for the targeted problem; described in Chapter 5)

Stage 3. Intervention Recommendations (described in Chapters 6 and 7)

Stage 4. Implementation of Recommendations (described in Chapter 7)

Stage 5. Evaluation (described in Chapter 8)

Stage 6. Follow-up (also described in Chapter 8)

Stage 1: Gaining Entry and Establishing Team Goals. The important outcome for the first stage is to establish informal relationships necessary to initiate a collaborative process. Determining the roles and responsibilities of various group members, conducting initial discussion of the problems or issues to be addressed, and disseminating information related to the rationale and benefits of Collaborative Consultation are activities typical of gaining acceptance among team members. At the end of this stage, collaborators typically focus on goals and objectives for the team to achieve. These goals and objectives might center around improving knowledge bases, interpersonal skills, or intrapersonal attitudes and beliefs. Sometimes individual collaborators will identify personal goals and objectives for themselves as well.

Stage 2: Problem Identification. During the second stage, collaborators assess the entry level needs and capacities related to the problem or issues to be addressed. The problem is defined and clarified, with all team members reaching consensus on the problem to be solved. The nature and parameters of the problem or issue are defined clearly and measured reliably. As a final part of this stage, the team develops goals and objectives for desired outcomes for resolution of the problem.

Stage 3: Intervention Recommendations. In this stage potential interventions for solving the problem are explored. Collaborators then analyze the feasibility of each recommendation, discussing the possible effects of the various suggested interventions. The possibilities are then prioritized in order to reach consensus on the best solution to the problem. Sometimes teams have to implement more than one solution, in which case they prioritize the order and the method of knowing when to move to a subsequent intervention. (Also see West, Idol, & Cannon, 1989, Modules 29 and 30.)

Stage 4: Implementation of Recommendations. In this stage the team generates a plan for how to implement the solution to the problem. This stage often involves two distinct steps. First, specific procedures are developed to be used to ameliorate the identified problem or issue designed to achieve the specified goals or objectives for solving the problem. Second, the collaborators specify how they will monitor the plan. (Also see West et al., 1989, Module 31.)

Stage 5: Evaluation. During the evaluation stage, the collaborators develop a method for monitoring the success of their implementation plan. Included are methods for measuring the immediate success of the plan for solving the targeted problem, as well as methods for evaluating changes in the collaborators themselves and the overall school system.

Stage 6: Follow-up. During this stage the evaluation data are used to assist collaborators in making decisions related to the success of the outcome of their plan. Decisions are made related to verifying and celebrating program successes in reaching specified goals and objectives, redesigning any interventions that were partially successful or not successful, reassessing the identified problem and related issues, or terminating the collaborative consultation process.

It should be noted that the stages are *not* mutually exclusive and the collaborative consultation process is recursive. Thus, collaborators can expect to overlap and cycle through the decision-making stages related to any given problem and can engage in similar activities throughout all the stages. For example, information gathering is a generic activity that can be important at every stage. Moreover, evaluation techniques often must be applied during the assessment stage.

COLLABORATIVE CONSULTATION AS A MODEL FOR SERVICE DELIVERY

In this book the authors have applied the process of Collaborative Consultation to the development of a model of service delivery referred to as the Collaborative Consultation Model. This service delivery model was originally conceptualized (in the first edition of this text published in 1986) in a broad manner to apply to any category of learner with special education needs who could be appropriately educated in a general education program with consultative support. Over the past decade the authors have applied the Collaborative Consultation Model in the education of learners with other types of special needs. These learners include those who may be at risk for school failure, learners who are enrolled in other types of remedial programs, learners who receive educational assistance because of cultural and language differences (e.g., through Chapter 1 or English as a Second Language programs), and learners who receive supportive speech and language instruction. The major outcome of the Collaborative Consultation Model is to provide comprehensive and effective programs for learners with special needs within the most appropriate context that is least restrictive of their civil rights and that enables them to achieve maximum constructive interaction with grade-level peers and grade-level curriculum, whenever possible.

DISTINCTIONS AMONG COLLABORATION, CONSULTATION, AND COOPERATION

The primary definition of collaboration comes from the Latin word *laborare* (to labor), and thus means to work together. However, some readers may be familiar with the connotation of collaboration as cooperation with the enemy. To overcome possible negative connotations, it may be helpful at this point to note the distinctions among collaboration, cooperation, and consultation. Cooperation within a social psychological construct of positive interdependence (D. Johnson & R. Johnson, 1987) relies on group members who are intent on reaching the same goals, who need specific information from each group member, or who receive the same rewards or consequences for the group's actions. A different yet informative perspective is offered by Hord (1986), who defined cooperation as a term that assumes two or more parties, each with separate and autonomous programs, who agree to work together in making more successful programs.

Consultation typically occurs when a consultant works with others to effect a beneficial change for the referred learner or issue, implying that the consultant has some knowledge or skill that the other person does not have. Although school consultation has often been perceived as relying on such an expert model, some school consultants have acknowledged a reliance on joint approaches—pooling of personal resources and shared responsibility that is a hallmark of collaboration. West et al. (1989) adapted an analysis developed by West (1985) from Babcock and Pryzwansky (1983). As shown in Table 1.1, collaborative processes of school consultants at each stage of the problem-solving process can be differentiated from the expert, medical, or mental health consultation models.

TABLE 1.1. Summary of Four Consultation Models at Five Stages of the Consultation Process

	Collaboration	Expert	Medical	Mental Health
Consultant goal	Work with a CEE to identify problem, plan/carry out recommendations	Plan/carry out recommendations for problem(s) identified by CEE	Identify problem/make recommendations for CEE to carry out	Increase CEE's ability to (fu
Problem identification	Both CEE and CST identify problem	CEE identifies problem	CST identifies problem	CST prc ing tior
Intervention recommendations	CEE and CST suggest intervention recommendations	CST plans intervention, which CEE carries out	CST offers recommendations for CEE to implement	CEE p with facilitator
Implementation	CEE and CST may each implement	CST implements	CEE implements recommendations developed by CST	CEE implements he or she developed
Nature and extent of follow-up	CEE and CST engage continuous follow-up to modify interventions if needed	None	CST may offer further advice to CEE	Further consultation may be initiated at CEE's request

Note. CEE = consultee; CST = consultant. Adapted from "Models of Consultation: Preferences of Educational Professionals at Five Steps of Service" by N. Babcock and W. Pryzwansky, 1983, *Journal of School Psychology, 22,* pp. 359–366.

Although the consultation or problem-solving stages are similar (i.e., goal setting, problem identification, intervention development, implementation, and evaluation or follow-up), people who use a collaborative model have clearly different role responsibilities when compared to those who use other consultation models (e.g., expert, advocacy, mental health, or medical models). For a comprehensive review and discussion of the research, theory, and practice related to these models, see West and Idol (1987) and West et al. (1989).

As demonstrated in this text, the emphasis may be placed on collaboration, which implies equally valued knowledge and skills distributed among equally skilled participants (after Lanier, 1980). This results in a mutual exchange of knowledge and skills as outcomes are developed together.

BENEFITS OF THE COLLABORATIVE CONSULTATION MODEL

The Collaborative Consultation Model has several benefits. In the course of our 50 combined years of practicing consultation, we have experienced these benefits both formally, as a result of data-based investigations, and informally, as a result of anecdotes and self-reports. Benefits occur at all levels (i.e., changes can occur for systems, adults, and learners).

First, all members of a collaborative consultation group (support staff, special educators, and general educators) are able to share expertise because of their mutual responsibility for the education of all learners. Second, the consultant role is practiced reciprocally by all members of the team, resulting in increased communication among diverse professional disciplines. This leads to an increased sharing of material and human resources. Third, Collaborative Consultation facilitates appropriate and beneficial liaison with other community agencies and parents.

Fourth, Collaborative Consultation facilitates the provision of instructional services based on academic and social learning needs rather than on categories of exceptionality, thus avoiding traditional territorial domains.

Fifth, Collaborative Consultation is a learner-centered process that requires all collaborators to develop creative and effective programs. As noted by Idol (1993), the referred learner, the collaborators, building principals, and the parents of the referred learners benefit from effective Collaborative Consultation. The referred learners benefit by receiving systematic instruction for academic or social problems in the least restrictive environment. Teachers and parents receive the benefits of support while implementing effective programs in their natural settings such as the classroom or the home. Administrators benefit from a more cost-effective provision of special services as well as from access to quantifiable records that document the results of Collaborative Consultation.

Using Collaborative Consultation avoids several pitfalls of more unidirectional consultation models that suggest a deficit on the part of the consultee, fail to promote equity or parity, and often achieve less than satisfactory outcomes as reported by Johnson, Pugach, and Hammittee (1988). Within a collaborative interaction, a multidirectional process is experienced. All members of the group have opportunities to be an expert and to serve in the dual role of giver and receiver of information or skills. And all members of the group have opportunities to increase and improve their conceptual and technological knowledge as well as their interpersonal skills and intrapersonal attitudes. Many members change their underlying beliefs and values, particularly in relation to the education of learners with special needs and those who are at risk for school failure.

Because Collaborative Consultation relies on the shared expertise of group members, members of the group are more likely to acquire one another's skills. For example, Thousand, Nevin, and Fox (1987) reported such increases as a function of a collaborative inservice education program. Increased group cohesiveness and willingness to work together on future projects often occurred when practitioners used cooperative or collaborative structures (D. Johnson & R. Johnson, 1987). For example, Thousand et al. (1986) found that classroom teachers who collaborated to integrate learners with severely challenging needs often reported that "they have *more say* in what local education programs look like; [and] they feel *more comfortable* asking for and receiving the material, technical and emotional support from colleagues to educate more challenging students" (p. 11). Thousand and Villa (1990) found that adults who practiced collaborative consultation processes have experienced the phenomenon of *process gain* (generating new ideas through group interaction that are not generated while working alone) or *collective induction* (inducing general principles that none induce alone) similar to learners who work cooperatively as reported in D. Johnson and R. Johnson (1989).

EFFECTIVENESS OF COLLABORATIVE CONSULTATION

Although the lack of a collaborative ethic in public schools has been lamented (Phillips & McCullough, 1990) and collaboration in school-based consultation has been called a "myth in need of data" (Witt, 1990, p. 367), many aspects of school-based consultation processes have been studied (see reviews by Evans, 1991; Idol & West, 1987; Tindal, Shinn, & Rodden-Nord, 1990; West & Idol, 1987). It is clear that there are major complexities and confounding variables related to implementing and evaluating collaborative consultation processes. Researchers and evaluators must conduct their work within the changeable and changing conditions of naturalistic settings like school systems. Moreover, the comprehensive nature of the requisite underlying knowledge base, interpersonal skills, and intrapersonal attitudes make it difficult to identify just which variables are most influential. Continued and expanded research and evaluation efforts are vital for the advancement of collaborative consultation programs.

Since the first edition of *Collaborative Consultation* in 1986, the collaborative consultation processes have been suggested for teachers of learners with visual handicaps (Erin, 1988), to improve educational services for learners with hearing impairments (Luckner, Rude, & Sileo, 1989), for learners with severely handicapping conditions (Nevin et al., 1990), for learners with mild handicaps or who are at risk for school failure (Schulte, Osborne, & McKinney, 1990; West & Idol, 1990), and to facilitate better programs for learners with limited English proficiency (Harris, 1991). In addition, collaborative consultation processes have been recommended as helpful for a transition planning process (Sileo, Rude, & Luckner, 1988), as a tool for school restructuring (Thousand & Villa, 1992), as a method for improving instructional effectiveness (Luckner et al., 1989; Merrell, 1989), and as a process for effecting educational collaboration (Idol & West, 1991).

Recent studies that may provide support for collaborative consultation processes use a variety of research methodologies. For example, Peck, Killen, and Baumgart (1989) conducted multiple baseline studies showing the direct and generalized effects of a nondirective consultation process on increasing the implementation of special education instruction in mainstream preschools. Patriarca and Lamb (1990) used a qualitative methodology to study the collaborative interactions of secondary education teachers and their student teacher interns as they used a reflective decision-making process to develop interventions for learners with special needs. Gersten, Darch, Davis, and George (1991) conducted a naturalistic study comparing the activities of consulting teachers who did and did not complete an apprenticeship. Johnson and Pugach (1991) conducted a comparative study of elementary and middle school teachers who used a peer collaboration process to effectively solve mutually defined problems.

Collaborative Consultation has been studied at the secondary school level (Florida Department of Education, 1989, 1990; Patriarca & Lamb, 1990; Tindal, Shinn, Walz, & Germann, 1987), the elementary school level (Adamson, Cox, & Schuller, 1989; Givens-Ogle, Christ, Colman, King-Streit, & Wilson, 1989; Givens-Ogle, Christ, & Idol, 1991; Saver & Downes, 1991; Schulte et al., 1990; Sumner Elementary School Staff, 1991), the preschool level (Peck et al., 1989), and the adult level (Cross & Villa, 1992; Patriarca & Lamb, 1990; Vlasak, Goldenberg, & Idol, 1992). Findings are shown in Table 1.2. At least three conclusions can be formed from this growing data base. First, learners with special education needs can be effectively served when their teachers collaborate to generate interventions. Second, school personnel can acquire the related skills and knowledge to collaborate with each other. Third, collaborators can expect changes at all three levels (changes in systems, adult collaborators, and learners).

TABLE 1.2. Evaluation Reports of Collaborative Consultation Effectiveness at Various Levels

Study	Findings
Preschool Level	
Peck, Killen, & Baumgart (1989)	Teacher prompts and learner responses related to IEP objectives of 6 preschoolers with mild to moderate developmental delays were measured. Frequencies improved systematically across multiple baseline measures; teachers reported increased confidence and willingness to implement specialized instruction related to IEP objectives.
Elementary Level	
Adamson, Cox, & Schuller (1989)	Measures of behaviors of 6 preschoolers with mild to moderate developmental delays improved when effectively instructed in general education classrooms with consultation services.
Givens-Ogle, Christ, Colman, King-Streit, & Wilson (1989)	Of the 79 learners (58 identified as learners with special education needs, 21 at risk), 75% increased to grade-level competence as a result of various collaboratively designed curriculum-based interventions (group instruction, tutorials, and one-to-one instruction).
Schulte, Osborne, & McKinney (1990)	Sixty-seven elementary students with learning disabilities were assigned to one of four groups (1 or 2 hours of resource room services, consultation with direct instruction, or consultation only). All learners showed improvements on the Woodcock-Johnson Tests of Achievement in reading, math, or language. Those in the consultation with direct-instruction group made greater academic gains, whereas the consultation-only group made comparable gains to those receiving resource room services.
Saver & Downes (1991)	K–6 elementary school with diverse cultural, academic, and behavioral differences implemented a Peer Intervention Team to generate solutions for teacher-identified instructional problems; effective action plans resulted in fewer, more appropriate referrals for special education placement. Measures included increases in learner population, decreases in numbers of learners tested and placed in special education, and increases in numbers of referrals

TABLE 1.2. Continued

Study	Findings
	to the team. By restructuring support staff assignments to general classes during reading and math instructional times, *all* learners (with and without special needs) are being instructed at appropriate levels of difficulty.
Sumner Elementary School Staff (1991)	Three hundred twenty K–6 students with 30 staff members scheduled weekly collaborative meetings for all staff regrouped into four teaching teams (K, 1–2, 3–4, 5–6), including all support staff with the result that all learners with special education needs were effectively mainstreamed.

Secondary Level

Study	Findings
Florida Department of Education (1989)	Teachers of 114 learners with mild handicaps received consulting services to develop, implement, and monitor IEPS; although there were no changes in grades, teachers reported improved communications between general and special education teachers.
Florida Department of Education (1990)	A comprehensive evaluation of the Cooperative Consultation Model implemented at elementary, middle, and high school levels included pre- and postmeasures of participants' knowledge; administrator and teacher satisfaction ratings; teacher and learner perceptions and attitudes; and performance data on learners (number of hours of special education classes, GPA, number of discipline referrals, and grades in the targeted classes). Learner academic data at the high school level showed that there was little change in GPA, although 47% maintained a C average.

Adult Change

Study	Findings
Cross & Villa (1992)	Forty-three percent of Winooski (Vermont) School District staff attributed their increased competence to teach learners with severe handicaps to the collaborative processes used to develop, implement, and monitor programs.
Givens-Ogle, Christ, & Idol (1991)	Extension of Givens-Ogle et al. (1989) to include description of teacher training in collaborative processes. Teams of elementary resource specialists, building principals, and classroom teachers completed two full courses to implement

TABLE 1.2. Continued

Study	Findings
	a collaborative problem-solving process for developing, implementing, and evaluating educational programs.
Lutkemeier (1991)	Survey of staff (59% return rate) in an urban southwest school district with broad cultural and ethnic diversity among the 10% to 15% non-Caucasian learner population and about 2.5% of both groups identified as needing services for learning disabilities and speech/language needs. Results showed an average of 60% of all respondents supported district implementation of a Collaborative Consultation Model, while 70% to 85% of the general education respondents indicated strong support.
Vlasak, Goldenberg, & Idol (1992)	Twenty-seven elementary and 11 junior high resource teachers (grouped by level of training: fully trained, minimally trained, no training) completed consultation logs documenting the services they provided to collaborating teachers. Data were collected on average monthly hours spent providing direct instruction, consulting, testing, planning, demonstration teaching, and developing materials. Trained teachers provided more direct service *and* more consultation services than minimally trained or untrained teachers.

SUMMARY

Collaborative Consultation is an interactive process that enables groups of people with diverse expertise to generate creative solutions to mutually defined problems. The outcome is enhanced and altered from original solutions that group members would produce independently. As a service delivery model, the Collaborative Consultation Model can be applied in school situations to improve a variety of school-based practices such as services to learners with special needs and learners who are disadvantaged or at risk for school failure. The empirical evidence and the benefits of collaborative consultation processes were discussed. In building a conceptual understanding of Collaborative Consultation, distinctions can be made among collaboration, consultation, and cooperation.

Effective Collaborative Consultation relies on the parity and equity of contributions from all collaborators. To use the Collaborative Consultation

Model effectively, group members should continually acquire expertise in the following three areas: (a) an underlying knowledge base; (b) interpersonal communicative, interactive, problem-solving skills; and (c) intrapersonal attitudes.

The six stages of Collaborative Consultation include (a) Gaining Entry and Establishing Team Goals (establishing formal relationships, initial identification of reasons to collaborate, establishing team and personal goals, and disseminating information related to the rationale and benefits of Collaborative Consultation), (b) Problem Identification, (c) Intervention Recommendations, (d) Implementation of Recommendations, (e) Evaluation, and (f) Follow-up.

In Chapter 2 we delineate the skills and knowledge required for the effective use of the Collaborative Consultation Model. We describe the scientific knowledge base, the artful base of interpersonal communication and problem-solving skills, and the intrapersonal attitudes needed for successful implementation.

STUDY QUESTIONS

1. Why is Collaborative Consultation an "interactive process?"

2. What three areas of expertise are needed for successful Collaborative Consultation?

3. Name the six stages of a collaborative problem-solving process and how the stages are related to the chapters in this book.

4. From the point of view of a collaborative consultant, compare the major differences between a collaborative model and two of the following models: expert, mental health, or medical.

5. Discuss two of the five benefits of the Collaborative Consultation Model that appeal to you most. Explain why the Collaborative Consultation Model is likely to "avoid several pitfalls of more unidirectional consultation models."

6. What is the evidence for the effectiveness of the collaborative consultation process?

REFERENCES

Adamson, D., Cox, J., & Schuller, J. (1989). Collaboration/consultation: Bridging the gap from resource room to regular classroom. *Teacher Education and Special Education, 12*(1–2), 52–55.

Babcock, N., & Pryzwansky, W. (1983). Models of consultation: Preferences of educational professionals at five steps of service. *Journal of School Psychology, 21*, 359–366.

Chalfant, J., & Pysh, M. (1989). Teacher assistance teams: Five descriptive studies. *Remedial and Special Education, 10*(6), 49–58.

Cross, G., & Villa, R. (1992). The Winooski School District. In R. Villa, J. Thousand, W. Stainback, & S. Stainback (Eds.), *Restructuring for caring and effective education: An administrative guide to creating heterogeneous schools* (pp. 219–237). Baltimore: Brookes.

Erin, J. (1988). The teacher-consultant: The teacher of visually handicapped students and Collaborative Consultation. *Education of the Visually Handicapped, 2*(2), 57–63.

Evans, S. (1991). A realistic look at the research base for collaboration in special education. *Preventing School Failure, 35*(4), 10–13.

Florida Department of Education. (1989). *Evaluating effectiveness, usefulness, practicality of cooperative consultation—1987–1988 pilot study in Florida secondary schools* (Research Report 10). Tallahassee, FL: Author.

Florida Department of Education. (1990, November). *Cooperative consultation regional training 1989–1990)* (Research Report 12). Tallahassee, FL: Author.

Gersten, R., Darch, C., Davis, G., & George, N. (1991). Apprenticeship and intensive training of consulting teachers: A naturalistic study. *Exceptional Children, 51*(3), 226–237.

Givens-Ogle, L., Christ, B., Colman, M., King-Streit, & Wilson, L., (1989). Data-based consultation case study: Adaptations of researched best practices. *Teacher Education and Special Education, 12*(1–2), 46–52.

Givens-Ogle, L., Christ, B., & Idol, L. (1991). Collaborative Consultation: The San Juan Unified School District Project. *Journal of Educational and Psychological Consultation, 2*(3), 267–284.

Harris, K. (1991). *A descriptive study of collaboration between bilingual and special educators* (USOE research grant award). Phoenix: Arizona State University West.

Hord, S. (1986). A synthesis of research on organizational collaboration. *Educational Leadership, 44,* 22–26.

Idol, L. (1990). The scientific art of classroom consultation. *Journal of Educational and Psychological Consultation, 1*(1), 3–22.

Idol, L. (1993). *Special educator's consultation handbook* (2nd ed.). Austin, TX: PRO-ED.

Idol, L., & West, J. F. (1987). Consultation in special education. Part II: Training and practice. *Journal of Learning Disabilities, 20,* 474–493.

Idol, L., & West, J. F. (1991). Educational collaboration as a catalyst for effective schooling. *Intervention in School and Clinic, 27*(2), 70–78.

Idol, L., & West, J. F. (1993). *Effective instruction of difficult-to-teach students.* Austin, TX: PRO-ED.

Johnson, D., & Johnson, R. (1987). *Learning together and alone.* Englewood Cliffs, NJ: Prentice-Hall.

Johnson, D., & Johnson, R. (1989). *Cooperation and competition: Theory and research.* Edina, MN: Interaction Book Co.

Johnson, L., & Pugach, L. (1991). Peer collaboration: Accommodating students with mild learning and behavior problems. *Exceptional Children, 57*(5), 454–461.

Johnson, L., Pugach, M., & Hammittee, D. (1988). Barriers to effective special education consultation. *Remedial and Special Education, 2*(6), 41–47.

Lanier, J. (1980). Collaboration session. In G. Hall, S. Hard, & G. Brown (Eds.), *Exploring man in teacher education: Questions for future research* (pp. 405–411). Austin, TX: Research and Development Center for Teacher Education.

Luckner, J., Rude, H., & Sileo, T. (1989). Collaborative Consultation: A method for improving educational services for mainstreamed students who are hearing impaired. *American Journal for the Deaf, 5,* 301–304.

Lutkemeier, D. (1991). Attitudes and practices regarding the implementation of collaborative educational services. *The Consulting Edge, 3*(2), 1–2.

Merrell, K. (1989). Collaborative consultation and instructional effectiveness: Merging theory and research into practice. *British Columbia Journal of Special Education, 13*(3), 259–266.

Nevin, A., Thousand, J., Paolucci-Whitcomb, P., & Villa, R. (1990). Collaborative consultation: Empowering public school personnel to provide heterogeneous schooling for all or, Who rang that bell? *Journal of Educational and Psychological Consultation, 1*(1), 41–67.

Paolucci-Whitcomb, P., & Nevin, A. (1985). Preparing consulting teachers through a collaborative approach between university faculty and field-based consulting teachers. *Teacher Education and Special Education, 8*(3), 132–143.

Patriarca, L., & Lamb, M. (1990). Preparing secondary education teachers to be collaborative decision makers and reflective practitioners: A promising model. *Teacher Education and Special Education, 13*(3–4), 200–224.

Peck, C., Killen, C., & Baumgart, D. (1989). Increasing implementation of special education instruction in mainstream preschools: Direct and generalized effects of nondirective consultation. *Journal of Applied Behavior Analysis, 22*(2), 197–210.

Phillips, V., & McCullough, L. (1990). Consultation-based programming: Instituting the collaborative ethic in schools. *Exceptional Children, 56*(4), 291–305.

Saver, K., & Downes, B. (1991). PIT crew: A model for teacher collaboration in an elementary school. *Intervention in School and Clinic, 27*(2), 116–122.

Schulte, A., Osborne, S., & McKinney, J. (1990). Academic outcomes for students with learning disability in consultation and resource programs. *Exceptional Children, 57*(2), 162–171.

Sileo, T., Rude, H., & Luckner, J. (1988). Collaborative consultation: A model for transition planning for handicapped youth. *Education and Training in Mental Retardation, 23*(4), 333–339.

Sumner Elementary School Staff. (1991). Collaborative teaming: Building success for all. *The Consulting Edge, 3*(1), 1–4.

Thousand, J., Fox, T., Reid, R., Godek, J., Williams, W., & Fox, W. (1986). *The Homecoming Project: Educating students who present intensive educational challenges within regular classroom environments* (Monograph No. 7–1). Burlington: University of Vermont Center for Developmental Disabilities.

Thousand, J., Nevin, A., & Fox, W. (1987). Inservice training to support education of learners with severe handicaps in their local schools. *Teacher Education and Special Education, 10*(1), 4–14.

Thousand, J., & Villa, R. (1990). Sharing expertise and responsibilities through teaching teams. In W. Stainback & S. Stainback (Eds.), *Support networks for inclusive schooling: Interdependent integrated education* (pp. 151–166). Baltimore: Brookes.

Thousand, J., & Villa, R. (1992). Collaborative teams: A powerful tool in school restructuring. In R. Villa, J. Thousand, W. Stainback, & S. Stainback (Eds.), *Restructuring for heterogeneity: An administrative handbook for creating effective schools for everyone* (pp. 73–108). Baltimore: Brookes.

Tindal, G., Shinn, M., Walz, L., & Germann, C. (1987). Mainstream consultation in secondary settings: The Pine County model. *The Journal of Special Education, 20*(3), 94–106.

Tindal, G., Shinn, M., & Rodden-Nord, K. (1990). Contextually based school consultation: Influential variables. *Exceptional Children, 56*(4), 324–338.

Vlasak, L., Goldenberg, D., & Idol, L. (1992). Preparing resource/consulting teachers: Ongoing staff development and evaluation. *The Cutting Edge*, 4(1), 3, 5.

West, J. F. (1985). Regular and special educators' preferences for school-based consultation models (Doctoral dissertation, The University of Texas at Austin, 1985). *Dissertation Abstracts International*, 47(2), 504A.

West, F., & Idol, L. (1987). School consultation. Part 1: An interdisciplinary perspective on theory, models, and research. *Journal of Learning Disabilities*, 20, 474–494.

West, J. F., & Idol, L. (1990). Collaborative Consultation in the education of mildly handicapped and at-risk students. *Remedial and Special Education*, 11(1), 22–31.

West, J., Idol, L., & Cannon, G. (1989). *Collaboration in the schools: Communicating, interacting and problem solving.* Austin, TX: PRO-ED.

Witt, J. (1990). Collaboration in school-based consultation: Myth in need of data. *Journal of Educational and Psychological Consultation*, 1(3), 367–370.

CHAPTER 2

The Scientific, Artful, and Intrapersonal Bases

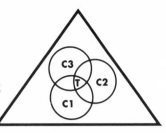

THE SUCCESSFUL IMPLEMENTATION OF Collaborative Consultation involves the simultaneous understanding of an appropriate underlying knowledge base, an artful base of interpersonal communication and problem-solving skills, and intrapersonal attitudes. Each area is discussed in detail in this chapter.

UNDERLYING KNOWLEDGE BASE

As stated in Chapter 1, the underlying knowledge base for the collaborative consultation process is what Idol (1990) defined as the scientific base of consultation. This content or knowledge base comprises the technical aspects of program implementation and includes techniques in assessment, instructional interventions, curricular and materials modifications and adaptations, and classroom and student management.

The scientific basis for the Collaborative Consultation Model involves several complex knowledge bases. In a recent study by Cannon, Idol, and West (1992) identified and validated teaching practices essential for effective teaching of mainstreamed learners with special needs. The 96 effective teaching practices were identified by a comprehensive literature search and validated by a panel of experts from both general and special education. Idol and West (1993) developed a related curriculum comprising 12 modules as listed in Table 2.1. It is important to note that these represent *current* best practices; collaborators must be willing to create improvements that lead to more best practices. In addition, it should be noted that effective teaching practices reflect the underlying knowledge base for effective Collaborative Consultation as elaborated below.

A second knowledge base collaborators can use comes from the conceptual framework and methods of behavior and curriculum task analysis used to identify the effects of educational programs on the progress of learners with special needs. The arrangement of the educational environments is emphasized in explaining learners' deficits as well as progress. Collaborators stop accounting for their learners' failure to achieve skills and knowledge in terms of inferred or inherent deficiencies of the learners. Instead, collaborators account for failure to achieve in terms of procedural and systems problems

19

TABLE 2.1. Essential Components of the Underlying Knowledge Base

Module	Component
1	Elements of Effective Instruction
2	Effective Instructional Decision Making
3	Student Portfolio Assessment
4	Curriculum-Based Student Assessment
5	Observation of Instructional Environments
6	Strategic and Cognitive Instruction
7	Curriculum Adaptation
8	Instructional Adaptation
9	Educational Materials Evaluation and Selection
10	Effective Classroom Management and Discipline
11	Management of the Teaching and Learning Environment
12	Student Progress Evaluation

Note. From *Effective Instruction of Difficult-to-Teach Students* (p. iii) by L. Idol and J.F. West, 1993, Austin, TX: PRO-ED.

that they then attempt to correct or ameliorate (Idol, 1990; Idol-Maestas, Lloyd, & Lilly, 1981). Similarly, reinforcement principles and practices can be applied to improve skills, knowledge, and attitudes of all group members. When collaborators learn and apply reinforcement principles to ameliorate and accelerate the academic and social progress of learners with special needs, they can apply those same principles to their own interpersonal interactions; as they "catch each other being good," they learn new skills more effectively.

A third knowledge base focuses on developing a philosophy of teaching that provides expanded educational opportunities for all learners. Collaborators can discard philosophies and beliefs that emphasize those aspects that they can do little to change (e.g., central nervous system pathology and noxious prenatal experiences). A classic philosophy proposed by Brown and York (1974) urged educators to aim their efforts at "the creation or arrangement of an environment that produces specific changes in the behavioral repertoire of students" (p. 12), especially those learners with special needs who cannot perform skills or display behaviors that other learners can. They suggested that such a philosophy requires teachers to be (a) instructional determinists (by specifying exactly which learning outcomes their learners will acquire), (b) instructional environmentalists (by specifying exactly how they intend to reach those outcomes), and (c) instructional empiricists (by measuring whether their learners acquire the expected outcomes).

A fourth knowledge base beneficial to members of the collaborative consultation group focuses on learning about the methods that have *not* worked well in special education so as to avoid them. For example, some researchers have conducted research reviews showing that learners with special needs in segregated programs do not demonstrate better academic progress than similar learners who have remained in general education programs (e.g., Dunn, 1968; Knight, Meyers, Paolucci-Whitcomb, Hasazi, & Nevin, 1981; Lipsky & Gartner, 1988; Miller & Sabatino, 1978).

More importantly, collaborators can learn about existing educational programs that allow them to directly affect the learning progress of learners with special needs. They can capitalize on collaborative and cooperative management structures that allow peers to learn from each other (e.g., Idol & West, 1993; D. Johnson, & R. Johnson, 1980; Nevin, 1990; West, 1985). They can learn about general education techniques that have proved to be beneficial for all students such as cooperative learning (e.g., D. Johnson & R. Johnson, 1987b, 1987c), mastery learning procedures (e.g., Bloom, 1981), cognitive learning (e.g., Idol & Jones, 1991; Jones & Idol, 1990), and so on. (See Chapters 6 and 7 for an elaboration of educational practices effective for integrated classrooms.)

GENERIC PRINCIPLES OF COLLABORATIVE CONSULTATION

Another goal within the Collaborative Consultation Model is to improve and maintain the competencies of all personnel as they are involved in educating groups of learners including those with special needs. The full implementation of the model relies on collaborators who are willing to acquire the appropriate interpersonal communicative, interactive, and problem-solving skills that represent behaviors collaborators may use to enhance and facilitate the problem-solving process—"the artful base of Collaborative Consultation" (Idol, 1990, p. 5). The generic principles of Collaborative Consultation that underlie these interpersonal communicative, interactive, and problem-solving skills are listed in Table 2.2 and discussed below.

Team Ownership of the Identified Problem

Unlike some consultation models that lead the consultee or the consultant to own the problem, the Collaborative Consultation Model requires that all members of the team own the problem. Accountability for the success or failure of the programs developed for the learner with special needs is shared. This is particularly important given the traditional nature of special education in relation to the general education system, which has a long history of associating problems with grade level, category of exceptionality, or academic subject matter.

Collaborative consultation processes avoid hierarchical communication from an expert to other team members. Rather, equity and parity among team members is created. Parity requires acknowledgment, mutual respect, and

---

TABLE 2.2.   Generic Principles of Collaborative Consultation (Interpersonal, Communication, Problem-Solving Skills)

---

1. Collaborative Consultation requires team ownership of the identified problem.
2. Implementing change involves recognition of individual differences in developmental progress.
3. Situational leadership guides the implementation of Collaborative Consultation.
4. Cooperative conflict resolution processes underlie Collaborative Consultation.
5. Collaborative Consultation relies on people who use appropriate interviewing skills.
6. Active listening facilitates meaningful interactions among all participants.
7. Oral and written communication must rely on common, nonjargon and positive, nonverbal language.

---

reliance on one another's unique contributions. Equity is simply equal treatment of each team member.

Parity means all members function at the same hierarchical level regardless of differences in knowledge, skills, attitudes, or position. It is demonstrated as each team member's skills and knowledge are combined with the different skills and knowledge of other team members resulting in new designs and solutions. Equity is demonstrated when each team member's ideas are equally respected and used to develop and evaluate team outcomes. Equity and parity are components of the term *reciprocity*. Reciprocity means "allowing all parties to have equal access to information and the opportunity to participate in problem identification, discussion, decision making, and all final outcomes" (West, Idol, & Cannon, 1989, p. 25).

The major goal of implementing the Collaborative Consultation Model is to provide comprehensive and effective programs for all learners with special needs within the most appropriate context, thereby permitting maximum constructive interaction with all other learners. This requires a cross-categorical emphasis; that is, the programs must be designed for the entire spectrum of special needs. As noted by Lates (1975), "educators must be willing to incorporate effective procedures into their own competencies and must learn to communicate with persons from many different and often specialized fields" (p. 48). This implies reciprocal interactions among highly trained personnel from a wide range of disciplines. Effective collaborative consultation teams depend on the ability of each person to explain opinions, to paraphrase perspectives, to encourage contributions from other team members, and to arrive at a team consensus. In short, recognition and appreciation of each person's expertise is imperative. At the same time, release from that expertise is necessary to make room for new ideas and practices to emerge.

The empirical determination of effectiveness of interventions may show that some team recommendations are effective whereas others are not. In fact, experimentation, or trial periods, may be needed to determine whether the intervention is worth the effort to implement. (See Chapter 8 for the recommended knowledge base for responsive evaluation of programs.) The degree of effectiveness is dependent on the idiosyncrasies of the situation, the special needs of the learners, the resources available, the intensity and frequency of the intervention procedures, and the many different types of skills of the collaborators. Thus, the effectiveness or ineffectiveness of team-determined procedures should in no way be used as the sole basis for evaluating the effectiveness of the implementers. In the spirit of assuring accountability, team members agree to collect and share evaluation data so as to improve team-developed services. All information provided by team members within the framework of parity should be treated with confidentiality to create a respectful and supportive environment.

Recognition of Individual Differences in Developmental Progress

Implementation of the Collaborative Consultation Model requires changes through multiple levels or stages of growth and development for both educators and administrators. These changes involve planning, learning new behaviors, and adapting to new routines. Because change is a personal experience, it involves a wide range of individual differences in rate of implementation, feelings, and reactions. Thus, in implementing Collaborative Consultation, it is important that all concerned be sensitive to the various aspects of change as they affect the student served and all members of the collaborative consultation team.

The Concerns-Based Adoption Model (CBAM) developed by Hall (1981) is a useful model for understanding developmental changes. The predictable patterns that appear as individuals become more knowledgeable and skillful in implementing changes are described as involving seven stages of concern with specific feelings and behaviors associated with each one, as follows (Hall & Loucks, 1978, p. 36):

- *Awareness* (Stage 0). Little concern about or involvement with change is indicated.
- *Informational* (Stage 1). A general awareness of the change and interest in learning about it in detail is indicated; the person seems to be unworried about self in relation to the change and is interested in substantive aspects of the innovation (for example, general characteristics, effects, and requirements for use) in a selfless manner.
- *Personal* (Stage 2). The person is uncertain about the demands of the change, personal adequacy to meet those demands, and role with respect to the change. This stage involves analysis of the person's role in relation to reward structure of the organization, the person's decision-making process, and the person's potential conflicts with existing structures or personal commitments; financial

or status implications of the program for self and colleagues may also be involved.

- *Management* (Stage 3). Attention is concentrated on the processes and tasks of using the change and on the best use of information and resources; issues related to efficiency, organization, management, scheduling, and time demands are paramount.
- *Consequences* (Stage 4). Attention focuses on the impact of the innovation on [learners] in one's immediate sphere of influence; the emphasis is on relevance of the innovation for the [learners]; evaluation of [learner] outcomes, including performance and competencies; and the changes needed to improve [learner] outcomes.
- *Collaboration* (Stage 5). The focus here is on coordination and cooperation with others in the use of the new procedures.
- *Refocusing* (Stage 6). Consideration is given to ways of generating more universal benefits from the change, including the possibility of inducing other major changes or replacing behaviors with more powerful alternatives; here the person has definite ideas about alternatives to the proposed or existing form of the change.

People typically use CBAM to determine where they are individually and where they are as a team. They use the instrument at the beginning of a change effort and 6 to 9 months later, or at some agreed time, to recognize and celebrate the changes (or lack thereof) noted. Within a developmental framework for understanding change, collaborators can reassure all participants as they react individually to implement the steps necessary to change programs and procedures on behalf of all learners. All collaborators can expect to experience any or all of the stages of concern as the Collaborative Consultation Model is implemented. An example of such changes has been researched by Pedron and Evans (1990), who used CBAM to trace classroom teachers' acceptance of a consulting teacher model. Participants were provided self-instructional modules related to information (CBAM Stage 1), management (CBAM Stage 3), and consequences (CBAM Stage 4) of consulting teacher models. All three groups showed significant reduction of concern, with those receiving the management module showing the greatest reduction. The results suggest that teachers in the early stages of implementing a consulting teacher approach may "profit more from practical 'how-to' detail than general theory and broad conceptual information" (p. 196).

Situational Leadership to Guide Implementation of Collaborative Consultation

The leadership process in Collaborative Consultation is defined as influencing relationships among mutually dependent team members (D. Johnson & F. Johnson, 1987). When two or more people depend on each other to reach a goal, leadership must be demonstrated by each person to influence the others.

In Collaborative Consultation, leadership is operationally distributed among the participants in a give-and-take fashion. Rather than having a designated leader, all the participants help the team to achieve its goal (e.g., the development and implementation of a successful program for the referred learner) and to maintain positive relationships among the team members. Two important outcomes of such distributed leadership are (a) all resources are used, and (b) there is a commitment to the team's decisions. (For a fuller description of the distributed functions theory of leadership, see D. Johnson & F. Johnson, 1987). As decisions are made, implemented, and revised, team members complete certain functions to operate effectively. These functions include setting mutual goals, enabling the team to proceed toward goals, providing necessary resources, and ensuring that team members are satisfied. Effective leadership depends on flexible behaviors from all team members.

Within a mutually interdependent team structure, principles of situational leadership can be applied. As defined by Hersey and Blanchard (1988), situational leadership requires flexibility in style of presentation and implementation, depending on the skill and attitudes of the participants. Various leadership styles (telling, selling, participating, and delegating) can be used to collaborate more effectively. For example, when a collaborator is inexperienced or insecure and does not have the requisite skill or attitude, other collaborators can use Leadership Style 1 (telling) by providing specific information (even to the point of modeling the task until it is demonstrated accurately by the one in need) and by closely supervising the resulting performance. When the collaborator is inexperienced but has a positive attitude about the required process, another collaborator can use Leadership Style 2 (selling) by providing the necessary information, allowing an opportunity for clarification and accurate demonstration while concurrently beginning to thin the schedule of supervision.

When a collaborator has demonstrated the necessary skills but is insecure or has a less than positive attitude about being able to complete the required process successfully, Leadership Style 3 (participating) can be used. Here all collaborators share ideas and help facilitate progress. When collaborators have demonstrated all of the necessary skills and have positive attitudes about completing the required process effectively, efficiently, and affectively, Leadership Style 4 (delegating) is appropriate. Here collaborators rely on their own skills and positive attitudes to complete the process successfully. When any one collaborator demonstrates the effective use of a variety of the suggested techniques, the other collaborators move from the role of instructor to the role of supporter.

Cooperative Conflict Resolution Processes

The collaborative consultation process can be designed to identify both areas of strength and areas of needed improvement for each collaborator to deliver the appropriate educational intervention for identified learners. Within a cooperative framework, disagreements and arguments are valued as opportunities for constructive interaction to elicit the most useful information. As collaborators feel comfortable with controversy and as they learn specific skills in negotiating conflicts, a conflict resolution process can lead to better plans, compared to those that might have emerged if the controversy were avoided or suppressed (see D. Johnson & R. Johnson, 1987c, 1989; and West, Idol, & Cannon, 1989, Module 23, for specific strategies that enable teams to identify and improve their conflict strategies).

Many participants view controversy as a negative influence; they tend to perceive conflict as an *I win, you lose* situation. Typically, arguments over territory take the form of categorical turf building (e.g., individuals might say, "That's a special education problem" or "That's a speech problem"). This inadvertently relegates the solution to the educator who is responsible for only those learners, that is, the learners with the particular label or category of exceptionality. Every effort to rephrase such problems into common language increases ownership of the problem by the team rather than by the persons assigned to teach those learners. Using language that refers to team ownership (e.g., saying, "These are our learners" or "This is our problem") allows for the best possible solution to emerge while maintaining positive working relationships.

Reviews of the research on controversy (D. Johnson & R. Johnson, 1987a) indicate that effective management of controversy results in increased motivation among the team members involved in the conflict. It produces increased perspective taking, higher levels of cognitive reasoning, more creativity, increased quality in problem solving, and higher levels of satisfaction among the team members who make decisions and follow through with them. Educators who become comfortable and skilled in dealing constructively with controversy and conflict will notice similar benefits arising from the collaborative consultation process.

The key to effective conflict management is an understanding of the controversy cycle. As described by D. Johnson and R. Johnson (1987a), constructive controversy relies on team members who can proceed from categorizing, organizing, and deriving conclusions from present information and experiences to having that conclusion challenged by other team members as they present opposing viewpoints and positions. Team members must by able to experience a state of internal conceptual conflict, uncertainty, and disequilibrium and then actively seek more information, new experiences, and a more adequate cognitive perspective and process of reasoning about the problem in hopes of resolving their uncertainty. Finally, they should be able to reach new or reorganized conclusions that take into account the reasoning and perspectives of others.

Team members can improve their individual conflict management effectiveness by becoming aware of the variety of strategies they can invoke, depending on the type of conflict. The team members must keep in mind two major concerns in any conflict: The first to achieve the goal; the second is to maintain good working relationships with the other team members. D. Johnson and R. Johnson (1987a) identified five strategies for managing conflict (withdrawing, forcing, smoothing, compromising, and confronting) that correlate with relative attention to achieving task and relationship goals. All collaborators can influence positive changes by attending to these variables as they manage interpersonal conflicts that arise during the collaboration process.

Appropriate Interviewing Skills

During their interactions collaborators have a variety of goals to achieve as they together develop an effective program for the identified target problem. Interviewing skills aid in receiving and giving specific information, in expressing and discovering feelings or emotions, in planning for future action, and in problem solving. Such skills are defined generally as the ability to conduct oral interactions that are purposeful and direct and in which one person may take the responsibility for the development of the conversation (Molyneaux & Lane, 1982). In directed interviewing the members of the collaborative consultation team garner the information necessary for changing the targeted learner's behaviors. For example, Wiederholt, Hammill, and Brown (1982) relied on the interview process to obtain teacher perceptions about current and past problems of referred learners. Sources of such information included parent and sibling interviews, classmate interviews, and interviews with other specialists. Similarly, Lippitt and Lippitt (1986) suggested an interview data collection procedure in which the results of the interview reflect the mutual interaction of both parties. Clearly, such interview skills are needed by all members of a collaborative consultation team (see West et al., 1989, Module 19, for an instructional module related to interview skills).

Understanding and accommodating for the effects of diverse cultures on interpersonal interactions is an important function for the interviewer. Collaborators can develop constructive ways of interviewing each other so as to serve learners from ethnically diverse cultures (see Harris, 1991; Morsink, Thomas, & Correa, 1991). Harris (1991) reviewed the literature related to competencies necessary for expanding the effectiveness of consultants who design programs for culturally and linguistically diverse learners with special needs. Interviewing techniques may need to be adapted to gather the kinds of information needed. For example, "understanding own perspective" includes the specific competencies such as "willing to learn from bilingual educators as well as share expertise with them" and "expressing beliefs regarding the abilities of various ethnic minorities and [knowing] the basis for those beliefs" (p. 27). Another competency focuses on using appropriate assessment (and by implication, evaluation) strategies including specific competencies such as incorporating "language and cultural considerations when making decisions" (p. 27).

Active Listening to Facilitate Meaningful Interactions

When implementing collaborative consultation processes, it is important to minimize the misunderstandings and distortions that often occur in interpersonal communication. Feedback systems require active listening that provides the sender with tangible evidence about how the receiver has decoded the message. Gordon (1980) developed an effective communication system with a series of techniques that ensures that messages are being accurately received. Collaborators benefit from the use of techniques such as door openers (an invitation to talk), passive listening (keeping quiet), and acknowledgment responses (evidence, e.g., eye contact and nodding, to indicate that the listener is attending to the message).

All collaborators benefit from implementing active listening principles during each stage of Collaborative Consultation. Experienced school consultants confirm that active listening facilitates the consultation process (Idol-Maestas & Ritter, 1985). Idol (1989) analyzed communication behaviors that were considered important in consulting. Over 30% of the behaviors involved active listening skills such as receiving in a nonjudgemental fashion, questioning to clarify messages, restating, paraphrasing, and summarizing. Specific training information on active listening can be found in Kroth (1978) and West et al. (1989), Module 14.

Oral and Written Communication Based on Common, Nonjargon and Positive, Nonverbal Language

Effective communication involves using common, nonjargon language. The members of the collaborative consultation team must use a language system that is understood or that all involved are willing to learn. Organizationally, common conceptual frameworks can be developed through inservice training of all personnel. Villa (1988) discussed model inservice programs that allow adequate time (at least 2 years) and interactive peer coaching or mentoring processes for learning the language and the practice of new conceptual frameworks.

On an interpersonal level, Verderber (1981) described the communication process as dynamic or in constant motion, as ongoing with no fixed beginning or end, and as transactional, with simultaneously occurring events between people who are interdependent. This conceptualization of communication includes seven elements: people, context, rules, messages, channels, noise, and feedback. It should be noted that this discussion reflects the prevailing Anglo culture in North American schools and may need to be adjusted to fit the communication norms for schools in which other cultures are predominant.

Collaborators in a communication interaction must assume mutually interdependent roles as senders and receivers. The physical and social setting establishes the context for the communication and can impact both the meaning (semantics) of the communication and the expectations and behaviors of the team members.

Rules or norms that are established or perceived to be established change and solidify as the communicators become better acquainted. For example, when working together, collaborators use languages and behaviors that are different from those they might use with a class of students or with a district administrator, or others at different hierarchical levels.

The message constitutes the content of the interaction; it involves meaning (semantics), symbols, and organization. In any specialized group, jargon terms tend to slip in inadvertently. These terms are intended to make communication more efficient, but to the uninitiated they tend to give it an element of exclusivity and distance. A way to check written and oral language for jargon is to ask a layperson to read and listen to it for comprehension and then to revise it as points of confusion surface. For example, some collaborators may have differing ideas about materials and teaching/learning procedures that can be helpful to other collaborators in accelerating the progress of target learners. On the other hand, collaborators can experience satisfaction in seeing progress or guilt about failure to identify helpful changes. In both areas, communication awareness will lead to more effective and efficient interactions.

Feedback tells the person sending a message whether the message was heard, seen, or understood. If the verbal or nonverbal response tells the sender that the communication was not received, was received incorrectly, or was misinterpreted, the sender can rephrase the message to ensure that the meaning the sender intended to share is the same meaning received by the listener. Collaborators must develop methods to provide each other with continuous feedback regarding the accuracy of their understanding of each other's messages and their feelings regarding the content and process of consultation. Open and honest feedback helps to ensure that the ideas that are shared are adapted appropriately and will be utilized.

Nonverbal language involves a vast array of actions and postures including proximity, territory, temperature, lighting, personal style, dress, time management, kinesics, gestures, affect, regulators, adaptors, paralanguage, and vocal interferences. Although much of nonverbal communication is not easily controlled, it can be understood and manipulated more easily by those who understand its various aspects. Each of the terms will be explained in the following pages.

The channel of communication may involve such elements as facial expressions, gestures, or movements. For example, a firm handshake or gentle touch on the shoulder may be as important as what is seen or heard in the consultation process. Distracting noise that interferes with sharing the meaning of messages can come from external as well as internal sources. A distracting external noise might be the sound of colleagues talking in the hallway while the collaborators are trying to evaluate their progress. Distracting internal noise might intrude, for example, when one collaborator starts thinking about dinner while another describes the target issue under discussion or a learner's responses to certain foods as potential reinforcers.

The physical actions of those involved in Collaborative Consultation convey important communications. For example, a message about parity that is communicated when one team member sits in a chair across from or beside another member may be quite a different message when it is communicated with a table or desk between the two team members. The most important aspect of nonverbal communication is the ability to perceive such subtleties and to check them with other team members. Such perception checking enhances the listener's understanding of the sender's nonverbal cues. The purpose of checking out a perception is to give one the opportunity to deal with that perception, that is, to verify it or correct it. It is important to emphasize that perception checks are descriptive rather than judgmental.

The following list of the elements of nonverbal language (adapted from Verderber, 1981) includes specific suggestions to improve the skill of perception checking.

- *Proximity.* Proximity refers to the space around us or the space we are occupying at the moment. In the United States, distances up to 1½ feet are considered appropriate for intimate conversation with close friends, parents, or young children; 1½ feet is considered appropriate for personal, casual conversation; 4 to 12 feet is considered appropriate for impersonal, business contacts such as job interviews; and more than 12 feet is an appropriate distance for public communications. When a person we do not know or like violates the appropriate intimate distance in conversation, we tend unconsciously to move away. This is important information for collaborators who wish to increase their members' comfort levels as they focus on problem-solving tasks related to identified problems.

- *Territory.* Territory is space over which a person claims ownership. The classroom is the teacher's territory. How other collaborators arrange to be invited into that territory is of vital importance in the helping relationship.

- *Temperature and lighting.* Temperature can act either as a stimulant or as a deterrent to communication. The ideal ambient temperature for communication is one that is perceived as being neither too high nor too low (by all collaborators). Americans seem most comfortable when the temperature is between 68 and 75 degrees Fahrenheit.

  Lighting can also act as either a stimulant or a deterrent to communication. In lecture halls and reading rooms, bright light is expected;

it encourages listening and comfortable reading. It is often helpful for collaborators to check the comfort level of both the temperature and the lighting. Color has also been identified as an element that may affect our behavior. Red is supposed to be exciting and stimulating, blue is believed to be comfortable and soothing, whereas yellow is said to be cheerful and jovial. Thus, we can create various communication climates by adjusting temperature, lighting, and color.

- *Personal style.* Certain aspects of personal style are related to body shape, clothing, and the way we treat time. Three basic body types are hypothesized: endomorph (soft, round, and fat), mesomorph (muscular, hard, and athletic), and ectomorph (thin, fragile, and brittle). Often, people draw unconscious initial conclusions based on body type alone. Technical ability and willingness to work with people can help overcome such first impressions. In any event, it is important that collaborators have access to information that may be causing others to perceive and respond in certain ways.

- *Time management.* Although we sometimes have little control over the amount of available time, how we manage the time we have and how we react to others' use and management of time are important elements of nonverbal communication. Collaborators need to determine both the length of time that is appropriate for meeting with each other and the time of day that is mutually convenient. Collaborators must be sensitive to their own as well as others' perceptions of time. In this way, the variable of time can be used to facilitate rather than inhibit communication.

- *Kinesics.* Kinesics, that is, nonverbal body motions—such as facial expressions, eye contact, gestures, posture, and movements of the limbs and body—are important elements in the consultation process. The display of thumbs up (everything is "go"), the extension of the first and second finger in a V sign (peace in America), the waved hand ("hi"), a shaking of the head (no), and nodding (yes) are all examples of body motions called emblems. Emblems are considered most effective when a person is too far away for speech to be heard, when there is too much noise to be heard, or when the person just does not feel like verbalizing. (Note: Emblems are culture dependent.)

- *Gestures.* Gestures that are used to accent or emphasize what is being said verbally are referred to as illustrators. Any body motion that emphasizes, shows a pattern of thought, points, describes, or mimics is an illustrator. It is important that collaborators be aware of the potential strengths and weaknesses of such gestures so that they can determine when and how to use them appropriately.

- *Affect.* Affect displays are facial configurations or some concurrent body response that is emitted when one feels some strong emotion. We reveal a great deal about ourselves through unconscious body motions. Although affect displays tend to be automatic, they are usually conditioned by a set of cultural, familiar, and personal norms. Collaborators can learn a lot about each other by observing each other's affect displays.

- *Regulators*. Regulators are nonverbal acts that regulate the flow of conversation by telling the speaker to continue, repeat, elaborate, hurry up, and so on. They include cues such as shifting eye contact, slight head movements, shifts in posture, raised eyebrows, and a nodding of the head.

- *Adaptors*. Adaptors involve adaptive efforts to satisfy needs, perform actions, manage emotions, or develop social contacts. They constitute a class of nonverbal movements that are difficult to code. For example, when people uncross their arms or face a person directly, the action is often interpreted as indicating acceptance of the person and the message the person is communicating. Awareness of adaptors can help collaborators adjust their behaviors in response to others.

- *Paralanguage*. Paralanguage refers to the sounds that we hear in communication, for example, the way something is said rather than what is said. Four major characteristics of paralanguage are pitch (highness or lowness of tone), volume (loudness), rate (speed), and quality (the sound of the voice). Each of these by itself or in concert with one or more of the others can complement, supplement, or contradict the words used in the communication.

- *Vocal interferences*. Vocal interferences are sounds that interrupt or intrude in verbal speaking, causing distraction and, occasionally, complete communication breakdown. Vocal interferences—such as "uh," "er," "well," and "OK"—are speech habits that are developed over a period of time. Verderber (1981) noted that vocal interferences are often caused by a fear of momentary silence. He suggested that we become aware of our use of such interferences, practice not using them, and then note the improvements in our communication results.

In summary, the generic principles of Collaborative Consultation include a complex array of interpersonal, communication, and problem-solving skills that have emerged from a variety of knowledge bases. The skills needed to practice the "art" of Collaborative Consultation are subsumed under seven generic principles: (a) team ownership of the identified problems; (b) recognition of individual differences in the systematic progression through multiple developmental stages; (c) situational leadership to guide the implementation of Collaborative Consultation; (d) cooperative conflict resolution processes to manage confrontations; (e) appropriate interview skills to guide information gathering; (f) active listening to facilitate meaningful interactions; and

(g) oral/written communication based on common, nonjargon, and positive nonverbal language patterns.

INTRAPERSONAL ATTITUDES

As collaborators implement the generic principles of Collaborative Consultation and practice the underlying knowledge base described above, they will begin to understand the importance of articulating and delineating various aspects of the collaborative consultation process. Their intrapersonal attitudes will be needed at each stage of the decision-making process to overcome any barriers in proceeding to the next stage.

In this section we delineate several intrapersonal attitudes, which include beliefs, values, and experiences that may be unique to each individual collaborator, yet that impact greatly on the group process. The statements shown in Table 2.3 are intended to serve as a guide to each collaborator in the development and growth of a personal set of self-preservation and survival attitudes so as to increase self-enhancement and growth, as well as to positively influence the collaborative group. Each attitude is defined in terms of its relevance to Collaborative Consultation.

Facing Fear

Fear is a feeling of anxiety and agitation caused by the presence or nearness of danger, terror, or fright. FEAR has also been characterized by Robbins (1986) as an acronym for False Evidence Appearing Real. Fear can be experienced when collaborators learn new ideas or engage in new ways of interacting or teaching (e.g., being educationally accountable for learners with more

---

TABLE 2.3. Some Intrapersonal Attitudes Relevant to Collaborative Consultation

1. Face fear.
2. Share a sense of humor.
3. Behave with integrity.
4. Live with joy.
5. Take risks.
6. Use self-determination.
7. Think longitudinally.
8. Create new norms.
9. Respond proactively.
10. Adapt upward.
11. Use self-differentiation.

challenging learning needs). Fear can be experienced by some collaborators when they are expected and/or encouraged to acquire and use different philosophies or methods of responding to learners with special needs (e.g., using behavioral or medical interventions).

Sharing Humor

Humor is the ability to perceive, appreciate, or express what is funny, amusing, or ludicrous. Collaborators can increase their enjoyment in working together by sharing a sense of humor as they face mutual challenges in improving educational opportunities for their learners. The appropriate use of humor enables collaborators to move from using inappropriate humor such as sexist and racist jokes to a level of humor that is respectful. Humor that is spontaneous is often based on the funny and heart-warming situations that collaborators have experienced.

Behaving with Integrity

Integrity is a state of being honest and sincere. Acting with integrity requires collaborators to search within themselves to find the highest level of moral development and respond in kind. Acting with integrity requires being honest with oneself as well as others about what we're thinking and feeling. Collaborators who act with integrity accept individual (personal) accountability for maintaining one's self-respect. This can be enhanced by being honest with other collaborators. Learning to trust oneself and to respond in a trustworthy manner is essential. Integrity also involves saying yes or no to assignments (self- or group-imposed) and to keep one's word in following through on agreed commitments.

Another aspect of integrity is stress management. Maintaining health (food, sleep, exercise) and balance in personal and professional relationships is essential in facilitating a person's ability to manage stress. This in turn impacts on the person's ability to function as an effective group member with integrity.

Living with Joy

Joy is a glad feeling, happiness, pleasure, and delight. Living with joy means creating opportunities in life that are joyful and delightful and increasing the frequency of those opportunities in our daily lives (Roman, 1986). Sometimes joy results from struggling through something that was thought to be impossible (e.g., writing an Individualized Education Program or a book) or unwanted (e.g., confronting someone when it might lead to an angry response). There is a higher probability that collaborators will experience joy in their group process if they adopt joy as a guiding principle, acknowledge its presence, and strive to increase its frequency.

Taking Risks

Taking risks means exposing oneself to potential injury, damage, or loss. Risks related to Collaborative Consultation include the potential loss of expert or position power, the potential for added responsibilities, the potential for failure to get intended results, working with others with whom you may not agree, fear of doing the wrong thing for learners with special needs, and so on.

When collaborators risk giving up familiar or previously successful ways of thinking and behaving, they are embarking on a voyage into the unknown. However, when they equip their launch with best and promising practices, they increase the probability they will effectively create a teaching/learning environment that is better than the one they left behind. For example, historically, persons with special needs were exiled, sacrificed, exploited, and segregated. Now, because others were willing to take risks, many persons with special needs can succeed in the mainstream of society in ways that promote growth for themselves, as well as for their service providers, families, and friends.

Using Self-Determination

Self-determination is the concept that people have the right to make decisions that affect their personal and professional lives as long as those decisions do not cause physical, mental, or emotional harm to others. In cases where decisions related to self-determination may cause other people harm, then all potentially affected group members need to define the problems(s) and solution(s) that are mutually beneficial to all those involved. For example, a collaborator who consumed large amounts of alcohol was confronted by her teammates about the effects of that behavior on her ability to function as an effective group member. The concept here is that, although alcohol consumption is an individual choice, it becomes a team problem when and if the resulting behavior hinders team performance. This is one of the most challenging intrapersonal growth and development practices, because the lines between self-determination and team determination are often blurred. Each team has the right and responsibility to determine if they are willing and/or able to continue as they are or if they need to make changes.

Thinking Longitudinally

Time management, timing, and time scarcity represent frequently mentioned barriers to effective consultation. Collaborators must be consciously respectful of keeping their word about time agreements and must consciously account for how the group's time is managed. More importantly, collaborators can reinforce each other for the changes that they notice in each other's knowledge, interpersonal skills, and intrapersonal attitudes that have been acquired over specific time periods. By planning in 6-week, 1- or 2-semester, or 2- to 5-year cycles, successful collaboration groups can yield evidence of substantial progress in individual and group achievements. (Also refer to West & Idol, 1990, for examples of ways collaborative teams have created more time for team decision making.)

Creating New Norms

Norms are those practices and underlying expectations that form the basis of a group culture. When entering and maintaining collaborative consultation groups, collaborators can consciously decide to establish new norms so as to replace prevailing norms that are counterproductive to the group's overall goals. For example, a prevailing norm in most North American schools is to segregate and separate learners and faculty (e.g., by tracking learners, by providing pullout special services, and by assigning single teachers to specified groups of learners). Teachers under prevailing norms often speak in derogatory ways about their learners in the safety of the teacher's lounge. Collaborators can adopt a norm to only speak publicly and positively about a learner's strengths. Traditionally, the collaborative ethic has not been the norm in American schools, and educators have not been expected nor have they been trained to interact in collaborative ways. The adoption of the collaborative consultation process will require consistent practice of new norms.

Responding Proactively

Another intrapersonal attitude is that of responding proactively to situations requiring changes in behavior, situations, or systems. To respond proactively is to respond by planning for anticipated changes, rather than to respond reactively to those changes. A proactive responder views anticipated changes as challenges that provide opportunities for empowerment, rather than as obstacles to which a reaction is needed. Empowerment, a term meaning actions or sanctions that enable certain persons to make decisions, is currently being applied in school reform efforts centered around site-based management. In this example, certain teachers are empowered to work with the building principal in making site-based management decisions. The idea behind this movement is the legitimization of power, such as the empowerment of decision making given to those who are most directly involved in the arena for which the decisions are being made.

When collaborators think proactively, they view dilemmas, barriers, and problems as challenges that can be solved, thus further enabling the collaborative process. Proactive responses set a tone for the collaborative group that centers on thinking in advance about future problems that might arise as a result of a particular intervention being planned for a targeted problem.

Adapting Upward

Upward adaptation is an intrapersonal attitude that refers to a practice recommended by Friedman (1985) in his writings of systems that function effectively. The premise is that for the good of all in any system, those who are functioning poorly in the group process should be challenged to adapt upward. According to Friedman, in systems of all types, adaptation tends to be downward rather than upward, with the well functioning tending to adapt to those who function poorly, rather than the other way around.

This problem frequently occurs in collaborative decision-making groups. For example, a group might have a member who sees everything negatively and has a tremendous need to be correct on every issue. A typical outcome might be that an individual's behavior becomes somewhat contagious, with the entire group beginning to react negatively and to need to be right! If upward adaptation is used, it is expected that all group members would adapt their own behaviors and attitudes to more closely match those of the better-functioning member(s) of the group. Hopefully, this results in a more positive orientation to problem solving and more willingness to negotiate for consensual agreement.

Using Self-Differentiation

Another important intrapersonal attitude that is interrelated to upward adaptation is self-differentiation, which has to do with the ability to differentiate oneself from the group or the system. According to Friedman (1985), self-differentiation means the capacity of a person to define his or her own life's goals and values apart from surrounding pressures, and the capacity to take maximum responsibility for his or her own destiny and emotional being. This includes the capacity to maintain a relatively nonanxious presence in the midst of anxious systems. To return to the above example of upward adaptation, a strong collaborator is able to self-differentiate from the group and especially from the group member who sees everything negatively and a strong need to be right, reflecting the capacity to be an "I" while remaining connected to the other group members.

Consciously choosing to practice intrapersonal attitudes such as these can enable team members to better facilitate the collaborative consultation process. When teams consciously decide to practice attitudes that are new and challenging (e.g., facing fear), discussion of subjects thought to be uncomfortable or even taboo can emerge (e.g., discussion of what it might be like to be blind in a sighted world). When team members share what their individual intrapersonal attitudes and beliefs are, others are more likely to understand their behaviors. Such results can lead to friendships, as well as to a renewed commitment for working together on other tasks.

SUMMARY

Collaborative Consultation is an interactive process that enables groups of people with diverse expertise to generate creative solutions to mutually defined problems. There is a scientific as well as an artful base related to effective Collaborative Consultation. Additionally, there is an evolving knowledge base regarding important values or intrapersonal attitudes.

Effective Collaborative Consultation relies on the parity and equity of contributions from all collaborators. To use the collaborative consultation process effectively, group members should continually acquire expertise in the following three areas: (a) a technological knowledge base, (b) interpersonal communicative/interactive problem-solving skills, and (c) intrapersonal attitudes.

The underlying knowledge base (the science of Collaborative Consultation) focuses on specific areas, including (a) the application of reinforcement principles to improve instruction for learners with special needs; (b) a philosophy of teaching that provides expanded educational opportunities for all learners; (c) avoidance of methods that have not worked well in special or general education; and (d) use of the existing educational programs that foster effective instruction of learners with special needs.

The communicative, interactive, and problem-solving skills (the art of Collaborative Consultation) build on seven generic principles: (a) team ownership of the identified problem, (b) recognition of individual differences in the systematic progression through multiple developmental stages, (c) situational leadership to guide the implementation of Collaborative Consultation, (d) cooperative conflict resolution processes to manage confrontations, (e) appropriate interview skills to guide information gathering, (f) active listening to facilitate meaningful interactions, and (g) oral/written communication based on common, nonjargon and positive, nonverbal language patterns.

The intrapersonal attitudes are beliefs, values, and experiences that are unique to each collaborator yet may positively impact the group. They include (a) facing fear, (b) sharing humor, (c) behaving with integrity, (d) living with joy, (e) taking risks, (f) using self-determination, (g) thinking longitudinally, (h) creating new norms, (i) responding proactively, (j) adapting upward, and (k) using self-differentiation.

Collaborative consultants must be like weavers using many colored threads. The tapestry of their work is varied by the scientific knowledge bases, the generic principles of Collaborative Consultation, and the intrapersonal attitudes of each collaborator. In the chapters that follow, these various threads continue to be woven as we show how collaborative consultation teams complete multiple tasks and successfully negotiate the stages of the collaborative consultation problem-solving process. In the next chapter, the history and rationale for the emergence of the Collaborative Consultation Model is traced, and its empirical, legal, ethical, ecological, and sociological contexts are discussed.

STUDY QUESTIONS

1. The authors make distinctions between the "scientific" and the "artful" bases for the Collaborative Consultation Model. Please explain in your own words what these distinctions mean to you.

2. Consider each of the seven generic principles of Collaborative Consultation. Describe two major underlying knowledge bases for each of them that you think are important to know and practice.

3. Consider the intrapersonal attitudes discussed by the authors. Describe three intrapersonal attitudes that are important to you. Compare and contrast them with those of the authors.

4. What is meant by best practices? Describe two best practices that you know about that are not mentioned by the authors and discuss why consultants should know about them. How can collaborative consultation teams be kept informed about new best practices?

5. Think of a classroom or school-based situation that is considered to be a problem. Describe how the three areas of expertise important for successful collaborative consultants (i.e., the intrapersonal attitudes, scientific bases, and artful bases of each person involved) might be used to improve the situation.

REFERENCES

Bloom, B. (1981). *All our children are learning: A primer of parents, teachers, and other educators.* New York: Holt, Rinehart & Winston.

Brown, L., & York, B. (1974). Developing programs for severely handicapped students: Teacher training and classroom instruction. *Focus on Exceptional Children, 6,* 1–11.

Cannon, G., Idol, L., & West, J. F. (1992). Educating students with mild handicaps in general classrooms: Essential teaching practices for general and special educators. *Journal of Learning Disabilities, 25,* 300–317.

Dunn, L. (1968). Special education for the mildly handicapped: Is much of it justifiable? *Exceptional Children, 35,* 5–22.

Friedman, E. H. (1985). *Generation to generation: Family process in church and synagogue.* New York: Guilford.

Gordon, T. (1980). *Leadership effectiveness training.* New York: Wyden.

Hall, G. (1981). The concerns-based perspective on personnel preparation program development and dissemination *Teacher Education and Special Education, 4*(2), 51–60.

Hall, G., & Loucks, S. (1978). Teacher concerns as a basis for facilitating and personalizing staff development. *Teachers College Record, 80*(1), 36–53.

Harris, K. (1991). An expanded view on consultation competencies for educators serving culturally and linguistically diverse exceptional students. *Teacher Education and Special Education, 14*(1), 25–29.

Hersey, P., & Blanchard, K. H. (1988). *Management of organizational behavior: Utilizing human resources.* Englewood Cliffs, NJ: Prentice-Hall.

Idol, L. (1989). The resource/consulting teacher: An integrated model of service delivery. *Remedial and Special Education, 10*(6), 38–49.

Idol, L. (1990). The scientific art of classroom consultation. *Journal of Educational and Psychological Consultation, 1*(1), 3–22.

Idol, L., & Jones, B. F. (1991). *Educational values and cognitive instruction.* Hillsdale, NJ: Erlbaum.

Idol, L., & West, J. F. (1993). *Effective instruction of difficult-to-teach students.* Austin, TX: PRO-ED.

Idol-Maestas, L., Lloyd, S., & Lilly, M. S. (1981). Implementation of a noncategorical approach to direct service and teacher education. *Exceptional Children, 48*(3), 213–219.

Idol-Maestas, L., & Ritter, S. (1985). A follow-up study of resource/consulting teachers. *Teacher Education and Special Education, 8*(3), 121–131.

Johnson, D., & Johnson, F. (1987). *Joining together: Group skills.* Englewood cliffs, NJ: Prentice-Hall.

Johnson, D., & Johnson, R. (1980). The key to effective inservice: Building teacher-teacher collaboration. *The Developer,* pp. 223–236.

Johnson, D., & Johnson, R. (1987a). *Creative controversy: Intellectual challenge in the classroom.* Edina, MN: Interaction.

Johnson, D., & Johnson, R. (1987b). *Learning together and alone.* Englewood Cliffs, NJ: Prentice-Hall.

Johnson D., & Johnson, R. (1987c). *A meta-analysis of cooperative, competitive, and individualized goal structures.* Hillsdale, NJ: Erlbaum.

Johnson, D., & Johnson, R. (1989). *Cooperation and competition: Theory and research.* Edina, MN: Interaction.

Jones, B. F., Idol, L. (1990). *Dimensions of thinking and cognitive instruction.* Hillsdale, NJ: Erlbaum.

Knight, M., Meyers, H. W., Paolucci-Whitcomb, P., Hasazi, S., & Nevin, A. (1981). A four year evaluation of consulting teacher services. *Behavior Disorders, 6*(2), 92–100.

Kroth, R. (1978). *Communicating with parents of handicapped students.* Denver, CO: Love.

Lates, B. J. (1975). IEP training in a large urban school system. *Periscope: Inservice and preservice preparation* (pp. 45–49). Reston, VA: Council for Exceptional Children.

Lippitt, G., & Lippitt, R. (1986). *The consulting process in action.* San Diego: University Associates.

Lipsky, D., & Gartner, A. (1988). *Beyond separate education.* Baltimore: Brookes.

Miller, T., & Sabatino, D. (1978). An evaluation of the teacher consultant model as an approach to mainstreaming. *Exceptional Children, 45,* 86–91.

Molyneaux, D., & Lane, V. W. (1982). *Effective interviewing techniques and analysis.* Boston: Allyn & Bacon.

Morsink, C., Thomas, C., & Correa, V. (1991). *Interactive teaming: Consultation and collaboration in special programs.* New York: Macmillan.

Nevin, A. (1990). Cooperative learning for adults. *Teaching Exceptional Children, 21*(3), 66–67.

Pedron, N., & Evans, S. (1990). Modifying classroom teachers' acceptance of the consulting teacher model. *Journal of Educational and Psychological Consultation, 1*(2), 189–200.

Robbins, A. (1986). *Unlimited power: The new science of personal achievement.* New York: Simon & Schuster.

Roman, S. (1986). *Living with joy.* Tiburon, CA: H. J. Kramer.

Verderber, R. F. (1981). *Communicate.* Belmont, CA: Wadsworth.

Villa, R. (1988). Model public schools inservice program—Do they exist? *Teacher Education and Special Education, 12*(4), 173–176.

West, J. F. (1985). Regular and special educators' preferences for school-based consultation models (Doctoral dissertation, The University of Texas at Austin, 1985). *Dissertation Abstracts International, 47*(2), 504A.

West, J. F., & Idol, L. (1990). Collaborative consultation in the education of mildly handicapped and at-risk students. *Remedial and Special Education, 11*(1), 22–31.

West, J., Idol, L., & Cannon, G. (1989). *Collaboration in the schools: Communicating, interacting, and problem solving—An inservice and preservice curriculum for teachers, support staff, and administrators.* Austin, TX: PRO-ED.

Wiederholt, J., Hammill, D., & Brown, V. (1982). *The resource teacher* (2nd ed.). New York: Allyn & Bacon.

CHAPTER 3

History and Rationale

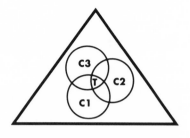

GENERAL AND SPECIAL EDUCATORS have had to develop new working relationships to enable learners with special education needs and their classmates to
reap the benefits of current mandates. Although the content of this chapter
draws from the research and practice in providing effective instruction for
learners with special education needs, we believe the results have implications for learners who are at risk for failure within general education programs.
Specifically, since educational change can take place only if teachers implement effective programs, classroom teachers have become increasingly involved
in providing special education. Special educators also have assumed new supportive relationships with general educators, in addition to continuing to provide direct service for learners with special education needs.

/ Many of the early consultation preparation programs at the University
of Vermont Consulting Teacher Program (e.g., Paolucci-Whitcomb & Nevin,
1985) and the University of Illinois Resource/Consulting Program (e.g., Idol,
1993) served as models for the design and structure of replications such as
Project ConSEPT at Pacific Lutheran University (Gerlach & Reisberg, 1986).
As noted by West and Brown (1987), 26 states had included consultation as
a formal service delivery option for special education services by 1987.

The success of these collaborative/consultative personnel preparation
models has been evidenced by the increased capacity of teachers to provide
effective programs for learners with special needs. The common element shared
by these exemplary programs is the collaborative support provided to educators. In this chapter, we examine the context in which the need for a Collaborative Consultation Model between general and special educators has
developed. In turn, the history of special education, the impetus behind the
relevant legislation and litigation, the empirical evidence, and the sociological
and ecological context for a mainstream classroom approach to special education are considered.

THE HISTORICAL CONTEXT

A detailed history of the special education movement is beyond the scope
of this book; the interested reader is referred to Hewett and Forness (1977),
who provided a comprehensive and succinct history of special education within
the conceptual framework of four historical determinants that they suggest

have led to improved treatment of persons with special needs. The first determinant, threat to survival, results primarily from harsh treatment by the environment. The second determinant, superstition, is related primarily to the appearance and behavior of persons with special needs. The third, science, refers to attempts to study exceptionality in a natural, lawful, and objective manner. The fourth determinant, service, includes the care, humane treatment, and social acceptance of persons with special needs. Hewett and Forness described how these four determinants have affected the treatment of persons with special needs through seven major historical periods. They noted that, during each historical period, a great range of variability and discrepancy could be seen in the kinds of treatment extended to persons with special needs, from cruel to humane, from exile to inclusion, from rejection to acceptance (see Table 3.1). This range can be accounted for by a variety of influences: nature, irrational and rational beliefs, social and economic conditions, religion, governance (law), and knowledge generated by specific individuals. Indeed, they suggested that:

> the current concerns with mainstreaming exceptional learners into regular education whenever possible contrast sharply with the historical practice of segregating them. Over two thousand years ago Plato specified, "If any one is insane, let him not be seen openly in the city." Commenting on treatment of handicapped children at birth, "Those of inferior parents and any children of the rest that are born defective will be hidden away, in some appropriate manner, that must be kept secret." Following this philosophy, custodial care institutions were built apart from major cities even up to recent times, and the earliest educational plans for exceptional learners placed them in self-contained classrooms, removed from their normal peers. (Hewett & Forness, 1977, p. 80)

TABLE 3.1. Historical Determinants of the Treatment of Individuals with Handicaps

Survival	Superstition	Science	Service
Harsh physical environment	Sacrifice	Natural explanation	Exploitation
Infanticide	Witch-burning	Categorization	Humane treatment
Eugenics	Torture	Objective study	Custodial care
Harsh treatment	Trephining	Psychological theory	Education
Exile	Exorcism	Mental measurement	Social acceptance
	Demonology	Research	
	Worship		

Note. Adapted from *Education of Exceptional Learners* (2nd ed.) by M. Hewett with S. R. Forness, 1977, Austin, TX: PRO-ED. Used by permission.

Unfortunately, many of these attitudes still prevail today, and must be addressed. To this end, Wolfensberger (1972) developed a philosophy and set of practices designed to expose and remove attitudinal, programmatic, and physical barriers that limit the provision of more normalized environments for all citizens with special needs.

A major determinant of treatment for learners with special needs lies in the theoretical constructs that underlie administrative and managerial practices. Reynolds (1962) described the array of educational services that public school systems have traditionally provided for their learners with special needs, as administrative alternatives to the previous "two-box" model of special-versus-general educational placement. This "cascade of services" model, shown in Figure 3.1, illustrates that (a) the greatest number of students *can* be served within the general public school structure; (b) the more severe the special need, the more restrictive or segregated the environment; and (c) the principle of least restrictive placement is feasible.

As school districts have become more proficient in developing the continuum of educational placements, and as technologies and innovative practices have been developed and translated into less restrictive environments, Reynolds (1977) suggested a new perspective, called "the instructional cascade," which contains fewer specialized places and more diverse general education places (see Figure 3.2). In the instructional cascade, special education services are not based primarily on administrative placement issues but are focused instead on procedures to transfer effective components, identified in specialized, more restrictive environments, to less restrictive environments.

Personnel who work in specialized environments can contribute information and skills that can be replicated or adapted for nonspecialized environments. In short, educators in both specialized and general environments must be capable of collaboratively consulting to acquire and adapt the information and skills that have been identified as salient aspects of effective instructional and organizational interventions. This was characterized by Idol (1990) as the "scientific art of classroom consultation" (p. 5). School personnel have the responsibility of collaborating to transfer the technical content of their knowledge base through the collaborative interactions that Idol (1990) referred to as "the artful component of classroom consultation" (p. 5) or the interpersonal process of communicating, interactive problem solving, and consensual decision making.

All educators are encouraged to identify and implement the salient aspects of effective treatments. Important differences in how special education personnel interact with general educators can then be discussed within the context of new roles for all educators. Collaboration skills are necessary to fulfill the consultation role required to maximize the implementation of such an instructional cascade of services.

FIGURE 3.1.   The Special Education Cascade.

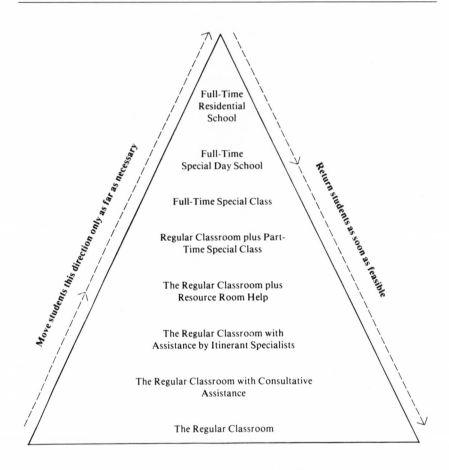

Full-Time
Residential
School

Full-Time
Special Day School

Full-Time Special Class

Regular Classroom plus Part-
Time Special Class

The Regular Classroom plus
Resource Room Help

The Regular Classroom with
Assistance by Itinerant Specialists

The Regular Classroom with Consultative
Assistance

The Regular Classroom

Move students this direction only as far as necessary

Return students as soon as feasible

**Limited Educational Environments
Outside of the School**

Special Treatment and Detention Centers
Hospitals
"Home-bound" Instructors

Note. From "The Instructional Cascade" by M. C. Reynolds in *The Least Restrictive Alternative,* A. Rehman and T. Riggen (Eds.), 1977, Minneapolis, MN: Minneapolis Public Schools. Copyright 1977 by Minneapolis Public Schools. Reprinted by permission.

FIGURE 3.2. The Changing Cascade: Fewer specialized places, more diverse general education places.

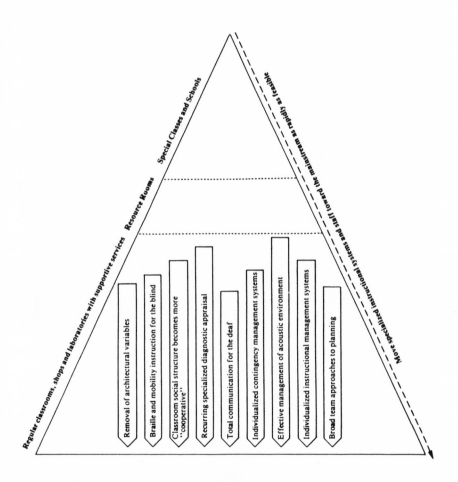

Note. From ''The Instructional Cascade'' by M. C. Reynolds in *The Least Restrictive Alternative,* A. Rehman and T. Riggen (Eds.), 1977, Minneapolis, MN: Minneapolis Public Schools. Copyright 1977 by Minneapolis Public Schools. Reprinted by permission.

THE LEGISLATIVE AND LITIGATIVE CONTEXT

Legal Principles

Both P.L. 99-457 (1986) (the Individuals with Disabilities Education Act [IDEA]) and P.L. 94-142 (1975) (formerly known as the Education for All Handicapped Children Act [EHA]) guarantee a free appropriate public education in the least restrictive environment. Such national legislation represents the culmination of several decades of litigation and legislation at the state level (Weintraub & Abeson, 1974). The major purpose of this national legislation was the provision of educational programs for millions of learners who had previously been excluded from special education services and major revisions of current delivery systems for learners already receiving services.

Five principles can be seen to underlie P.L. 94-142: the right to education, a zero reject philosophy, least restrictive placement, parental involvement, and protection from discriminatory evaluation and assessment practices. Several court decisions culminated in the formulation of P.L. 94-142 as described below. Public schools were required to (a) provide a full range of services for all learners with special needs, (b) protect the procedural and substantive due process of the learners with their parents, (c) incorporate procedures for placement within the least restrictive alternative, and (d) develop and monitor Individualized Education Programs (IEPs) on the basis of non-discriminatory testing procedures. States were required to develop state plans and regulations to enable such legislation to be effective. Of course, these rules and regulations must be recognized when implementing any consultation model. In the following discussion of each of the five basic principles cited above, it should be kept in mind that relevant state regulations should be consulted regarding local implementation.

Right to Education.   The right-to-education mandate is based on the landmark case *PARC* (Pennsylvania Association for Retarded Citizens) *v. The Commonwealth of Pennsylvania* (1971), which resulted in a court order for the commonwealth to provide all children diagnosed with mental retardation a free appropriate public education. Basically, because state law and the Pennsylvania constitution provided education to all children, the state could not then deny educational programs to its children diagnosed with mental retardation, who were being denied access to free public day school programs. A similar case was successfully brought on behalf of children who had been diagnosed as having hyperactivity, emotional disturbance, and behavior disorders, as well as mental retardation, in *Mills v. Board of Education of the District of Columbia* (1972).

Zero Reject Philosophy.   The legal cases cited above reflect a zero reject philosophy, which states that public schools cannot turn away any of their learners, regardless of their special needs. Prior to these legal decisions, it was the responsibility of the parent or guardian to prove that the learner could appropriately benefit from instruction. On the basis of the testimony and evidence presented in these court cases, however, the educational community was importuned to develop programs for all of its learners, on the basic assumption that the opportunity for instruction cannot be denied to some if it is offered to all.

Least Restrictive Placement. The legal doctrine of the least restrictive environment, elegantly detailed by Bergdorf (1975), can be summarized as follows. Basically, the principle states that learners with special needs should be educated in a setting as much like the normal classroom environment as appropriate (Bergdorf, 1975, p. 146). Court decisions have referred to this principle as "less drastic means for achieving the same purpose" (*Shelton v. Tucker*, 1960), "least restrictive means" (*Smith v. Sampson*, 1972), and "the least burdensome method" (*Ramirez v. Brown*, 1973). This has direct implications for any method that segregates or separates learners with special needs from the normal program. It is based on the *Brown v. Board of Education* (1954) decision that "the doctrine of separate but equal has no place . . . separate educational facilities are inherently unequal." The direct result of this principle is the inclusion of learners who had previously been educated in separate institutions, as well as those learners placed in special classes within public schools.

Parental Involvement. Parental involvement was a basic outcome of these court decisions and mandates, in that it was typically a parent or a parent advocacy group that initiated the class action suits. Furthermore, most state legislation, as well as P.L. 94-142, requires that parents or guardians be informed and give informed consent when a learner is referred for educational assessment, placement in a program, and evaluation of progress. Parental involvement and consent must also be obtained when exiting a learner from special services. Due process procedures must be in place to ensure that dissatisfied parents are provided an appropriate forum for review and reconsideration of disputed decisions. Prior to these protections, learners were admitted, placed, and discharged from special educational programs without necessarily obtaining such consent. More importantly, P.L. 94-142 stresses a collaborative relationship. For example, in 1986, a congressional committee "received overwhelming testimony . . . pointing out the critical need for parents and professionals to function in a collaborative fashion" (U.S. House Committee on Education and Labor, 1986, p. 20).

Protection from Discriminatory Evaluation and Assessment Practices. Protection in assessment and evaluation procedures is another underlying principle that has been determined by litigation. The landmark case is *Larry P. v. Riles* (1972), which documented that there was an overrepresentation of black learners in classes for learners with retardation and that IQ tests administered to classify learners as retarded resulted in a racial imbalance, an operational definition of discrimination. *Diana v. State Board of Education* (1970) similarly noted imbalances on behalf of Mexican-American, Spanish-speaking learners who were placed in classes for learners with educable mental retardation on the basis of scores from IQ tests given in English. Such inappropriate testing practices have been consistently challenged and have resulted in the development of important due process procedures to ensure fairness in the evaluation of learners.

Legal Definitions and Intent

The following excerpts provide an overview of the intent of P.L. 94-142 and its specific requirements regarding learners with special needs. In the following citations, please note the former language of P.L. 94-142 referring to "handicapped children" has been changed to match current usage reflected in its new name, the Individuals with Disabilities Education Act. The term "learner with special education needs" reflects a shift from a focus on the disability to a focus on the person first.

It is the purpose of this Act to ASSURE that all learners with handicapping conditions have available to them . . . a FREE APPROPRIATE PUBLIC EDUCATION and related services designed to meet their unique needs, to assure that the rights of learners with handicapping conditions and their parents or guardians are protected, to assist states and localities to provide for the education of all learners with handicapping conditions, and to assess and assure the effectiveness of efforts to educate learners with handicapping conditions. (16) The term "special education" means specially designed instruction at no cost to parents or guardians, to meet the unique needs of a learner with handicapping conditions, including classroom instruction, instruction in physical education, home instruction, and instruction in hospitals and institutions. (17) The term "related services" means transportation and such developmental, corrective, and other support services (including speech pathology and audiology, psychological services, physical and occupational therapy, recreation, and medical and counseling services, except that such medical services shall be for diagnostic purposes only) as may be required to assist the learner in benefiting from special education, and includes the early identification and assessment of handicapping conditions in children. (18) The term "free education and related services" which (A) have been provided at public expense, under public supervision and direction, and without charge, (B) meet the standards of the state educational agency, (C) include an appropriate preschool, elementary or secondary school education in the state involved, and (D) are provided in conformity with the individualized education program required under section 614(a)(5). (19) The term *"individualized education program"* means a written statement for each learner with handicapping conditions developed in any meeting by a representative of the local education agency or an intermediate educational unit who shall be qualified to provide, or supervise the provision of, specially designed instruction to meet the unique needs of learners with handicapping conditions, the teacher, the parents or guardians of such child, and, whenever appropriate, such child, which statement shall include (A) a statement of the present levels of educational performance of such child, (B) a statement of annual goals, including short term instructional objectives, (C) a statement of the specific educational services to be provided to such child and the extent to which such child will be able to participate in regular educational programs, (D) the projected date for initiation and anticipated duration of such services, and appropriate objective criteria and evaluation procedures and schedules for determining, at least on an annual basis, whether instructional objectives are being achieved. (Congressional Federal Register (CFR) 45, 121a, 340–349)

P.L. 99-457 (IDEA) and P.L. 94-142 (EHA) call for explicit detailed provisions for educational programs, explained in the following sections. Again, notice the changes in language with the learner referenced first, followed by a reference to the handicapping condition or special education need.

The Individualized Education Program (IEP)

The following terms and requirements are specifically relevant to implementation of an Individualized Education Program (IEP).

Physical Education. Specially designed physical education services, if necessary, must be made available to every learner with special needs receiving a free appropriate public education. Furthermore, each learner must be afforded an opportunity to participate in the general physical education program (CFR 121a. 307). Where appropriate, adaptive physical education must be prescribed in the IEP (CFR 121a. 346).

Least Restrictive Environment. A salient aspect of both federal and state legislation is the requirement to educate learners with special needs in the "least restrictive environment." Within the context of an available continuum of program options, public schools are to ensure that learners with handicapping conditions, including children in public or private institutions or other facilities, are educated with same-age peers to the maximum extent appropriate. Special classes, separate schooling, or other removal of learners with special needs from the general educational environment should occur only when the nature or severity of the handicap is such that education in general classes with the use of supplementary aids and services cannot be achieved satisfactorily (CFR 121a. 550). Individuals with exceptional needs must be provided the opportunity to participate with same-age peers in nonacademic and extracurricular services and activities as well as academic activities (CFR 121a. 553).

Participation in the General Education Program.   The IEP must indicate the extent to which the learner will be educated in the general educational program. One way of meeting this requirement (according to the U.S. Office of Special Education) is to indicate the percentage of time the learner will be spending in the general education program with general education learners. Another way is to list the specific general education classes the learner will be attending. In a special note regarding integration of learners with severe handicaps, the IEP may include any noncurricular activities in which the learner can participate with same-age peers, such as lunch, assembly periods, club activities, and other special events (CFR 46).

Modifications of the General Education Program.   If modifications—that is, supplementary aids and services of the general education program—are necessary to ensure the learner's participation in that program, those modifications must be described in the IEP. For example, if a learner with a hearing impairment required special seating arrangements in the general education classroom, this should be specified in the IEP. This applies to any general education program in which the student may participate, including physical education, art, music, and vocational education (CFR).

Comprehensiveness of the IEP.   Regarding the comprehensiveness of the IEP, the U.S. Office of Special Education has noted that the IEP is required to include only those matters concerning the provision of special education and related services and the extent to which the learner can participate in general education programs (CFR). The regulations define "special education" as specially designed instruction to meet the unique needs of a learner with special needs and "related services" as those that are necessary to assist the learner to benefit from special education (CFR 121A. 14; 121A. 13).

Classroom Teacher's Role in IEP Development and Implementation.   When a learner with special needs is enrolled in both normal and special education classes, the learner's special education teacher should attend the IEP meeting. At the option of the educational agency or the parent, the learner's classroom teacher may also attend (CFR). The U.S. Office of Special Education suggests that if the classroom teacher does not attend the meeting, the agency should either provide this teacher with a copy of the IEP or inform the teacher of its contents. Further, it is recommended that the special education teacher or other support personnel consult with and be a resource to the learner's classroom teacher (CFR). The authors recommend that classroom teachers be encouraged to attend these meetings.

Implementation Timeline and Accountability.   Federal and state legislation specifically address the issue of Individualized Education Program timelines and accountability. Once completed, the IEP should be implemented as soon as possible (CFR 121a. 342). The IEP is not intended to be a performance contract that can be held against a teacher or agency if a learner with special needs does not meet the IEP objectives. However, the special education and related services must be provided in accordance with the IEP (CFR 121a. 349).

The implementation and administration of change in the context of rapidly changing social policies has been a continuing concern of the public school system. For example, the civil rights movement resulted in broad revisions of general educational practices. Since the 1954 *Brown v. Board of Education* decision, which ruled that separate education systems were unequal, the policies and actions of American public schools have been increasingly challenged by the courts. The landmark court decisions indicate that many policies relating to all learners (e.g., racially segregated schools and ability tracking) violate the equal protection clause of the Fourteenth Amendment of the U.S. Constitution.

Similar arguments presented in court decisions such as *PARC v. The Commonwealth of Pennsylvania* (1971) and *Mills v. Board of Education of the District of Columbia* (1972) show that these policies and practices have been related to learners with special needs. Specifically, what is provided for some people or learners must be provided for all on equal terms unless a compelling cause for such differential treatment can be demonstrated. The provision of due process for the educational placement and programming of learners with special needs requires that schools select the setting that is least restrictive of the learner's civil rights.

Since the implementation of P.L. 94-142, the courts have been used as a means for defining appropriate education. Osborne (1992) traced the early decisions that ruled that appropriate did not mean the best (*Springdale School District v. Grace,* 1981; *Rettig v. Kent City School District,* 1981). Furthermore, the existence of a better program did not render a placement inappropriate (*Buchholtz v. Iowa Department of Public Instruction,* 1982; *Age v. Bullitt County Public Schools,* 1982). More recent distinctions include the notions that beneficial educational progress, not trivial educational advancement, must be a likely result of an IEP (*Board of Education of East Windsor Regional School District v. Diamond,* 1986) and that learners with disabilities must be provided an education that has meaningful benefit (*Polk v. Centra, Susquehanna Intermediate Unit 16,* 1988). It is within this legal context that the collaboration between general and special educators and administrators becomes a sine qua non of providing successful services for learners with special needs in more normalized environments.

THE EMPIRICAL CONTEXT

In this section, the empirical context for Collaborative Consultation is historically traced. For a discussion of the research evidence from 1986 through 1992, refer to Chapter 1.

Researchers in special education began to seriously question the efficacy of segregated special class placement as early as 1960. At that time, Blatt (1960) noted that "it has yet to be demonstrated that the special class offers a better school experience for retarded children than does regular class placement" (p. 54). Dunn (1968) importuned both special and general educators to stop past and present practices that "we know now to be undesirable for many of the children we are dedicated to serve" (p. 5). Such criticisms culminated in an article by Lilly (1970), calling for a change in the basic structure of traditional special education by changing from a focus on exceptional children to a focus on exceptional situations within the school. Deno (1970) also called for a new conceptualization of special education as "developmental capital." This was later expanded by Burrello, Tracy, and Schultz (1973) into the notion of "experimental education." Lilly (1971) proposed a training-based model in which special educators serve in a training and support role with classroom teachers, who maintain primary responsibility for the education of all but those with severe handicaps. Deno (1972) provided a collection of data-based models, indicating that such a training-based model is a valid approach that could yield appropriate and effective services for learners with special needs in general education classrooms. In 1975, a triadic model of consultation provided a theoretical and empirical basis for specialists to consult with teachers.

The triadic model had three components: the target (T), the mediator (M), and the consultant (C) (Tharp, 1975; Tharp & Wetzel, 1969). This model (see Figure 3.3) placed the consultee as the mediator of change between the consultant and the person in whom the behavior change is sought. In our earlier adaptation of the model (Idol, Paolucci-Whitcomb, & Nevin, 1986), the target is the referred learner with an academic or social problem. The mediator is typically the classroom teacher, the person with the available means of social influence for achieving the goal of ameliorating the learner's problem behavior. The consultant is typically the person with the knowledge or skills to mobilize the mediator's influence, although in the actual implementation of this model the mediator often influences and informs the consultant. Consultants and mediators are general educators, special educators, speech therapists, aides, principals, parents, physicians, and so on. The consultant and mediator together share knowledge about appropriate content, processes, and reinforcers that may be mobilized to ameliorate the problem.

Early empirical evidence comparing a segregated special education approach to a consultation training–based approach has been provided by Jenkins and Mayhall (1976); Miller and Sabatino (1978); Knight, Meyers, Paolucci-Whitcomb, Hasazi, and Nevin (1981); and Lew, Mesch, and Lates (1982). Specifically, Miller and Sabatino (1978) showed that academic gains were equivalent for both models, whereas teacher behaviors were judged slightly better under the consultation model. The Knight et al. (1981) study showed statistically significant increased progress of learners receiving services in districts where consulting teachers had worked with classroom teachers for more than 6 years. Moreover, the increased skills of the teachers were partially responsible for the improvement.

FIGURE 3.3. Triadic consultation: A conceptual model.

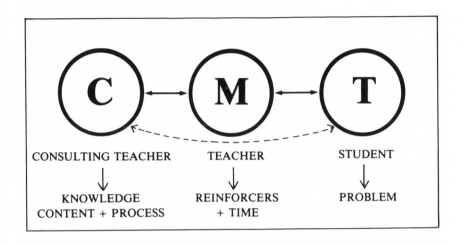

Note. Adapted by Idol et al. (1986) from *Psychological Consultation in the Schools: Helping Teachers Meet Special Needs* (p. 137) by C. Parker (Ed.), 1975, Reston, VA: Council for Exceptional Children. Adapted by permission.

As shown in Table 3.2, all aspects of the process to serve learners with special needs are affected by the implementation of a consultation model. Compared to teachers in schools without a consultation approach, those in schools with a consultation approach assumed more direct roles and engaged in more direct activities with learners with special needs—from referral through assessment, curriculum development, implementation of teaching/learning activities, and evaluation. Similar reports of empirical validation of the effectiveness of classroom teachers in collaboration with special educators were provided by Idol (1993) for Champaign-Urbana, Illinois; by Nelson and Stevens (1981) in Kentucky and Deno and Gross (1972) for the Minneapolis, Minnesota, area; and by Lew et al. (1982) for Boston, Massachusetts. These reports showed the effectiveness of this approach for urban as well as rural areas over the entire range of elementary, junior, and senior high schools; see Knight et al. (1981) and Lates (1975).

An example of a functional analysis of effectiveness is described by Hawkes and Paolucci-Whitcomb (1980). In this study, a special educator collaborated with a classroom teacher to implement a well-articulated peer tutoring program. The program was effective in accelerating the academic and social progress of several learners with special needs. Idol (1993) described more than 40 data-based interventions developed for learners with special needs. Similarly,

TABLE 3.2.   Changes in Procedures in Schools with a Consultation Approach

Procedure	Schools with Consultation Approach	Traditional School Not Using Consultation Approach
Referral	1. Classroom teacher assumes primary role in referral. 2. Classroom teacher assumes primary responsibility for IEP development. 3. Staffing process allows general education personnel opportunity to provide referral input.	1. Special educator or guidance counselor assumes primary role in referral. 2. Special educator assumes primary responsibility for IEP development. 3. Staffing process allows special education personnel to obtain approval of referral.
Assessment	1. Basic staffing team shares responsibility for test selection and interpretation. 2. Criterion-referenced tests used. 3. Basic staffing team assumes responsibility for diagnosis.	1. Special educator assumes primary responsibility for test selection and interpretation. 2. Norm-referenced tests used. 3. Special educator assumes responsibility for diagnosis.
Curriculum	1. Staffing process allows mainstream education personnel opportunity to share in development of skill sequences. 2. Locally developed skill sequences used. 3. Curriculum referenced to school specific standards.	1. Staffing process allows special education personnel to obtain approval of selected skill sequences. 2. Commercially developed skill sequences used. 3. Curriculum referenced to classroom specific standards.
Teaching and learning	1. Classroom teacher assumes primary responsibility for instruction. 2. No student spends more than 10% of time outside of general classroom. 3. Staffing process allows mainstream education personnel opportunity to provide instruction input.	1. Special educator assumes primary responsibility for instruction. 2. Some learners spend more than 10% of time outside of mainstream classroom. 3. Staffing process allows special education personnel to obtain approval of instruction.
Evaluation	1. Classroom teacher assumes primary responsibility for measures. 2. Measures usually same as measures used for most learners in classroom.	1. Special educator assumes primary responsibility for measures. 2. Measures usually different than measures used for most learners in classroom.

TABLE 3.2. Continued

Procedure	Schools with Consultation Approach	Traditional School Not Using Consultation Approach
	3. Staffing process allows mainstream education personnel opportunity to evaluate learner progress.	3. Staffing process allows special education personnel to obtain confirmation of evaluation.

Note. From "A Four-Year Evaluation of Consulting Teacher Services" by M. Knight, H. Meyers, P. Paolucci-Whitcomb, S. Hasazi, and A. Nevin, 1981, *Behavioral Disorders, 6*, pp. 95–96. Copyright 1981 by Council for Children with Behavioral Disorders. Reprinted by permission.

Mainer, Stahlbrand, Knight, Paolucci-Whitcomb, and Nevin (1982) collaborated with a paraprofessional to institute a self-recording procedure to improve the paraprofessional's administration of contingent positive feedback. A multiple baseline design across three eighth-grade learners with special needs was used to evaluate effectiveness. The paraprofessional increased her frequency of correctly administering contingent positive oral feedback for each learner only when she implemented a simple self-recording procedure that was subsequently monitored by another member of the team. In addition to increased enjoyment among the participants in the small-group tutorial program, the paraprofessional observed a greater consistency in the amount of time the learner remained on task and an unexpected increase in the learners' positive comments about their instructional time with her. Clearly, a functional analysis of the effects of the collaborators is important in documenting successful implementation of collaborative consultation interventions.

The literature shows a clear relationship between instructional support to improve the skills of educators and accelerated growth of learners with special needs. Moreover, there is a growing body of research on "effective schools," indicating that public school personnel are designing achievement-oriented environments for all learners. Based on the work of Edmonds (1979), Brookover et al. (1982), and Hersh (1981), the characteristics of effective schools may be summarized as shown in Table 3.3. These characteristics are (a) instructional leadership, (b) expectations for learner achievement, (c) the monitoring of learner progress, (d) orderly and safe environments, and (e) an emphasis on those teaching variables that permit increased academic learning time.

Educational researchers have identified certain mastery learning and individualized instruction techniques that are successful in increasing achievement for all students (Block, 1975; Guskey, 1985). Other techniques used by classroom teachers can positively interact with successful techniques identified by special educators. For example, the effects of cooperative learning as an

TABLE 3.3. Attributes of Effective Schools

Social Organization	Instruction Curriculum
Clearly specified academic and social behavior goals	High academic learning time
Order and discipline	Frequent monitoring of homework
High expectations	Frequent monitoring of student progress
Teacher efficacy/confidence	Tightly coupled curriculum
Pervasive caring	Variety of teaching/learning strategies
Public rewards/incentives	Opportunity for expanding learner responsibilities
Administrative leadership	
Community support	

instructional methodology have been well researched and documented. Johnson and Johnson (1987), Johnson, Maruyama, Johnson, Nelson, and Skon (1981), Sharan (1980), and Slavin (1984) have conducted comprehensive and detailed reviews of the literature. As shown in Table 3.4, the research findings support the use of cooperative learning for increasing student achievement, improving positive race relations in desegregated schools, increasing mutual concern among learners, improving learner self-esteem and acceptance of differences, and ensuring positive interactions among learners with and without special needs in mainstreamed academic settings. Both general and special educators have much to share in collaboratively articulating the elements that produce effective educational programs. For more detailed descriptions of classroom-based programs that have been collaboratively developed by general and special educators, see Chapters 5, 6, 7, and 9. In addition, the more recent empirical evidence is detailed in Chapter 1.

THE ETHICAL CONTEXT

Ethical considerations can impel collaborators to respond to a variety of issues. Any time a person differs in some respect (as in ethnic background, race, sex, class, sexual orientation, culture, or special learning needs) and that difference is negatively valued by the majority of others in society, that person can be subject to the effects of bias. Bias in that regard has serious effects on human behavior (Eitzen, 1992; Faludi, 1991; Fineman, McCormick, Carroll, & Smith, 1991; Gibbs, 1992; Kozol, 1991; Rowan, 1990). Although this book was specifically written to assist educators in becoming more effective in teaching learners with special needs and who are at risk for school failure, we encourage collaborating team members to challenge themselves and each other regarding prejudice (attitudes) and discrimination (differen-

TABLE 3.4. Research Outcomes for Cooperative Learning

Cognitive Outcomes	Affective Outcomes
Increased academic achievement	Improved racial and ethnic relationships
Higher retention	Increased self-esteem
Higher levels of thinking (e.g., analytic reasoning)	More positive attitudes about school and subject matter
More varied strategies to solve problems	Increased acceptance of differences, including learners with special needs
Increased use of metacognitive strategies	Increased group membership skills
Increased frequency of new ideas	More frequent helping behaviors

tial treatment). For, as Zastrow and Kirst-Ashman (1991) stated, "Our country has always been racist and ethnocentric. Discrimination continues to have tragic consequences for those who are victims" (p. 549). We need to create teaching/learning environments where adults and learners feel free to share their thoughts and values and can be positively challenged to change negative views so that people's diversity can become understood and valued rather than feared and deplored (Latting, 1990). Learning to acknowledge the effects of our socialization and being willing to change are the first steps toward facilitating equality.

Lilly (1975) and Blankenship and Lilly (1981) described a competency base that calls for specified roles and responsibilities in providing special education within general education classrooms. Reynolds (1977) developed a detailed description of competencies for training classroom teachers at the preservice level. The competencies and responsibilities of all educators must also be considered within the context of ethical practices and protections that should be extended to teachers who learn to implement programs for learners with special needs. Egner (Nevin) and Paolucci (1975) proposed that each teacher develop a personal ethical statement within the individual professional context. In a larger context, however, they noted that some rights may be said to be universal:

- *The right to have support systems.* Teachers must be recognized as individual learners. They have the right to have access to a variety of training options, incentive systems, and released time arrangements.

- *The right to appropriate special education training.* Teachers must develop competence and confidence by directly teaching learners with special needs. They have the right to learn concepts and models that allow them to make effective teaching and learning decisions. They have the right to clarify their values in relation to an advocacy role as well as in the development of a philosophy of teaching that emphasizes what the teacher can do to effect learning. They have the right to include progressively more learners with special needs as long as the instructional outcomes are equivalent to or better than those provided elsewhere.

- *The right to professional discharge of responsibility.* Teachers have the right to participate actively in identifying effective educational programs; planning, evaluating, and redesigning programs on team teaching; and making budget and funding decisions. Teachers have the right to practice affirmative action by publicly specifying who are the learners with special needs to be educated in their classrooms. They have the right to legal protections when they advocate services that their data show are appropriate on behalf of learners with special needs. Finally, they have the right to appropriate recognition of their professional expertise.

Recently, the Council for Exceptional Children (CEC) adopted a common core of knowledge and skills essential for all beginning special education teachers (Swan & Sirvis, 1992), which is based on the CEC Code of Ethics. This ethical code includes a commitment to

- developing the highest educational and quality of life potential of exceptional individuals.

- maintaining a high level of competence and integrity in practicing the profession.

- exercising objective professional judgment in the practice of the profession.

- advancing the knowledge and skills regarding the education of individuals with exceptionalities.

- working within the standards and policies of the profession, upholding and improving where necessary the laws, regulations, and policies for delivery of special education and related services and the practice of the profession.

- avoiding condoning or participating in unethical or illegal acts or violating professional standards. (p. 17)

Beginning special education teachers are expected to be effective in collaborative partnerships with learners, parents, other teachers, school and community personnel, and in working in collaboration with team members. An important skill they are expected to demonstrate is to "collaborate with [classroom] teachers, administrators, and other school personnel about characteristics and needs of students with specific exceptional learning needs" (Swan & Sirvis, 1992, p. 20).

THE SOCIOLOGICAL AND ECOLOGICAL CONTEXT

Bogdan and Knoll (1988) described the ecological perspective to understanding people with disabilities as "psychology informed by sociology" (p. 459). In contrast with laboratory approaches, ecological studies examine people's societal roles, the match between individual and environmental demands, and the interplay of complex forces on individual behaviors. How meaning is ascribed to individuals through labeling and stereotyping and how all aspects of a culture pervade its treatment of individuals with disabilities form the comprehensive context for understanding the sociology of disability. Pernicious and pervasive evidence of handicapism—the prejudicial, discriminatory treatment of individuals with disabilities—can be found at all levels of interaction (interpersonal, community, state, and national) and for all types of human services (judicial, medical, educational, recreational). Even professionals who provide services to people with disabilities can contribute to the perpetuation of handicapism. Constant vigilance must be practiced to change systems, textbooks, assumptions, and practices so as to eradicate or at least reduce the effects of handicapism.

Collaborative models help to empower underrepresented populations by ensuring their views are solicited and acted on. Peck et al. (1989) described an ecological process for implementing the least restrictive environment (LRE) mandate in designing services for students with special education needs in early childhood programs. As they noted:

> Segregated special education programs were not invented, nor have they ever been justified, as a pedagogically superior arrangement for meeting the needs of children. Rather, they have historically represented a socially and politically acceptable response to pressures from parents and other advocates seeking access to services for a traditionally disenfranchised group of children. (p. 296)

In the ecological model described by Peck et al., services are developed within a collaborative framework in which the needs of teachers, parents, administrators, community members, and children are taken into account. Special attention is focused to ensure fair representation of all views (convergent and divergent interests), shared control of influence as well as resources, and public dissemination of all results. Their successes are tempered with an understanding that the LRE principle challenges "closely held cultural assumptions about the worth and appropriate treatment of human beings who have disabilities" and cannot "be resolved by narrowly pedagogical means" (Peck et al., 1989, p. 297).

Other ways to ameliorate the effects of handicapism include changing the administrative and organizational assumptions within which services are developed and implemented. Skrtic (1991) argued that school professionals must make a paradigm shift to organize from a bureaucratic to an adhocratic model. In an interview with Thousand (1990), Skrtic stated, "Professionals mutually adjust their collective skills and knowledge to invent unique, personalized programs for each student" (p. 32). What is needed is a dynamic structure that enables novel services to be crafted to meet unique learner needs. As noted by Skrtic in the interview (Thousand, 1990),

The value of the adhocracy is that it is configured for diversity whereas the professional bureaucracy is configured for homogeneity, and so must remove diversity from the system through means like special education and other pull-out programs. (p. 32)

Collaborative consultation teams are typically organized as an adhocracy. Another form of adhocracy is the *teaching team* (Thousand & Villa, 1990), "an organizational and instructional arrangement of two or more members of the school and greater community who distribute among themselves planning, instructional, and evaluation responsibilities for the same students on a regular basis for an extended period of time" (p. 152). All school personnel are reassigned based on knowledge and skills needed for the learners to achieve progress, including those learners who need intensive instructional support. The change to an adhocracy is facilitated through removal of categorical labels for professionals (e.g., speech therapists and special educators are referred to as teachers) and systematic inservice training of all school personnel in skills, knowledge, and collaborative competencies that assist them to effectively educate learners with educational challenges (see Villa, 1989).

SUMMARY

All participants of a collaborative consultation team need encouragement and support as they develop their personal ethical statements regarding the learners with special needs they serve, expand their special education skills and knowledge bases, and develop new working relationships to ensure the development of the most appropriate educational system. Within the relevant historical, legislative, empirical, and ethical contexts, collaboration among personnel with varied expertise becomes the sine qua non of providing successful services in more normalized environments for learners with special needs. To this end, by mobilizing research evidence and experience from both general and special educators, key elements that produce effective educational programs can be identified.

In Chapter 4, we begin the journey through the stages of the collaborative consultation problem-solving processes. We describe how collaborators gain entry to establish their collaborative interactions and how they establish team goals and responsibilities.

STUDY QUESTIONS

1. What historical factors in the treatment of persons with disabilities (refer to Table 3.1) are evident in how learners with special needs are served in your local setting?

2. What are the six basic legal principles that underlie the Education for All Handicapped Children Act (EHA, Public Law 94-142, now known as IDEA, or Individuals with Disabilities Education Act)?

3. What is meant by the "empirical context" for deciding how learners with special needs should be educated? Why is it important?

4. Explain the ethical context for providing collaborative consultation services.

5. How are the sociological and ecological contexts different from the historical, empirical, legal, and ethical contexts?

REFERENCES

Age v. Bullitt County Public Schools, 673 F.2d 141, 3 Ed. Law Rep. 303 (6th Cir. 1982).

Bergdorf, R. L. (1975). The doctrine of the least restrictive alternative. In R. A. Johnson, R. F. Weatherman, & A. M. Rehman (Eds.), Handicapped youth and the mainstream educator. Vol. 4, Leadership Series in Special Education (pp. 143-155). Minneapolis: University of Minnesota, Audio-Visual Library Service.

Blankenship, C., & Lilly, M. S. (1981). Mainstreaming students with learning and behavior problems. New York: Holt, Rinehart & Winston.

Blatt, B. (1960). Some persistently recurring assumptions concerning the mentally subnormal. Training School Bulletin, 57, 48-59.

Block, J. (Ed.). (1975). Schools, society, and mastery learning. New York: Holt, Rinehart & Winston.

Board of Education of East Windsor Regional School District v. Diamond, 808 F. 2d 987, 36 Ed. Law Rep. 1136 (3d Cir. 1986).

Bogdan, R., & Knoll, J. (1988). The sociology of disability. In E. Meyen & T. Skrtic (Eds.), Exceptional children and youth: An introduction (3rd ed., pp. 449-478). Denver: Love.

Brookover, W., Beamer, L., Efthim, J. H., Hathaway, D., Lezotte, L., Miller, S., Passalacqua, J., & Tornatsky, L. (1982). Creating effective schools: An inservice program for enhancing school learning climate and achievement. Holmes Beach, FL: Learning Publications.

Brown v. Board of Education, 347 U.S. t83 (1954).

Buchholtz v. Iowa Department of Public Instruction, 315 N.W.2d 789, 2 Ed. Law Rep. 848 (Iowa 1982).

Burrello, L., Tracy, M., & Schultz, E. (1973). Special education as experimental education: A new conceptualization. Exceptional Children, 40, 29-34.

Deno, E. (1970). Special education as developmental capital. Exceptional Children, 37, 129-237.

Deno, E. (Ed.). (1972). Instructional alternatives for exceptional children. Reston, VA: Council for Exceptional Children.

Deno, S., & Gross, J. (1982). The Seward-University Project: A cooperative effort to improve school services and university training. In E. Deno (Ed.), Instructional alternatives for exceptional learners (pp. 104-123). Reston, VA: Council for Exceptional Children.

Diana v. State Board of Education, Civil No. c-70, 37RFP (N.D. CA, Jan. 7, 1970 and June 18, 1973).

Dunn, L. (1968). Special education for the mildly handicapped: Is much of it justifiable? Exceptional Children, 35, 5-22.

Edmonds, R. (1979). Some schools work and more can. *Social Play, 9*(5), 28–32.

Egner, A., & Paolucci, P. (1975). For the sake of the children: Some thoughts on the rights of teachers who provide special education within regular classrooms. In A. Rehman, R. Johnson, & R. Weatherman (Eds.), *Handicapped youth and the mainstream educator. Vol. 4, Leadership Series in Special Education* (pp. 29–47). Minneapolis: University of Minnesota, Audio-Visual Library Service.

Eitzen, D. S. (1992). Problem students: The sociocultural roots. *Phi Delta Kappan, 73*, 584–588.

Faludi, S. (1991). *Backlash: The undeclared war against American women.* New York: Crown.

Fineman, H., McCormick, J., Carroll, G., & Smith, V. E. (1991, May 6). The new politics of race. *Newsweek,* pp. 22–26.

Gerlach, K., & Reisberg, L. (1986). *General competencies for Project ConSEPT.* Unpublished document, Pacific Lutheran University, Tacoma, WA.

Gibbs, N. (1992, March 9). The war against feminism. *Time,* pp. 50–54.

Guskey, T. (1985). *Implementing mastery learning.* Belmont, CA: Wadsworth.

Hawkes, K., & Paolucci-Whitcomb, P. (1980). A consultation model: Helping teachers use peer tutoring. *The Pointer, 24*(3), 47–55.

Hersh, R. (1981). *What makes some schools and teachers more effective?* Eugene: University of Oregon.

Hewett, F., & Forness, S. (1977). *Education of exceptional learners* (2nd ed.). Boston: Allyn & Bacon.

Idol, L. (1990). The scientific art of classroom consultation. *Journal of Educational and Psychological Consultation, 1*(1), 3–22.

Idol, L. (1993). *Special educator's consultation handbook* (2nd ed.). Austin, TX: PRO-ED.

Jenkins, J., & Mayhall, W. (1976). Development and evaluation of a resource teacher program. *Exceptional Children, 43*, 21–29.

Johnson, D., & Johnson, R. (1987). *Learning together and alone.* Englewood Cliffs, NJ: Prentice-Hall.

Johnson, D. W., Maruyama, G., Johnson, R., Nelson, D., & Skon L. (1981). Effects of cooperative, competitive, and individualistic goal structures on achievement: A meta-analysis. *Psychological Bulletin, 89*(1), 47–62.

Knight, M., Meyers, H., Hasazi, S., Paolucci-Whitcomb, P., & Nevin, A. (1981). A four-year evaluation of consulting teacher services. *Behavioral Disorders, 6*, 92–100.

Knight, M., Willard, J., Stahlbrand, K., Moore, A., Oaks, D., & Meyers, H. (1981). Impact: Interactive model for professional action and change for teachers. *Journal of Personnel Development, 2*(2), 103–113.

Kozol, J. (1991). *Savage inequalities: Children in America's schools.* New York: Crown.

Larry P. v. Riles, Civil No. c-71-2270, 343F Supp. 1306 (N.D. CA, 1972).

Lates, B. J. (1975). IEP training in a large urban school system. In *Periscope: Inservice and preservice preparation* (pp. 45–49). Reston, VA: Council for Exceptional Children.

Latting, J. K. (1990). Identifying the "isms": Enabling social work students to confront their biases. *Journal of Social Work Education, 26*(1), 36–44.

Lew, M., Mesch, D., & Lates, B. J. (1982). The Simmons College generic consulting teacher program: A program description and data-based application. *Teacher Education and Special Education, 5*(2), 11–16.

Lilly, M. S. (1970). Special education: A teapot in a tempest. *Exceptional Children, 37*, 43–49.

Lilly, M. S. (1971). A training-based model for special education. *Exceptional Children, 37*, 745–749.

Lilly, M. S. (1975). Special education in transition: A competency base for classroom educators. In A. Johnson, R. Weatherman, & A. Rehman (Eds.), *Handicapped youth and the mainstream educator. Vol. 4, Leadership Series in Special Education* (pp. 48–66). Minneapolis: University of Minnesota, Audio-Visual Library Service.

Mainer, P., Stahlbrand, C., Knight, M., Paolucci-Whitcomb, P., & Nevin, A. (1982). *The effects of self-recording on a paraprofessional's administration of contingent positive feedback and the related effects on eighth grade students in a small group tutorial setting* (Master's research study). Department of Special Education, Social Work and Social Services, College of Education and Social Services, University of Vermont, Burlington.

Miller, T., & Sabatino, D. (1978). An evaluation of the teacher consultant model as an approach to mainstreaming. *Exceptional Children, 45,* 86–91.

Mills v. Board of Education of the District of Columbia, 348 F. Supp. 866 (D.D.C., 1972).

Nelson, M., & Stevens, K. B. (1981). An accountable consultation model for mainstreaming behaviorally disordered children. *Behavior Disorders, 6,* 82–91.

Osborne, A. (1992). Legal standards for an appropriate education in the post-Rowley era. *Exceptional Children, 58,* 488–494.

PARC v. The Commonwealth of Pennsylvania, 344 F. Supp. 1257 (E.D. PA, 1971).

Paolucci-Whitcomb, P., & Nevin, A. (1985). Preparing consulting teachers through a collaborative approach between university faculty and field-based consulting teachers. *Teacher Education and Special Education, 8*(3), 132–143.

Peck, C., Richarz, S., Peterson, K., Hayden, L., Mineur, L., & Wandschneider, M. (1989). An ecological process model for implementing the least restrictive environment mandate in early childhood programs. In R. Gaylord-Ross (Ed.), *Integration strategies for students with handicaps* (pp. 281–298). Baltimore: Brookes.

Polk v. Central. Susquehanna Intermediate Unit 16, 853 F. 2d 171, 48 Ed. Law Rep. 336 (3d Cir. 1988).

Ramirez v. Brown, 9 c.3d 199, 107 Ca.R. 137, J07 P.dd 1345, 1353 (1973).

Rettig v. Kent City School District, 539 F. Supp. 768, 4 Ed. Law Rep. 1083 (N.D. Ohio, 1981), aff'd inpt. vac'd and rem'd i pt. 720 F. 2d 463, 14 Ed. Law Rep. 445 (6th Cir. 1983), on rem'd (unpublished opinion), rev'd 788 F. 2d 328, 31 Ed. Law Rep. 759 (6th Cir. 1986), cert. den'd 106 S. Ct 3297, 33 Ed. Law Rep. 35 (1986).

Reynolds, M. (1962). A framework for considering some issues in special education. *Exceptional Children, 28,* 267–270.

Reynolds, M. (1977). The instructional cascade. In A. Rehman & T. Riggen (Eds.), *The least restrictive alternative. Vol. 4, Leadership Series in Special Education* (pp. 37–48). Minneapolis: University of Minnesota, Audio-Visual Library Service.

Rowan, C. T. (1990, December). Racism: It's an easy thing to be against, but what should you be for? *USA Weekend* pp. 4–5.

Sharan, S. (1980). Cooperative learning in small groups: Recent methods and effects on achievement, attitudes, and ethnic relations. *Review of Educational Research, 50*(2), 241–271.

Shelton v. Tucker, 364 U.S. 479, 483 (1960).

Skrtic, T. (1991). *Beyond special education.* Denver: Love.

Slavin, R. (1984). Review of cooperative learning research. *Review of Educational Research, 50*(2), 315–342.

Smith v. Sampson, 349 F. Supp. 368 (DN.H., 1972).

Springdale School District v. Grace, 656 F. Supp. 300 (8th Cir. 1981), vac'd and rem'd 102 S. Ct. 3504 (1982), on rem'd 693 F. 2d 41, 7 Ed. Law Rep. 509 (8th Cir. 1982).

Swan, W., & Sirvis, B. (1992). The CEC common core of knowledge and skills essential for all beginning special education teachers. *Teaching Exceptional Children*, Fall, 16–20.

Tharp, R. (1975). The triadic model of consultation. In C. Parker (Ed.), *Psychological consultation in the schools: Helping teachers meet special needs* (pp. 133–151). Reston, VA: Council for Exceptional Children.

Tharp, R. G., & Wetzel, R. J. (1969). *Behavior modification in the natural environment*. New York: Academic Press.

Thousand, J. (1990). Organizational perspectives on teacher education and renewal: A conversation with Tom Skrtic. *Teacher Education and Special Education*, *13*, 30–35.

Thousand, J., & Villa, R. (1990). Sharing expertise and responsibilities through teaching teams. In W. Stainback & S. Stainback (Eds.), *Support networks for inclusive schooling: Interdependent integrated education* (pp. 151–166). Baltimore: Brookes.

U.S. House Committee on Education and Labor. (1986). *Education of the Handicapped Act Amendments of 1986* (H. Rpt. 99-860). Washington, DC: U.S. Government Printing Office.

P.L. *94-142: The Education for All Handicapped Children Act*. (Federal Register). (1975). United States Department of Education. Washington, DC: U.S. Government Printing Office.

P.L. *99-457* (Federal Register). (1986). United States Department of Education. Washington, DC: U.S. Government Printing Office.

Villa, R. (1989). Model public school inservice programs: Do they exist? *Teacher Education and Special Education*, *12*, 173–176.

Weintraub, F., & Abeson, A. (1974). New education policies for the handicapped: The quiet revolution. *Phi Delta Kappan*, *58*(8), 526–529.

West, J. F., & Brown, P. (1987). State departments' of education policies on consultation in special education: The state of the states. *Remedial and Special Education*, *8*(3), 45–51.

Wolfensberger, W. (1972). *Normalization: The principle of normalization in human service*. Toronto, Canada: National Institute on Mental Rehabilitation.

Zastrow, C., & Kirst-Ashman, K. (1991). *Understanding human behavior and the social environment*. Chicago: Nelson-Hall.

CHAPTER 4

Gaining Entry and Establishing Team Goals

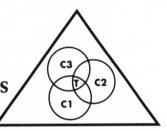

OVER TIME AND IN DIFFERENT disciplines, experts in school consultation have identified this stage as the Entry/Goal stage and as being a first and essential step in the consultation process (e.g., Idol, Paolucci-Whitcomb, & Nevin, 1986; Kurpius & Robinson, 1978; Sarason, 1982; also see Chapter 1 of this book). In the Collaborative Consultation Model, the primary purpose of the Entry/ Goal stage is "to develop parity between special and classroom teachers, resulting in shared ownership of learning and management problems of exceptional and nonachieving students participating in general classroom instruction" (West, Idol, & Cannon, 1989, p. 34). In using a collaborative problem-solving process, the primary purpose of this first stage is for team members to achieve acceptance of all group members and to establish initial rapport among team members. Collaborators accomplish this task by defining and agreeing on what their respective roles and responsibilities are going to be throughout the collaborative consultation process.

In this chapter we explain (a) how collaborators gain entry to the collaborative consultation process and, thus, gain acceptance of one another and (b) how they go about establishing goals for the team. The chapter is organized into three major sections (Principles of Problem Identification, Gaining Entry and Acceptance, and Establishing Team Goals). In each of the latter two sections is a rationale followed by descriptions of specific techniques for accomplishing entry and acceptance as well as specific methods for establishing team goals. Germane to these sections is a set of principles for facilitating the accomplishment of this first stage in the collaborative problem-solving process.

PRINCIPLES OF PROBLEM IDENTIFICATION

The process of gaining entry and establishing team goals requires the establishment of relationships in which all parties feel comfortable in expressing their ideas and feelings without fear of adverse judgments or rejection (Blake & Mouton, 1976). The generic principles of Collaborative Consultation described in Chapter 2 are especially important in facilitating this stage. Beyond that, there are at least 10 specific principles that can be employed to help collaborators gain acceptance and establish team goals. They are as follows:

1. *Treat others with respect.* Collaborators need to treat each other with respect (Corey & Corey, 1992; West et al., 1989). This is important throughout the consultation process, but it is especially important in gaining entry and building team goals. Collaborators can model respect for other people by listening to them, by sharing information, by engaging in joint problem solving, by maintaining confidentiality, and by treating one another in a mannerly fashion. Collaborators must listen to descriptions about what kind of special assistance other team members think they want and need. Likewise, collaborators need to explain what they think their own special skills are so that, together, they can determine how they can best work together to provide educational services. It is especially important that collaborators show respect for each other by keeping team information confidential (Brill, 1990; Lippitt & Lippitt, 1986; Shulman, 1984). Collaborators should never discuss other members of the team unless they have specific permission to do so.

2. *Share relevant information.* Collaborators need to share information about their own skills in assessment, instruction, and evaluation so they will be able to determine when and how to request one another's assistance (Friend & Cook, 1992; West et al., 1989). Brief, clear descriptions of assessment, instruction, and evaluation instruments and techniques will enable collaborators to gain some idea about how they might use each other's assistance (Idol, 1993; Lippitt & Lippitt, 1986; Montgomery, 1980; West et al., 1989).

3. *Use appropriate language.* Appropriate language increases the probability of shared meaning (Friend & Cook, 1992; Idol, 1993; Johnson, 1986; Verderber, 1981). Collaborators should be able to describe their program goals and special skills in a language that is familiar to other school personnel. Occasionally, it is appropriate for collaborators to use a new term because it is the most effective and accurate way of describing a behavior, procedure, or material. When that happens, it is important for the sender to explain the new term and the purpose for its use so that it can quickly become shared information and therefore a part of all of the team members' repertoire.

4. *Listen to others.* Collaborators can use appropriate listening skills in at least two ways: First, they can model passive listening by just keeping quiet and really listening to what others say. Second, they can use active listening by providing feedback on what they think others have said. This feedback process provides others with the opportunity either to confirm that they heard correctly or to correct any inaccuracy in the interpretation of their original message (Conoley & Conoley, 1982; Gordon, 1980; Johnson, 1986, 1990; Montgomery,

1980; Verderber, 1981). West et al. (1989, Module 14) have offered training opportunities on six specific appropriate listening and responding skills (acknowledging, paraphrasing, reflecting, clarifying, elaborating, and summarizing).

5. *Model the use of interview skills.* Collaborators need to use specific interviewing skills so that they can gain information from others, share information, express and explore their feelings about working together, solve problems, and plan appropriate future action on behalf of learners. The interview process provides an opportunity for collaborators to model purposeful and directed verbal interactions that can help to increase a shared information base and a willingness to work with others. Later, classroom teachers can use those same skills when working with learners in their own classrooms (Benjamin, 1987; Molyneaux & Lane, 1982; West et al., 1989).

6. *Demonstrate a willingness to learn from others.* Collaborators must demonstrate a willingness to learn from others if they want others to learn from them (Montgomery, 1980). Collaborative Consultation is a problem-solving process in which the members have many chances to learn and teach one another. All members have specific, yet different, skills and knowledge to share. Some collaborators have knowledge about special education assessment and intervention techniques, while others have specific knowledge about curriculum, child development, content area specifics, and so on. Thus, collaborative consultation team members have different but equally valued knowledge and skills that need to be shared for the benefit of all learners (Gordon, 1980; Lippitt & Lippitt, 1986).

7. *Give and receive feedback.* Giving and receiving feedback is of vital importance to the change process (Conoley & Conoley, 1982; Friend & Cook, 1992; Hersey & Blanchard, 1988; Idol, 1993; Johnson, 1986; Verderber, 1981; West et al., 1989, Module 21). It is often helpful to identify at least two areas that deserve positive feedback: one area that needs improvement, and then one or two areas of strength. Feedback should be specific, immediate, and appropriate. Collaborators should engage in both giving and receiving feedback. One strategy for doing this is to say, "I think I did those two things very well, but it seems as if I need to improve here. However, it does make me feel good to know that identifying and adapting intervention techniques are two of my major strengths. How do you think I could improve those two techniques?" This situation provides an opportunity for collaborators to model both the process of self-evaluation and the process of requesting feedback. Collaborators also model the technique of requesting a perception check by obtaining their

team members' view of their own skills. Collaborators can give feedback by responding to others' views of their own strengths and areas in need of improvement. A major concept that is built through this process is that the focus of change is on behaviors, not people. There are no good or bad people or techniques but rather areas of strength or effectiveness and areas that need improvement. Patience, mutual respect, and shared skills can, however, make the process of giving and receiving feedback easier and more enjoyable.

8. *Give others credit for their ideas and accomplishments.* Collaborative Consultation is a shared process of responsibilities and rewards (West et al., 1989, Module 22). Collaborators can model the practice of giving others the credit for their ideas and accomplishments. That includes providing credit for ideas in written materials, as well. This practice increases the probability that collaborators will share their knowledge and rewards, thus providing increased strength and willingness to identify and solve more problems.

9. *Manage conflict and confrontation appropriately.* Conflicts or disagreements are inevitable in human relationships. The goal is for collaborators to model the appropriate use of confrontation skills so that a no-lose method of resolving conflict is utilized. When appropriate confrontation skills are used, both parties express their points of view and listen to each other. They use "I" messages to express their needs, feelings, and concerns, instead of blaming the other person for their conflicts. Finally, they search together for creative and mutually acceptable solutions (Friend & Cook, 1992; Gordon, 1980; Johnson, 1986, 1990; West et al., 1989, Module 23).

10. *Adapt situational leadership to Collaborative Consultation.* Collaborators need to determine the attitude and skill levels of the people they will be collaborating with, so that they can adjust their collaboration styles to match the maturity level of each member of the group. Maturity levels should be identified by determining each member's willingness, as well as skills, and knowledge to provide special or remedial services. The amount of special education coursework the collaborator has completed and the number of years the collaborator provided effective services are two possible indicators of their willingness and ability to work with learners with special needs. The concept of situational collaboration has been adapted from situational leadership, which was described in Chapter 1 and by Hersey and Blanchard (1988) and Toseland and Rivas (1984).

Following the general guidelines for situational leadership outlined in Chapter 2, when collaborators are inexperienced and insecure or do not have the requisite skills or attitudes, collaborators should use Leadership Style 1 (telling) by providing specific information, or even modeling the task of specifying objectives, until it is demonstrated accurately. In this process, collaborators should closely supervise one another's performance. When collaborators are inexperienced but have a positive attitude about specifying objectives, they should use Leadership Style 2 (selling), providing the necessary information and an opportunity for clarification and accurate demonstration. Only intermittent supervision is required at this time. When collaborators have demonstrated that they have the necessary skills but are insecure or have less than a positive attitude about being able to successfully complete the task of specifying objectives, Leadership Style 3 (participating) should be utilized. Here, collaborators mutually share ideas and help facilitate progress. Finally, when the collaborators have demonstrated that they have all of the necessary skills and a positive attitude toward effectively, efficiently, and affectively specifying instructional objectives, collaborators should use Leadership Style 4 (delegating). At this point, collaborators can rely on the skills and positive attitudes of the group to complete the task successfully.

When situational leadership is accurately and appropriately adapted for situational collaboration, one or more members of the collaborating group *do* serve as the experts for that particular task. In this case some of the collaborators may have had more training or experience in the task at hand. This is different from the expert consultant model where one person remains in the expert role throughout the consultation process. With the adaptation of situational leadership to collaboration, any members of the collaborating group may move in and out of the leadership position based on their expertise and the group's task and needs. The person with the most proficient knowledge serves as the group's leader for each particular task. This is an example of equity and parity among the group members. The goal is to enable and empower *all* group members to become highly proficient at all of the group's tasks and to accurately adapt situational leadership to the collaborative consultation process until Leadership Style 4 (delegating) becomes the most frequently needed style.

Sharing Information

Collaborators need to emphasize the importance of goals and objectives. They also need to take the time to determine what others, with whom they must work, think about goals and objectives. Collaborators can identify books, articles, and audiovisual materials to help clarify the importance of goals and objectives as well as how to specify them. Parents, administrators, and other teachers can often be very helpful in discussing the importance of goals and objectives and in providing examples or models of objectives that have been useful for their learners.

Educators need and deserve the right to debate the pros and cons of various educational issues, including the issue of specifying goals and objectives. Through the use of coursework, research, site visits, and discussions, educators can begin to acquire the need and desire to specify instructional objectives; such acquisition is worth a reasonable waiting period. All of the collaborators—the classroom teacher, special educator, building administrator, other support staff, and the parents of learners with special needs—must determine together what a reasonable waiting period should be. It should never be beyond an academic year; typically, it is 1 to 2 months. In this period, agreed-on activities and timelines must be delineated so that information sharing and decision making can be facilitated in an ongoing manner among the concerned parties.

GAINING ENTRY AND ACCEPTANCE

The first part of the initial stage in the collaborative problem-solving process is to gain entry and acceptance. People who use the Collaborative Consultation Model to serve learners with special needs rely heavily on interactive and cooperative teaming among school professionals at many different levels—among the collaborative team members themselves (micro level), among principals and other school staff at the building level (mezzo level), and among administrators and other educators at the district level (macro level)—that impacts on the policies and practices within the school system itself (also macro level). Certainly, the most important level for gaining entry and acceptance is among members of the collaborative team. But, it is also important to gain entry and acceptance at the building and district levels among key decision makers, policymakers, and school/community leaders.

In essence, entry and acceptance can be accomplished at any level: macro, mezzo, and/or micro. An exploration of various techniques used to accomplish the goal of gaining entry and acceptance is described next.

There are several techniques used to increase and improve entry and acceptance at macro, mezzo, and micro levels. The purposes of these collaborative consultation techniques are (a) to facilitate mutual acceptance among collaborators, (b) to establish clear and open lines of communication, and (c) to develop mutual understanding and agreement about how people work together. The techniques described in this section are:

1. Examining attitudes and beliefs of staff toward learners with special needs, particularly those who qualify for special education services

2. Reviewing and updating district materials

3. Participating in district meetings

4. Clarifying and defining the roles and responsibilities of each collaborator

5. Providing time for collaboration

6. Using Quality Circle problem-solving processes

7. Engaging parents and learners as partners

8. Planning and providing staff development opportunities for all involved staff

9. Disseminating program information

Examining Attitudes and Beliefs About Learners with Special Needs

Among the most important, yet often unspoken, issues influencing collaborative efforts are the attitudes and beliefs the individual collaborators have toward persons with special needs. Many people seem reluctant to discuss and share their attitudes and beliefs about what they think is appropriate or inappropriate regarding the inclusion of learners eligible for special education services. Often, as a result of this reluctance, perceptions sometimes become distorted, with people believing half-truths and falsities about one another. For example, consulting teachers have reported that classroom teachers do not want learners with special education needs in their classrooms (Idol-Maestas & Ritter, 1985).

In a nationwide survey of experts in school consultation (West & Cannon, 1988), a Delphi panel reached consensus on six essential competencies for Collaborative Consultation that relate to this issue. They concluded that collaborators should:

(1) facilitate equal learning opportunities by showing respect for individual differences in physical appearance, race, sex, handicap, ethnicity, religion, socioeconomic status, or ability.

(2) advocate for services that accommodate the educational, social, and vocational needs of all [learners], with and without handicaps.

(3) encourage implementation of laws and regulations designed to provide appropriate education for all [learners] with handicaps.

(4) use principles of the least restrictive environment in all decisions regarding [learners] with handicaps.

(5) modify myths, beliefs, and attitudes that impede successful social and educational integration of [learners] with handicaps into the least restrictive environment.

(6) recognize, respect, and respond appropriately to the effects of personal values and belief systems of self and others in the consultation process. (p. 60)

Specific modules for preparation and practice in these skills can be found in West et al. (1989, Modules 38–43).

In our experience we have found it to be very important for collaborative teams to reach consensus concerning what is appropriate educational programming for each individual learner in question, rather than creating general statements and policies that would automatically apply to an entire classification of learners.

Second, we have found it to be especially helpful for collaborators to distinguish between *social* inclusion and *academic* inclusion. In many cases, the disparity in belief and opinion is because one collaborator perceives that the discussion is about including a learner in a normal social environment with same-age peers, whereas another might perceive that the discussion concerns whether to include a particular learner in the academic tasks and activities in the general classroom. Again, such decisions must be made on an individual learner basis. It is essential that team members share their perceptions and define collaboratively what is the *most educationally enhancing environment* (see Idol, 1993; Idol & West, 1993) for the individual learner with special needs.

Reviewing and Updating District Materials

In the past, many professionals have emphasized the need for collaborators to review written information (Alpert, 1977; Bagley, 1977; Blake & Mouton, 1976; Lippitt & Lippitt, 1986; McKenzie, 1976). Often, reference manuals are available that explain the school district philosophy and provide background information about the various administrators, specialists, teachers, and learners within each school in the district. Such manuals usually include brief descriptions about the community and information about curriculum materials. Such background information can help collaborators gain important insights about school organizations. The information can be used to develop questions so administrators and other collaborators can be given the chance to correct or update the information. Collaborators demonstrate that they care about their districts by reading such information and then building on it through discussions with school personnel. Reviewing the latest annual reports and minutes of the previous year's faculty meetings helps to provide initial entry information that collaborators can use during their participation in district meetings.

Participating in District Meetings

By participating in school board and administrative-level meetings, collaborators can learn more about their work situations at the district (macro) level (Bagley, 1977; Carlson & Ackerman, 1991; Egner (Nevin) & Paolucci, 1975; McKenzie, 1976; Villa, Thousand, Stainback, & Stainback, 1992). These meetings provide opportunities to hear about administrators' expectations and styles of interacting; they also give collaborators a chance to discuss their program goals, planned activities, and evaluation processes. This initial sharing of ideas and expectations provides a chance to share and receive information and to negotiate discrepancies in expectations and policies as well as procedures. It is important for collaborators to be honest and open about their philosophies, expectations, and procedures. It is equally important that collaborators demonstrate their willingness and ability to adjust their expectations and procedures so that there is an initial, appropriate match and agreement with other collaborators with whom they must work. Collaborators who respect the entry level of district personnel are the ones who seem to gain acceptance and are encouraged to stay and work in those districts for the 5 to 7 years that it may take to facilitate effective change. Since there is typically a structured hierarchy in school districts, it is helpful for collaborators to meet and work with superintendents first, principals second, and teachers third. When collaborators follow that sequence, administrators are able to provide important information and to use their position power in positive ways to facilitate the acceptance of collaborative consultation processes.

Major outcomes of participation in district meetings are shared understandings of how the collaborators' philosophy of learning fits the district philosophy, which learners will be eligible for special services, how many learners will be served, which teaching/learning procedures may be utilized, and how the collaborative consultation services will be evaluated. It is also important to establish how and when each administrator wishes to receive progress reports from each collaborative consultation team (see Chapter 3).

When initiating the Collaborative Consultation Model in schools, it is helpful to have monthly progress meetings with superintendents and principals during the first year; after that, quarterly meetings may be sufficient. Administrators have expressed appreciation for one-page summary reports that show them at a glance how things are going. They seem to respond more positively when collaborators deliver the reports personally and spend 15 to 30 minutes discussing them. In turn, such discussions provide opportunities for collaborators to express positive accomplishments, brainstorm solutions to problems, and gain feedback from the administrator.

Administrators seem to appreciate that collaborators care about students and teachers and that they rely on oral and written data to help them make decisions about how best to work with teachers on behalf of their students. In our experience, when collaborators respect and request the creative assistance of administrators, they are seldom disappointed.

Clarifying Roles and Responsibilities

An essential part of establishing entry in collaborative relationships and creating a viable level of acceptance among all team members is to define the roles and responsibilities the individual collaborators will have in the proposed project. In the consultation literature this is commonly known as an integral part of the Entry/Goal stage.

Developing informal relationships prior to working together formally is a natural and necessary part of this process. For example, during this stage collaborators might agree that they will use a particular type of service delivery system for learners with special needs (see Idol & West, 1991). A collaborative team might decide to use a consulting teacher model with a special education teacher serving as a collaborative consultant to a classroom teacher who has some learners with special needs enrolled in the program. They would clarify that the classroom teacher would work directly with the learners and the consulting teacher and the classroom teacher would plan collaboratively the program of instruction and classroom management procedures.

Or, as another example, the team may decide to use cooperative teaching (Bauwens, Hourcade, & Friend, 1989) with the special education teacher joining the classroom teacher to collaboratively define, plan, and implement the instructional and child management program. Another example is that the classroom teacher might decide to take the problem to a teacher assistance team (comprising classroom and specialty area teachers) who would work together to plan and define the program, which the classroom teacher could implement.

A different example is when classroom teachers have had no formal preparation or experience in working with learners with special needs and need more relationship support and technical assistance from their collaborative teammates, especially at the beginning of a project. Here, the adaptation of situational leadership (Hersey & Blanchard, 1988) to situational collaboration may be helpful. Each collaborator must be encouraged to express his or her individual needs for support. These requests should be respected and responded to with the intention of facilitating each team member's ability and willingness to become an independent functioning member of the team through the participatory process.

There are many options for how to provide quality services to learners with special needs (e.g., see topical issues of *Remedial and Special Education*, Volume 10, Issue 6, 1989; Volume 11, Issue 1, 1990). For effective collaborative problem solving, the collaborators must reach agreement as to what their roles and responsibilities will be, making certain there is consistency and clarity among all collaborators. Through the process of defining roles and responsibilities, collaborators may find that written job descriptions for the school organization are obsolete, need to be updated, or need to be created.

Providing written descriptions of various types of roles to all school staff facilitates people exploring various options to solve a problem, rather than relying on the status quo or choosing more restrictive educational programs for certain learners with special needs simply because that is the way it has always been done.

Providing Time for Collaboration

Many educators identify the major barrier to collaboration as being lack of sufficient time to meet. In fact, consulting teachers report it to be the single most important barrier to serving as a school consultant (Idol-Maestas & Ritter, 1985). Time is a very important systems variable (at both macro and mezzo levels) that needs to be provided. In our experience we have found that most efforts to seek and provide sufficient meeting time evolve at the building (mezzo) level, in situations where the school principal supports the collaborative program.

The first aspect of time provision is having time for the school staff at large to have sufficient opportunity to consult and collaborate with support staff and other classroom teachers. West and Idol (1990) reported several different solutions for time release that they have observed in their field visits to school-based collaborative teams. They include:

(a) regularly bring large groups of [learners] together for special types of school experiences (e.g., guest speakers, films, plays) with fewer staff supervising;

(b) having the principal or other support staff/supervisor teach a period a day on a regularly scheduled basis;

(c) when [learners] are working on the same independent assignment or study activity, arranging for them to be clustered together in large groups (e.g., in the multipurpose room or library);

(d) hiring a permanent [rotating] substitute or two part-time substitutes for the same half-day (this may be done at no cost to the school district by business community school adopters);

(e) utilizing aides or volunteers to guide or supervise groups/classes of [learners] at class-changing time, lunch or recess, or music or physical education classes;

(f) utilizing volunteers (e.g., parents, grandparents, community business leaders, retired teachers);

(g) the principal assigning specific time each week for staff collaboration only (documentation required);

(h) altering the school day to provide staff collaboration time without [learners] (e.g., last Friday afternoon in each month);

(i) utilizing student teachers;

(j) the principal setting aside one day per grading period as "collaboration day" (no other activities can be substituted on this day);

(k) the faculty voting to extend their instructional day 2 days per week for 20 minutes to provide a collaboration period for staff (days can be staggered as well as time periods each day of the week to free staff on different days/times). (pp. 29–30)

Of course, West and Idol specified that none of these strategies will work successfully in every situation, nor are they needed in all. Each school faculty devises the options that work best for them, and that is how the above list has evolved.

A second aspect of time provision is having time for any support staff who are providing collaborative consultation time to be allocated to classroom teachers. Idol (1988) described six scheduling options for consulting teachers. Briefly, they are:

(a) using a 50/50 split in time between consulting and resource teaching within each school day;

(b) rotating the days and times of day when a collaborative consultant is available;

(c) assigning a collaborative consultant to selected full days per week, such as on Tuesdays and Thursdays;

(d) assigning a collaborative consultant to one classroom teacher (e.g., for language or mathematics class) per school term (found to be especially effective in the middle and secondary schools);

(e) assigning a collaborative consultant to a particular curricular division or unit in the school (found to be effective in middle and secondary schools);

(f) selecting two or three, high-need courses, across departments, that have large numbers of learners with special needs or at risk for school failure (primarily used at the middle and secondary levels). (pp. 55–56)

Again, these are only possible options, and time scheduling for consulting collaborators should be determined in each individual school at the mezzo level.

At the macro level, Whittaker (1992) described how a systemwide adoption of a collaborative consultation program is a necessary prerequisite for change. Whittaker reminded us that often establishing the need for consultation is the responsibility of the practitioner. Then, she says a dilemma occurs. Demonstrating the need for such a program frequently requires extending the normal workday. Such job expansion without job restructuring can result in teacher frustration and eventual burnout for the practitioner. Conscientious educators who try to "do it all" without job restructuring send an implicit message to administrators that changes in the job or the environment in which to do their jobs are basically unnecessary. The additional work can be done without providing more time to do it. Whittaker outlined some strategies for developing a systemwide collaborative program that includes the following: Enlist administrative support, form a collaborative consultation committee, use existing groups and vehicles, and establish a communication network.

Using Quality Circle Problem-Solving Processes

Some collaborators have adapted the Quality Circle (QC) problem-solving process to address long-term problems that need consistent attention. The

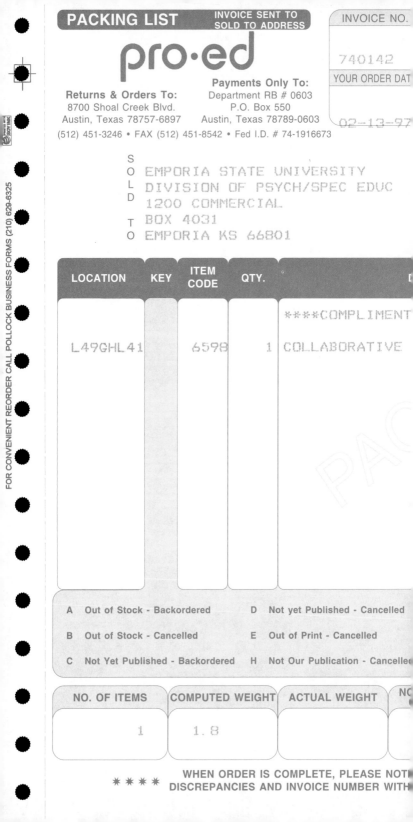

PACKING LIST   INVOICE SENT TO SOLD TO ADDRESS

pro·ed

INVOICE NO.	
	740142
YOUR ORDER DAT	
	02-13-97

Returns & Orders To:
8700 Shoal Creek Blvd.
Austin, Texas 78757-6897

Payments Only To:
Department RB # 0603
P.O. Box 550
Austin, Texas 78789-0603

(512) 451-3246 • FAX (512) 451-8542 • Fed I.D. # 74-1916673

S
O EMPORIA STATE UNIVERSITY
L DIVISION OF PSYCH/SPEC EDUC
D 1200 COMMERCIAL
T BOX 4031
O EMPORIA KS 66801

LOCATION	KEY	ITEM CODE	QTY.	D
				****COMPLIMENT
L49GHL41		6598	1	COLLABORATIVE

A   Out of Stock - Backordered   D   Not yet Published - Cancelled

B   Out of Stock - Cancelled   E   Out of Print - Cancelled

C   Not Yet Published - Backordered   H   Not Our Publication - Cancelled

NO. OF ITEMS	COMPUTED WEIGHT	ACTUAL WEIGHT	NO
1	1.8		

****   WHEN ORDER IS COMPLETE, PLEASE NOT
DISCREPANCIES AND INVOICE NUMBER WITH

FOR CONVENIENT REORDER CALL POLLOCK BUSINESS FORMS (210) 628-6325

TE	CUSTOMER NO.	YOUR PURCHASE ORDER NO.	
97	48649		
D VIA	SPECIAL INSTRUCTIONS/COMMENTS		PAGE
			1

S
H EMPORIA STATE UNIVERSITY
I DORIS COLE
P DIVISION OF PSYCH/SPEC EDUC
T 1200 COMMERCIAL
O BOX 4031
   EMPORIA KS 66801

	NET UNIT PRICE		NET AMOUNT
/****			
ATION (2E)	38.00	100	0.00

	SUB TOTAL	0.00
AYS; PAYABLE TO **PRO·ED**	SALES TAX	0.00
JNDS; ALL PRODUCTS	SHIPPING/HANDLING	0.00
30-DAY APPROVAL;	PAYMENT/CREDIT	0.00
SHIPPING ERRORS WITHIN	**AMOUNT DUE** ▶	0.00
IF CREDIT IS EXPECTED.		

NG S	PICKED BY	CHECKED BY	PACKED BY
	BH		

USINESS OFFICE. REPORT ANY SHIPPING
OF INVOICE DATE IF CREDIT IS EXPECTED.   ****

QC process provides a specifically structured way for people to collaborate by ensuring that everyone has opportunities to voice his or her opinions and thoughts regarding organizational improvements.

The QC process is one problem-solving technique that has been used in a variety of settings to help facilitate improvements at the mezzo and macro levels. This technique was first used in the business industry (Dewar, 1979; Gryna, 1981; Ingle, 1982; Ouchi, 1981; Pascale, 1981). It has also been adapted and utilized in human services (Campbell & Hatfield, 1982; Geldback, Klein, & Moore, 1981; Hatfield, 1982; Kahn, 1988; Middleman, 1984; Parness, 1982) and education (Bonner, 1982; Chase, 1983; Lindner, 1984; O'Hanlon, 1983).

The QC process consists of groups of people, from the same work area, who voluntarily meet to work as a team to identify and solve work-related problems. QC participants share their varied values, knowledge, and skills so that their collective expertise is greater than that of any one of the individuals. QC participants usually meet about 1 hour per week during the regular workday. Time is used to provide progress information to continually identify and work on problems.

The majority of organizations that have been successful in implementing the QC process have ensured that participation is voluntary. The number of persons that participate in QC teams range from two to 20; however, the most functional size seems to be about eight. Usually, people from one department start using the QC process and, as enthusiasm increases, more and more members get involved. Sometimes the people from entire organizations adopt this problem-solving process. Commitment to stay with one QC team from problem identification through solution implementation is encouraged so that members will have enough information to make informed decisions about future participation. (School applications of QC can be found in the November 1992 issue of *Educational Leadership*.)

There are usually at least four levels of personnel involved in the QC process: the circle members, a leader, a facilitator, and a steering committee. The leader is often the group's natural supervisor. QC members are expected to share their particular expertise. As a function of working on QC teams, they have on-the-job opportunities to increase their technical, interpersonal communication, and conceptual skills (having an understanding regarding the ecology of the organization). QC leaders provide direction and encouragement but must take turns just like other members during meetings. All members including the leader have only one vote when it comes to decision making. QC facilitators assist leaders by providing administrative support, keeping records, coordinating outside participation, and attending circle presentations. QC facilitators are important, higher level administrative support persons who provide assistance on request; they are more observers than participants.

A QC steering committee can be composed of representatives from all units or departments of an organization. Members are responsible for establishing objectives and roles, providing guidance and support, assisting with problems when requested, attending QC presentations, and helping to develop plans, budgets, and progress reports related to QC functions.

Certainly, various cautions must be considered by collaborators when implementing a QC program: (a) Responsible expectations need to be established, (b) training and commitment need to be provided at all levels, (c) implementation guidelines need to be developed to provide a balance of structure and flexibility, and (d) an evaluation system needs to be generated so that both formative and summative evaluation data can be used.

While QCs are by no means the only structured process for facilitating organizational change, they do provide a voice for all members of an organization. This is a specific type of problem-solving method that encourages the growth of its members through cooperation, collaboration, and shared responsibilities.

Engaging Parents and Learners as Partners

Collaborators should include parents of learners with special needs in the problem-solving process. In our opinion, if a child is having sufficient difficulties in the general classroom to warrant either (a) referral to any collaborative problem-solving group such as child study teams or (b) consideration of using the Collaborative Consultation Model as a means of providing an appropriate education, then parents should be informed and included in decision making.

An important case in point is an instance where prereferral consultation teams in San Diego City Schools were found in violation of a regulation regarding parental consent (Section 104.36) in Section 504 of the Rehabilitation Act of 1973 (see West, 1989). In this school system, site consultation teams (SCT) identified and provided intervention for learners experiencing one or more of a wide range of problems: education, health-related, psychological, social, or emotional. SCT members might include, in addition to the classroom teacher, the school psychologist, resource teacher, nurse, principal, counselor, and so on.

In brief, the SCT process worked like this. First, a learner was referred to the SCT by a parent, teacher, or other staff member. Next, the referring person completed a form providing basic information about the learner and a checklist to indicate all factors that described the difficulties the learner was experiencing. Third, the SCT coordinator gathered additional pertinent information from the learner's existing records (e.g., family history, academic and health history, academic skills test scores, other test scores, and history of parent contacts). This information was circulated among team members designated to participate in the SCT. The SCT did not conduct any testing. Their problem analysis and subsequent intervention plan to address the problem(s) identified were based on a review of existing student records.

The San Diego County Coalition for Learning Differences filed a formal complaint with the Federal Office of Civil Rights alleging that the SCT process was in violation. Following a districtwide investigation, the Office of Civil Rights found wide variability within the school district with regard to parental notification and opportunities for involvement in the SCT process. District decision makers believed that full due process rights were not required for SCT action until an actual special education evaluation was to be conducted by an IEP team. The final conclusion (Education for the Handicapped Law Report 353.238) was that (a) a prescreening process does constitute an evaluation process, (b) standards and procedures must be established for using such a process, and (c) parents must be provided with full procedural safeguards during the process.

An important element of using a collaborative process is to build and foster strong ties between schools and communities, and particularly between schools and homes. Any parent or guardian of a school-age child should be considered as an important resource to collaborators. Parents and guardians must be informed of special interventions and included in the decision-making process itself when appropriate.

Likewise, learners themselves should be involved in the collaborative decision-making process when appropriate. With older learners this becomes especially important. Villa and Thousand (1992) described the importance of including learners in the collaborative process as being essential in the creation and delivery of instruction in the 21st century. They see learners as members of instructional teams, as peer tutors, as peer advocates, and as decision makers *with* teachers, administrators, and parents. Some collaborators are involving learners in the interventions themselves by teaching them to use peer mediation skills (Johnson, Johnson, Dudley, & Burnett, 1992). Villa and Thousand (1992) stated,

> Educational assumptions and practices must be examined regularly in order to ferret out and eliminate those that impede students' opportunities to actively determine and be involved in their education, to practice being contributing members of society through real life experiences. (p. 139)

Saleebey (1992) criticized helping professionals for only giving lip service to the idea of building on clients' strengths. He challenged readers to view the whole person, not just the problem or named pathology. This is especially important for collaborators when creating educational programs for learners with special needs. In most cases, when those learners are respectfully included in the collaboration process, we find that they have many strengths—cognitive, physical, emotional, interpersonal, social, and spiritual—that can be utilized to further empower them. We must avoid the victim mind-set that is created when we focus only on a person's problems. The use of a strengths perspective is one vehicle for increasing the probability that we will empower rather than victimize our learners. The strengths perspective fits well with the concept of self-determination (respecting the right of individuals to make decisions about their own lives). Collaborators *must* include learners and parents in educational decisions that directly affect them.

Planning and Providing Staff Development Opportunities

A fatal flaw in attempting to build collaborative school programs is when staff have not been sufficiently prepared to collaborate. Because these skills are centered around humans solving problems together, it is sometimes assumed that skills in working with other people are simply pleasant aspects of some of our personalities or a product of our rearing. Quite the contrary, there are specific skills related to group problem solving and interacting, and interpersonal communication skills that are discernible and that people can learn to use in their professional practice, as described in Idol (1990).

For example, West and Cannon (1988) conducted an extensive, interdisciplinary review of the literature on consultation (school psychology, counseling, general education, and special education) to determine some of the process-oriented skills. The skills were then validated by a panel of experts on school consultation to determine those skills that were viewed as being essential to the consultation process. Forty-seven of the skills met these experts' standards for being essential and have been developed into a training curriculum for helping professionals develop and refine these process skills (West et al., 1989). The skills are categorized into eight general categories and are listed in Table 4.1.

Collaborators must receive preparation and supervised practice in developing and using communicative, interactive problem-solving skills (as detailed in Chapter 2), if they are expected to apply them and to be effective in their collaborative efforts. Information and appropriate staff development opportunities should be made available at all three levels (macro, mezzo, and micro) within a school organization where the collective vision includes collaborative decision making, as well as implementation of the Collaborative Consultation Model for learners with special needs.

It is important and helpful when administrators at the macro level (superintendents and program directors) and mezzo level (principals) are committed to developing effective educational programs for all learners. In many cases, administrators who have been traditionally educated have not received preparation and education that enables them to understand the importance of equally valuing and educating learners with special needs. Our experience indicates that when administrators have an opportunity to study the history of special education, to receive information about learners with special needs, and to review research and materials related to various educational service delivery models, they become advocates for learners with special needs (Nevin,

TABLE 4.1.   Essential Skills for the Process of Consultation

Consultation Theory Models

1. Practice reciprocity of roles between consultant and consultee in facilitating the consultation process.

2. Demonstrate knowledge of various stages/phases of the consultation process.

3. Assume joint responsibility for identifying each stage of the consultation process and adjusting behavior accordingly.

4. Match consultation approach(es) to specific consultation situation(s), setting(s) and need(s).

Research on Consultation Theory, Training, and Practice

5. Translate relevant consultation research findings into effective school-based consultation practice.

Personal Characteristics

6. Exhibit ability to be caring, respectful, empathic, congruent, and open in consultation interactions.

7. Establish and maintain rapport with all persons involved in the consultation process, in both formal and informal interactions.

8. Identify and implement appropriate responses to stage of professional development of all persons involved in the consultation process.

9. Maintain positive self-concept and enthusiastic attitude throughout the consultation process.

10. Demonstrate willingness to learn from others throughout the consultation process.

11. Facilitate progress in consultation situations by managing personal stress, maintaining calm in time of crisis, taking risks, and remaining flexible and resilient.

12. Respect divergent points of view, acknowledging the right to hold different views and to act in accordance with convictions.

Interactive Communication

13. Communicate clearly and effectively in oral and written form.

14. Utilize active ongoing listening and responding skills to facilitate the consultation process (e.g., acknowledging, paraphrasing, reflecting, clarifying, elaborating, summarizing).

15. Determine own and others' willingness to enter consultative relationship.

16. Adjust consultation approach to the learning stage of individuals involved in the consultation process.

17. Exhibit ability to grasp and validate overt/covert meaning and affect in communications (perceptive).

TABLE 4.1. Continued

---

18. Interpret nonverbal communications of self and others (e.g., eye contact, body language, personal boundaries in space) in appropriate context.

19. Interview effectively to elicit information, share information, explore problems, set goals and objectives.

20. Pursue issues with appropriate persistence once they arise in consultation process.

21. Give and solicit continuous feedback that is specific, immediate, and objective.

22. Give credit to others for their ideas and accomplishments.

23. Manage conflict and confrontation skillfully throughout the consultation process to maintain collaborative relationships.

24. Manage timing of consultation activities to facilitate mutual decision making at each stage of the consultation process.

25. Apply the principle of positive reinforcement to one another in the collaborative team situation.

26. Be willing and safe enough to say, "I don't know . . . let's find out."

Collaborative Problem Solving

27. Recognize that successful and lasting solutions require commonality of goals and collaboration throughout all phases of the problem-solving process.

28. Develop a variety of data collection techniques for problem identification and clarification.

29. Generate viable alternatives through brainstorming techniques characterized by active listening, nonjudgmental responding and appropriate reframing.

30. Evaluate alternatives to anticipate possible consequences, narrow and combine choices, and assign priorities.

31. Integrate solutions into a flexible, feasible, and easily implemented plan of action relevant to all persons affected by the problem.

32. Adopt a "pilot problem-solving" attitude, recognizing that adjustments to the plan of action are to be expected.

33. Remain available throughout implementation for support, modeling, and/or assistance in modification.

34. Redesign, maintain, or discontinue interventions using data-based evaluation.

35. Utilize observation, feedback, and interviewing skills to increase objectivity and mutuality throughout the problem-solving process.

Systems Change

36. Develop role as a change agent (e.g., implementing strategies for gaining support, overcoming resistance).

TABLE 4.1. Continued

37. Identify benefits and negative effects that could result from change efforts.

Equity Issues and Values/Beliefs Systems

38. Facilitate equal learning opportunities by showing respect for individual differences in physical appearance, race, sex, handicap, ethnicity, religion, SES, or ability.

39. Advocate for services that accommodate the educational, social, and vocational needs of all learners, handicapped and nonhandicapped.

40. Encourage implementation of laws and regulations designed to provide appropriate education for all learners with special needs.

41. Utilize principles of the least restrictive environment in all decisions regarding learners with special needs.

42. Modify myths, beliefs, and attitudes that impede successful social and educational integration of learners with special needs into the least restrictive environment.

43. Recognize, respect, and respond appropriately to the effects of personal values and belief systems of self and others in the consultation process.

Evaluation of Consultation Effectiveness

44. Ensure that persons involved in planning and implementing the consultation process are also involved in its evaluation.

45. Establish criteria for evaluating input, process, and outcome variables affected by the consultation process.

46. Engage in self-evaluation of strengths and weaknesses to modify personal behaviors influencing the consultation process.

47. Utilize continuous evaluative feedback to maintain, revise, or terminate consultation activities.

Note. From *Collaboration in the Schools* (pp. 299–301) by J. F. West, L. Idol, and G. Cannon, 1989, Austin, TX: PRO-ED. Reprinted by permission.

Thousand, Paolucci-Whitcomb, & Villa, 1990; Paolucci-Whitcomb, Carlson, & Bright, 1991).

It has also been our experience that when principals become members of collaborative leadership teams, comprising the principal, selected classroom teachers, and relevant support staff, their support of the Collaborative Consultation Model is garnered and enhanced (see Idol & West, 1991; West, 1990; West & Idol, 1990). Idol and West have used such building-based leadership teams in a train-the-trainer model to provide staff development opportunities for an entire school faculty. First, the leadership teams received staff development in collaborative teaming; second, each leadership team provided training opportunities to the school staff, using the *Collaboration in the Schools* staff development program (West et al., 1989) (see Table 4.1).

We recommend that all groups of collaborators expected to implement the Collaborative Consultation Model be afforded staff development opportunities to develop the necessary process skills. Some other sources for skill development in team decision making include Sher and Gottlieb (1989) as well as Thousand and Villa (1992). Fisher and Brown (1988) and Fisher and Ury (1981) are also reliable sources for developing skills in team decision making and, in particular, negotiation skills. Kraus (1984) as well as Zins and Ponti (1990) have provided suggestions for developing and maintaining collaboration in organizations, whereas several others have offered strategies for working consultatively within various levels of a system (e.g., Alpert, 1982; Brown, Pryzwansky, & Schulte, 1987; Brown, Wyne, Blackburn, & Powell, 1979; Conoley & Conoley, 1982; Gallessich, 1982; Lewis, 1986; Parsons & Meyers, 1984).

Disseminating Program Information

A variety of techniques and materials can be used for disseminating program information, including oral reports, written reports, slide shows, pamphlets, newsletters, films, books, articles, and conferences. All of these techniques are useful in the early stage of gaining entry and acceptance in school organizations. Often, collaborative consultants are introduced to school staff during group meetings prior to or at the beginning of the school year. Usually, at that time, they are asked to talk about their programs. In such meetings, a well-developed slide show or overhead transparency presentation can help provide clear, positive information and give administrators and teachers a better idea of how collaborators work together. Including descriptions of real cases and/or problems solved by the team is a powerful way to demonstrate effectiveness. Distribution of a brief, attractive brochure after the presentation is also helpful. Such a brochure should include information about which learners are eligible for services, how to refer learners, and how to contact other collaborators. Any special skills and interests should also be highlighted. The brochures should emphasize that collaborators provide special education services through a partnership approach. Collaborators do not remove learners from their classes; instead, they help teachers identify the most appropriate materials and techniques. The goal is to facilitate the progress of learners with special needs in mainstream classrooms.

During the acceptance stage of collaboration, it is important to acknowledge publicly when and where collaborators are scheduled to work, as well as the times that they will be available to answer questions or attend grade-level staff meetings and informal get-togethers (e.g., lunches and coffee breaks). School personnel appreciate knowing which days and times they can expect collaborators to meet. It is helpful to brainstorm a list of ways that collaborators can work together. This list can then be used or revised as collaborators start talking and working with one another. It is also recommended that the group brainstorm a list of ways that they think they can help meet the educational needs of all learners.

A major outcome of brainstorming and discussing lists of special skills and needs is a shared understanding of what all collaborators can contribute to improving the quality of education for all learners, especially those with special learning needs. This may help to pinpoint areas of need that district personnel cannot respond to individually. In such cases, district personnel may agree to request assistance from community resources such as psychologists, psychiatrists, social workers, and family counselors.

ESTABLISHING TEAM GOALS

It is essential at this stage for collaborators to reach consensus on a collective vision of their purpose(s) for working together at the micro level. This is not to be confused with establishing goals and objectives for the learners themselves, which is described in Chapter 5. Rather, at this stage collaborators celebrate their acceptance of one another and the informal formation of their team. A formalization of the team-building effort must culminate in the development of a collective vision of their purpose as a team.

Members of a collaborative consultation team plan and develop goals for improvement at three levels: personal, individual professional, and team professional. For example, at the *personal* level a collaborator might plan to improve one's ability to think divergently, to value dissonance and differences of opinion as opportunities to expand and grow, to take personal responsibility for one's own health and ability to remain relaxed, and to examine one's own beliefs about inclusion of people with special needs in society.

Examples of *individual professional* goals might be to learn new teaching or management techniques, to read the professional literature, to monitor the quality and quantity of how much one speaks during team meetings, to listen actively when other collaborators are speaking, to learn to manage confrontation and conflict rather than being intimidated or angered by it, and/or to meet one's own professional commitments. Examples of *team professional* goals might be to create a working climate where people enjoy themselves as they work together, to ensure that all learners achieve their annual goals, to monitor the quality of the interpersonal interactions in team meetings, to use meetings in a planned and efficient manner, and/or to include certain learners with special needs in general education programs.

The creation of a collective vision also happens at macro (school-system) and mezzo (school-building) levels. At the macro level, key decision makers may begin to build and support efforts and vehicles to use collaborative decision making within the system. For example, staff development monies may be spent to prepare various groups to make collaborative decisions and to implement collaborative plans. Some of these groups might include members of school boards, members of school/community/home committees and partnerships, members of site-based management teams, interdisciplinary teams, building-based teams, and entire school staffs (see related discussions in Bergman, 1992; Caldwell & Wood, 1992; Idol & West, 1991; Kessler, 1992; and Russell, Cooper, & Greenblatt, 1992). All of these vehicles become part of a macro-level vision of collaborative partnerships in schools.

At the building (mezzo) level, school staff can create their own vision of a collaborative school. Included in the schoolwide plan for improvement might be goals and objectives for (a) how to best use various organizational structures for collaborative decision making, (b) how to implement the Collaborative Consultation Model in a school, or (c) how to develop an inclusive school that includes all learners from a community and promotes learning in the *most educationally enhancing environment.*

Idol and West (1991) described in further detail what some of the various organizational structures might be in a collaborative school. In their vision of a collaborative school, the following components are included:

- A school-based management team

- Committees of education professionals to make decisions regarding curricula, textbooks, testing efforts, and so on

- Department and grade-level instructional teams

- A collaborative instructional program requiring coordination between special and general education and including the following: (a) consulting teacher services, (b) cooperative teaching in the classroom, and (c) supportive resource programs.

In addition to these components we would add:

- Integrated and inclusive neighborhood school programs for learners with severe mental retardation coupled with multiple handicapping conditions

- School/community/home partnership planning committees that prepare recommendations for specialized programs such as for drug prevention, sex education, and developing a curriculum for teaching peaceful decision-making practices to learners (e.g., McCarthy, 1992; Molnar, 1992)

As collaborators engage in this vision-building process and begin to formulate these various types of goals, it may be helpful to consider Svoboda's

(1993) view of how goals can be used. He views goals as a way of promoting success and subsequent motivation to achieve further successes by combining long-term and short-term goals. He classifies goals in several ways. The first type of goal enables people to achieve a dream. Another type of goal encourages exploration or divergent thinking about the goal to have, which is especially useful for those who don't have a clear dream to achieve. A third type of goal is a goal for having time to enjoy whatever goals are achieved, as well as the process or journey to achieving those goals.

Svoboda (1993) suggested that the most important goal of all is to enjoy every day to the fullest without sacrificing the future of the self or others. He provided a set of questions, if answered, that can help people formulate appropriate goals within this framework. First, ask why (before asking how): that is, answering the questions, Why should I do that? Is that the best or most important goal or thing to do? What are the reasons or values for this? Is that the best or most important goal or thing to do? What are the reasons or values for this? Svoboda recommended that these questions be answered before asking how the goal can be achieved. In answering the why questions first, clarity is achieved, alternative choices that are often superior are considered, and different perspectives, as well as consequences, are raised that can test the commitment to set the goal in the first place. From this discussion, it's clear that Svoboda has a very broad conceptualization of how goals might contribute to a person's achievements.

SUMMARY

This chapter focused on the first stage in collaborative problem solving: Gaining Entry and Establishing Team Goals. We explored some specific collaborative consultation principles to facilitate entry and acceptance, as well as to establish team goals, at three levels within school organizations: at the district or school system level (macro), at the building level (mezzo), and among the members of each collaborative team (micro). Specific techniques to help collaborators gain entry and establish team goals among themselves and within school organizations were described. The techniques can be used to facilitate an improved level of acceptance at macro, mezzo, and micro levels within a school system. Finally, discussion focused on the types of goals collaborators might generate at the macro, mezzo, and micro levels of their organizations.

In our experience, people who use Collaborative Consultation successfully must be leaders, trainers, listeners, and learners themselves. They must be willing to model the techniques that they expect teachers to use with their learners. These skills are continually tested, from the first day the collaborators begin working together to gain mutual acceptance until the day they complete their collaborative efforts.

Active administrative understanding and support for Collaborative Consultation is crucial. Collaborators must share with administrators the benefits of a collaborative training-based model and then, by gaining their assistance, support, and suggestions throughout implementation, learn how best to adapt and apply the model. Educational administrators who demonstrate their belief that students and teachers can improve and then set out to facilitate that improvement are invaluable partners for collaborators and become an essential part of the collaborative group.

Collaborators must define their roles and responsibilities in the Collaborative Consultation Model. Within the context of educating learners with special needs, collaborators become educational team members, instructional managers, behavioral managers, and learner advocates. Individual collaborators may of course be familiar with and skillful in only one or two roles and must then be encouraged to expand competencies in other, less familiar roles. Similarly, other collaborators may be more confident in their roles as student and program advocates, due to their familiarity with referrals, assessment, and IEP planning processes. They may be less confident in the role of instructional manager of large groups of students. In any case, through Collaborative Consultation, participants are expected and encouraged to teach and learn from each other.

Successful collaborators remember that administrators and others will vary considerably in their ability and willingness to provide services to students through Collaborative Consultation. It may take years until some administrators and teachers are willing, confident, and skilled at providing effective services. Gaining acceptance by administrators and teachers is just the first step in building a teaching/learning partnership with them. The principles for gaining acceptance and the techniques described in this chapter should help facilitate that partnership.

STUDY QUESTIONS

1. Why is it important to distinguish among macro-, mezzo-, and micro-levels of an organization at this stage of the collaborative consultation process?

2. In addition to the generic collaborative consultation principles advanced in Chapter 1, what are the principles that the authors suggest are important, in their experience, to facilitate the entry into a collaborative consultation relationship? Why, in your opinion, are these important?

3. Describe an example of your own actions in entering a macro-, mezzo-, or micro-level relationship and the principles you found to be helpful.

4. Compare and contrast one or two of the authors' specific strategies for establishing collaborative consultation at the macro-, mezzo-, or micro-levels of organizations with one or two of your own strategies for each level.

5. Who decides what goals and objectives are important at each level of an organization (macro, mezzo, and micro)?

6. Who decides what goals and objectives are important for a team that is implementing the Collaborative Consultation Model? Why?

REFERENCES

Alpert, J. L. (1977). Some guidelines for school consultation. *Journal of School Psychology,* 15(4), 308–319.

Alpert, J. L. (1982). *Psychological consultation in educational settings: A casebook for working with administrators, teachers, students and community.* San Francisco: Jossey-Bass.

Bagley, M. T. (1977). *Teacher consultant.* Woodcliff Lake, NJ: Educational Consulting Associates.

Bauwens, J., Hourcade, J. J., & Friend, M. (1989). Cooperative teaching: A model for general and special education integration. *Remedial and Special Education,* 10(2), 17–22.

Bergman, A. B. (1992). Lessons for principals from site-based management. *Educational Leadership,* 50(1), 48–51.

Benjamin, A. (1987). *The helping interview.* Boston: Houghton-Mifflin.

Blake, R. R., & Mouton, J. S. (1976). *Consultation.* Reading, MA: Addison-Wesley.

Bonner, J. S. (1982, June). Japanese Quality Circles: Can they work in education? *Kappan,* p. 681.

Brill, N. I. (1990). *Working with people: The helping process.* White Plains, NY: Longman.

Brown, D., Pryzwansky, W. B., & Schulte, A. C. (1987). *Psychological consultation: Introduction to theory and practice.* Boston: Allyn & Bacon.

Brown, D., Wyne, M. D., Blackburn, J. E., & Powell, W. C. (1979). *Consultation: Strategy for improving education.* Boston: Allyn & Bacon.

Caldwell, S. D., & Wood, F. H. (1992). Breaking ground in restructuring. *Educational Leadership,* 50(1), 41–44.

Campbell, D., & Hatfield, B. P. (1982, March/April). How Quality Circles work: An "inside look" at two different hospitals, with actual meeting notes. *Hospital Topics,* pp. 46–47.

Carlson, R., & Ackerman, G. (Eds.). (1991). *Educational planning: Concepts, strategies, and practices.* New York: Longman.

Chase, L. (1983, February). Quality Circles in education. *Educational Leadership,* pp. 18–26.

Conoley, J. C., & Conoley, C. W. (1982). *School consultation: A guide to practice and training.* New York: Pergamon.

Corey, M., & Corey, G. (1992). *Groups: Process and practice.* Belmont, CA: Brooks/Cole.

Dewar, D. L. (1979). *Quality Circles: Answers to 100 frequently asked questions.* Red Bluff, CA: Dewar.

Egner, A., & Paolucci, P. (1975). For the sake of the children: Some thoughts on the rights of teachers who provide special education within regular classrooms. In R. A. Johnson, R. F. Weatherman, & R. M. Rehmann (Eds.), *Handicapped youth and the mainstream educator. Vol. 4, Leadership Series in Special Education* (pp. 47–55). Minneapolis: University of Minnesota, Audio-Visual Library Service.

Fisher, R., & Brown, S. (1988). *Getting together: Building relationships as we negotiate.* New York: Penguin.

Fisher, R., & Ury, W. (1981). *Getting to YES: Negotiating agreement without giving in*. New York: Penguin.

Friend, M., & Cook, L. (1992). *Interactions: Collaboration skills for school professionals*. New York: Longman.

Gallessich, J. (1982). *The profession and practice of consultation: A handbook for consultants, trainers of consultants, and consumers of consultation services*. San Francisco: Jossey-Bass.

Geldback, P. L., Klein, W. F., & Moore, R. C. (1981). Quality control circles solving O R problems. *AORN Journal*, 34, 1029–1035.

Gordon, T. (1980). *Leader effectiveness training*. New York: Wyden.

Gryna, F. M. (1981). *Quality Circles: A team approach to problem solving*. New York: AMACOM A Division of American Management Associations.

Hatfield, B. (1982, March/April). Quality Circles in nursing. *Hospital Topics*, pp. 34, 40.

Hersey, P., & Blanchard, K. H. (1988). *Management of organizational behavior: Utilizing human resources*. Englewood Cliffs, NJ: Prentice-Hall.

Idol, L. (1988). A rationale and guidelines for establishing special education consultation programs. *Remedial and Special Education*, 9(6), 48–98.

Idol, L. (1990). The scientific art of classroom consultation. *Journal of Educational and Psychological Consultation*, 1(1), 3–22.

Idol, L. (1993). *Special educator's consultation handbook* (2nd ed.). Austin, TX: PRO-ED.

Idol, L.,. Paolucci-Whitcomb, P., & Nevin, A. (1986). *Collaborative consultation*. Austin, TX: PRO-ED.

Idol, L., & West, J. F. (1991). Educational collaboration: A catalyst for effective schooling. *Intervention in School and Clinic*, 27(2), 70–78, 125.

Idol, L., & West, J. F. (1993). *Effective instruction of difficult-to-teach students: An inservice and preservice professional development program for classroom, remedial, and special education teachers*. Austin, TX: PRO-ED.

Idol-Maestas, L., & Ritter, S. (1985). A follow-up study of resource/consulting teachers. *Teacher Education and Special Education*, 8(3), 121–131.

Ingle, S. (1982). *Quality Circles master guide: Increasing productivity with people power*. Englewood Cliffs, NJ: Prentice-Hall.

Johnson, D. W. (1986). *Reaching out: Interpersonal effectiveness and self-actualization*. Englewood Cliffs, NJ: Prentice-Hall.

Johnson, D. W. (1990). *Human relations and your career: A guide to interpersonal skills*. Englewood Cliffs, NJ: Prentice-Hall.

Johnson, D. W., Johnson, R. T., Dudley, B., & Burnett, R. (1992). Teaching students to be peer mediators. *Educational Leadership*, 50(1), 10–13.

Kahn, S. (1988). Use of social work skills in implementing Quality Circles. *Catch the wave: Organizational development at the crest of occupational social work* (Monograph). Boston: NASW Publication, 30–43.

Kessler, R. (1992). Shared decision making works! *Educational Leadership*, 50(1), 36–38.

Kraus, W. (1984). *Collaboration in organizations: Alternatives to hierarchy*. New York: Human Science Press.

Kurpius, D., & Robinson, S. E. (1978). Overview of consultation. *Personnel and Guidance Journal*, 56, 321–323.

Lewis, J. (1986). *Achieving excellence in schools*. New York: Wilkerson.

Lindner, J. (1984). Replacing lip service with participation. *The School Administrator*, 41(3), 10–14.

Lippitt, G., & Lippitt, R. (1986). *The consulting process in action.* San Diego: University Associates.

McCarthy, C. (1992). Why we must teach peace. *Educational Leadership, 50*(1), 6–9.

McKenzie, H. S. (1976). Higher education's role in mainstreaming: An example. In J. B. Jordan (Ed.), *Teacher, please don't close the door* (pp. 112–133). Reston, VA: Council for Exceptional Children.

Middleman, R. R. (1984). The Quality Circle: Fad, fix or fiction. *Administration in Social Work,* No. 1, Spring, 31–44.

Molnar, A. (1992). Too many kids are getting killed. *Educational Leadership, 50*(1), 4–5.

Molyneaux, D., & Lane, V. W. (1982). *Effective interviewing techniques and analysis.* Boston: Allyn & Bacon.

Montgomery, M. D. (1980). The special educator as consultant: Some strategies. In N. J. Long, W. C. Morse, & R. G. Newman (Eds.), *Conflict in the classroom* (pp. 177–179). Belmont, CA: Wadsworth.

Nevin, A., Thousand, J., Paolucci-Whitcomb, P., & Villa, R. (1990). Collaborative consultation: Empowering public school personnel to provide heterogeneous schooling for all—or, Who rang that bell? *Journal of Educational and Psychological Consultation, 1*(1), 41–67.

O'Hanlon, J. C. (1983, February). Theory Z in school administration? *Educational Leadership,* pp. 16–18.

Ouchi, W. (1981). *Theory Z: How American business can meet the Japanese challenge.* Reading, MA: Addison-Wesley.

Paolucci-Whitcomb, P., Carlson, R., & Bright, W. (1991). Interactive leadership: Processes for improving educational planning and implementation. In R. Carlson & G. Ackerman (Eds.), *Educational planning: A collection of insights* (pp. 295–314). New York: Longman.

Parness, M. I. (1982). Quality Circles as a management tool for hospital pharmacy. *American Journal of Hospital Pharmacy, 39,* 1189–1192.

Parsons, R. D., & Meyers, J. (1984). *Developing consultation skills: A guide to training, development, and assessment for human services professionals.* San Francisco: Jossey-Bass.

Pascale, R. T. (1981). *The art of Japanese management: Applications for American executives.* New York: Simon & Schuster.

Russell, J. J., Cooper, B. S., & Greenblatt, R. B. (1992). How do you measure shared decision making? *Educational Leadership, 50*(1), 39–40.

Saleebey, D. (Ed.). (1992). *The strengths perspective in social work practice.* White Plains, NY: Longman.

Sarason, S. B. (1982). *The culture of the school and the problem of change* (2nd ed.). Boston: Allyn & Bacon.

Sher, B., & Gottlieb, A. (1989). *Teamworks: Building support groups that guarantee success.* New York: Warner.

Shulman, L. (1984). *The skills of helping individuals and groups.* Hasca, IL: Peacock.

Svoboda, W. (1993). *52 ways to gain more control over your life—or, Thank God, It's Friday . . . Saturday, Sunday, Monday, Tuesday, Wednesday, Thursday!* Greensboro: Educational Resources Information Clearinghouse/Counseling Psychology and Counseling Personnel Services, University of North Carolina at Greensboro.

Thousand, J., & Villa, R. (1992). Collaborative teams: A powerful tool in restructuring. In R. Villa, J. Thousand, W. Stainback, & S. Stainback (Eds.), *Restructuring for a caring and effective education* (pp. 73–108). Baltimore: Brookes.

Toseland, R. W., & Rivas, R. F. (1984). *An introduction to group work practice.* New York: Macmillan.

Verderber, R. F. (1981). *Communicate.* Belmont, CA: Wadsworth.

Villa, R., & Thousand, J. (1992). Student collaboration: An essential for curriculum delivery in the 21st century. In S. Stainback & W. Stainback (Eds.), *Curriculum considerations in inclusive classrooms: Facilitating learning for all students* (pp. 117–142). Baltimore: Brookes.

Villa, R. A., Thousand, J. S., Stainback, W., & Stainback, S. (1992). *Restructuring for caring and effective education: An administrative guide to creating heterogeneous schools.* Baltimore: Brookes.

West, J. F. (Ed.). (1989). Prereferral consultation teams found in violation of Section 504 regulations. *The Consulting Edge, 1*(2), 1–3.

West, J. F. (1990). Educational collaboration in the restructuring of schools. *Journal of Educational and Psychological Consultation, 1*(1), 23–40.

West, J. F., & Cannon, G. (1988). Essential collaborative consultation competencies for regular and special educators. *Journal of Learning Disabilities, 21,* 28, 56–63.

West, J. F., & Idol, L. (1990). Collaborative Consultation in the education of mildly handicapped and at-risk students. *Remedial and Special Education, 11*(1), 22–31.

West, J. F., Idol, L., & Cannon, G. (1989). *Collaboration in the schools: An inservice and preservice curriculum for teachers, support staff, and administrators.* Austin, TX: PRO-ED.

Whittaker, C. (1992). Transitional consultation strategies: Finding the time to collaborate. *Journal of Educational and Psychological Consultation, 3*(1), 85–88.

Zins, J., & Ponti, C. (1990). Strategies to facilitate the implementation, organization, and operation of system-wide consultation programs. *Journal of Educational and Psychological Consultation, 1*(3), 205–218.

CHAPTER 5

Problem Identification: Assessment and Goal Setting

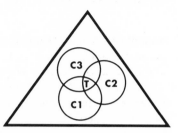

ONCE COLLABORATORS HAVE ESTABLISHED a working relationship, the most immediate task is to define accurately the identified problem. This step in the collaborative consultation process is essential for successful problem solving. If the collaborators move too quickly to problem remediation without first drawing the most accurate picture of the problem, the likely result is ineffective service. Collaborators need to develop a precise and consensual agreement as to the problem; otherwise, they might erroneously engage in making more and more assessment recommendations and never really get to solving the problem. Or, if collaborators fail to reach agreement on the nature of the problem, it is not likely that the interventions selected will solve the problem or that the team will be unified in the problem-solving effort.

The problem identification stage in collaborative problem solving is one that is sometimes overlooked or skipped over too quickly. For example, some teams spend a brief amount of time discussing the problem and engage in discussion of *how* to solve the problem before the problem is understood. Problem identification should be a consensual process where all team members contribute resources and information to aid in problem clarification. All information gathered belongs to the collaborative team. Parents of targeted learners should be informed and involved with the collaborative team as it figures out why those learners are having difficulty. All involved are committed to solving that problem.

In this chapter, we describe a collection of principles related to assessment that have been effective for both consulting and classroom teachers as well as school-based teams when using the Collaborative Consultation Model. We then describe several techniques for conducting assessments with the primary intent of solving problems occurring or likely to occur in general and inclusive classrooms.

Once the collaborative team gathers the relevant assessment data, they meet to reach consensus on the nature of the problem. We define consensus building as coming up with something that everyone on the team can live with, both morally and professionally. The team then writes a specific problem statement, with defining characteristics to provide clear examples of the problem. Sometimes, at this point, the team may collect a little more information to make certain that the agreed-on problem is, in fact, the problem. As an example, in the second case study in Chapter 9, a consulting teacher and a classroom teacher engaged in this second, problem-verification step.

After the problem statement and any necessary modifications are made, the collaborative team constructs a set of goals and objectives they would like the targeted learner(s) to accomplish. Later in this chapter, this goal-setting process is described, with discussion of some techniques that facilitate the process.

DEFINING THE TARGET PROBLEM

One barrier to successful classroom assessment is that teachers sometimes believe that formal assessment by a school psychologist—usually based on standardized intelligence, perceptual, and achievement tests—provides a sufficient assessment base. The thinking process goes something like this: "OK, we know this learner has learning disabilities, and because he has learning disabilities, he's going to fail in the classroom setting. So, what should we try to do to prevent his failure?" The missing step here is to define and describe precisely the problems and difficulties the learner is experiencing *in* the classroom environment. In such cases, it is anticipated that the collaborators will complete the assessment process as a team.

There is evidence to suggest, at least for learners labeled as having learning disabilities, that numerous tests are indeed given prior to placing learners in special programs (Thurlow & Ysseldyke, 1979; Ysseldyke, Algozzine, Potter, & Regan, 1980). Yet, it has been observed that teachers do not refer to the data from those tests either before or during intervention and, further, that such data do not differentiate successful from nonsuccessful learners (Ysseldyke et al., 1980). It thus appears that program eligibility decisions are made in spite of data (Ysseldyke, Algozzine, Shinn, & McGue, 1982). These investigators found no psychometric differences, on 49 different dependent measures, between low achievers and learners with learning disabilities. There was, in fact, a 96% overlap in the distributions of the scores earned by the two groups. Examination of placement team meetings suggested that there was little relationship between the type of information presented in the meetings and its applicability to various identification criteria currently being used (Ysseldyke et al., 1982). In fact, 83% of the statements made during the meetings were found to be irrelevant. These observational data provide little evidence to suggest that placement teams use specific criteria when making eligibility decisions.

The above observational data, collected through the University of Minnesota Institute for Research on Learning Disabilities, should lead collaborators to a reexamination of the assessment procedures they are currently using. If the collaborators do not refer to assessment data before or during intervention, the data themselves may *not* be relevant to the instruction being offered. If the data are not related to the criteria for program eligibility, teachers should formulate criteria that are relevant to instruction, and then select measures that accurately measure performance.

These problems should be carefully considered in relationship to the consultation process regarding all difficult-to-teach learners, even though the University of Minnesota data refer specifically to learner placement in programs for learning disabilities. Collaborators must devise an assessment system wherein, first, they decide if a learner needs consultation service and, second, determine how the learner is progressing compared to classroom teacher expectations. To determine these two criteria, the group members must mutually recognize the assessment strengths of all parties involved. Even though most classroom teachers are not well-versed in special education assessment, they are knowledgeable about evaluating learning performance in their classrooms, classroom curricular structure, instructional methodologies, group management, and child development. In addition to assessment expertise, special educators should bring to the collaborative group process a knowledge of task and curriculum task analysis, training in the formulation of specific objectives and goals, adaptations of curriculum and instruction, and learner management techniques. All of these skills are pertinent in designing appropriate assessment procedures.

Most special service teachers have a knowledge of remedial areas of instruction: reading, arithmetic, spelling, oral and written language, independent study skills, and behavior management. Some collaborators need to acquire a new knowledge base relevant to classroom instruction, classroom teacher expectations, and classroom curricula. This new knowledge should be merged with existing knowledge to assimilate better the new knowledge base. The new base should produce team members who view learning and behavior problems in relationship to the classroom environment in which the behaviors exist.

No longer should collaborative consultation team members initially accept that a learner has learning and behavior problems that are serious enough to warrant removal to special class for instruction. Instead, with the newly assimilated knowledge base, the team should be ready to examine the problems in relation to the learner performance expectancies of the classroom teacher, the teaching and management methodologies used by that teacher, and the curricula used in the classroom. After having examined the referral problem under these conditions, the collaborators are better able to decide which intervention procedures might prove to be most successful. It is recommended that, initially, collaborators select intervention procedures that can be implemented within the classroom setting, selecting the more stringent and restrictive option of special class placement only if several types of carefully planned and evaluated classroom programs have failed. (See Idol & West, 1993, for decision-making frameworks to aid collaborators in this process.)

An extremely important artifact of classroom-based assessment is produced during the collaborative consultation process. As the collaborators strive to understand more clearly the classroom milieu, all involved are affected. The process of knowledge assimilation facilitates a type of clarification for everyone. Prior to the process, the collaborators may have set some very general goals, or even merely vague goals, for certain learners in the class. The knowledge assimilation process can help to (a) form more realistic goals, (b) alter the number of goals, (c) clarify the goals, (d) differentiate goals for various types of learners in the class, and/or (e) form specific objectives that can be used to achieve those goals. (See the final section of this chapter for an in-depth discussion of goals and objectives.)

Our intent in this chapter is to describe the knowledge assimilation process, whereby collaborators work together to assess more clearly the learning and behavior problems that occur in classroom settings. The first section is a discussion of principles of Collaborative Consultation that should enhance the assessment process. Then the assessment process is examined via a series of techniques that are recommended as a means of accurately defining and measuring problems that occur in classroom settings.

ASSESSMENT PRINCIPLES

The principles of Collaborative Consultation discussed in Chapter 2 should be woven into the interactions that take place among collaborators as they begin the assessment process concerning classroom problems. Supplementing these general principles are several assessment principles that can be used to facilitate the collaborative consultation process. In this section we examine these principles:

- Collaborators should form an informal relationship prior to beginning a formal collaborative consultation project.

- Collaborators should perceive themselves as gatherers of information.

- The goals and objectives of the instructional interventions must be matched to the areas that are being assessed.

- Learner performance in the classroom curricula and learning environment must be carefully observed.

- Careful consideration must be given to the effect the classroom teacher has on the learner.

- Collaborators should take major responsibility for helping one another develop and administer assessments.

- Assessment techniques should be designed for adaptable use with either groups or individual learners.

- The developed assessment techniques should be usable with other learners after the collaborative consultation relationship has terminated.

- Collaborators must be willing to share assessment tools and techniques with other teachers who are using a similar curriculum.

Collaborators Should Form an Informal Relationship Prior to Beginning a Formal Collaborative Consultation Project

Collaborators should not begin the collaborative consultation process by initiating the assessment process. Rather, this step should be approached more naturally, after the collaborators have begun to form an informal relationship. This process of orientation is discussed in detail in Chapter 4, where we have identified some intra- and interpersonal goals and objectives, and have clarified roles and responsibilities. Group members (from outside the classroom) should avoid creating an impression that their primary function is to observe and assess. This impression is sometimes erroneously created when the first topic of conversation between the group members is, in fact, centered on problem definition and assessment. It is thus recommended that collaborators strive to establish an informal and friendly relationship before beginning formally to define problems and assess a target learner's skills.

Collaborators Should Perceive Themselves as Gatherers of Information

During the assessment process, the collaborator's role is to gather the most pertinent and definitive information possible. This information is collected from a variety of sources, such as classroom observations, criterion-referenced and norm-referenced test data, anecdotal reports from important others in the target learner's life, self-reports, and finally, the most important, reports from the classroom teacher, including learner portfolios. To collect, organize, and analyze this information accurately, the collaborators must be skilled in focusing on specifics, and in helping others to learn the same skill(s). Vague, impressionistic information must be transformed into clear statements of behavior and of antecedent and consequential events. The relevant clarifying interchanges that take place, especially between the collaborators, are essential in laying a sound framework for successful remediation programs.

The Goals and Objectives of the Instructional Interventions Must Be Matched to the Areas That Are Being Assessed

As collaborators meet to define identified problems, they develop a feeling for what the targeted learners need to achieve. In this process, the collaborators develop and extend these aims beyond a general feeling of what constitutes good and acceptable classroom behavior to goals and objectives that are discernible and achievable. Once *what* is expected of learners has been determined, a viable route for assessment has been established. The collaborators can then design an assessment system that tests the learners' skill areas in relation to the goals and expectations of the collaborative consultation team. As this process is developed, classroom teachers are likely to make adaptations in their original goals for certain learners; sometimes the end result is more stringent, sometimes it is less. However, once this level of specificity has been achieved, the learners are well on the way to mastering the concepts and skills they are ready to learn.

Learner Performance in the Classroom Curricula and Learning Environment Must Be Carefully Observed

To understand classroom problems, it is especially important to observe carefully student performance in the classroom curricula and learning environment. This exemplifies a general principle of Collaborative Consultation, namely, that exceptionality should be defined in the context in which it occurs. Thus, in Collaborative Consultation, any deviant classroom behavior must be examined in the classroom itself. This means examining learner performance in the curricula that are used in the general classroom and also examining the ways in which learners interact with curricula, teachers, and peers in that classroom.

Careful Consideration Must Be Given to the Effect the Classroom Teacher Has on the Learner

The ways in which classroom teachers interact with learners have a definite effect on student behavior. An extensive body of literature on classroom intervention studies has demonstrated the tremendous impact of contingent and positive teacher attention on decreasing disruptive classroom behavior and improving study behavior (Becker, Madsen, Arnold, & Thomas, 1967; Hall, Lund, & Jackson, 1968; Hall, Panyan, Rabon, & Broden, 1968; Idol, 1993; Thomas, Becker, & Armstrong, 1968). In addition, positive teacher attention has been found to generalize among learners (Broden, Bruce, Mitchell, Carter, & Hall, 1970), and learners have been taught to modify teacher attention by controlling their classroom behavior (Graubard, Rosenberg, & Miller, 1971).

Collaborators should be particularly concerned about the effect of teacher attention on learners with special needs because of the possible negative attitudes the teachers may have toward the learner. Several studies on teacher attitudes toward learners with special needs have revealed that teachers are indeed influenced by special education labels (Foster & Salvia, 1977; Foster, Schmidt, & Sabatino, 1976; Gillung & Rucker, 1977).

It is thus clear that teacher-learner interactions should be examined. The remaining question is how these interactions can be examined in a nonthreatening and comfortable way for the classroom teacher. One solution is always to focus the intent of the collaboration on modifying learner behavior, even though an eventual outcome may include collaborators deciding to modify their own behavior. An example of how this process occurred in an actual collaborative consultation situation is described by Idol (1993, pp. 192–201).

Collaborators Should Take Major Responsibility for Helping One Another Develop and Administer Assessments

Two seemingly insurmountable obstacles to classroom assessments arise with regard to finding sufficient time for preparation and testing. The first is *when do classroom teachers have the time to construct the assessment tools?*; the second is *how* can one assess all of the learners who really need to be tested? The first obstacle can probably be overcome if at least one collaborator's role is defined to include test preparation as a part of consultation time. The collaborators then mutually decide which skill areas to test. The majority of test construction would probably be completed by the designated assessor, who would check frequently to determine that all parties agree on various points in the decision-making process. The second obstacle, that of finding sufficient time for testing, is addressed by the following assessment technique.

Assessment Techniques Should Be Designed for Adaptable Use with Either Groups or Individual Learners

Ideally, whenever possible, curriculum-based assessments (CBAs) should be designed for group administration. In this case, outside collaborators (members of the team other than the classroom teacher) can offer valuable assistance and support by either administering the tests to individual learners or by taking over group instruction while the classroom teacher administers individual tests. A decided advantage of the latter choice is that it offers the classroom teacher the opportunity to become more familiar with learners' skills and limitations. It also affords other group members the opportunity to work with the larger group of learners. This experience could prove to be extremely helpful in subsequent designing and planning of realistic teaching and learning procedures to be used in general classrooms.

Under most circumstances and for most curricula, CBAs can in fact be administered to groups. It is even possible to test different learners on different skill levels simultaneously as long as time frames are of approximately equivalent lengths. It is anticipated that most group testing will be done by the classroom teacher. The testing could be done in short time periods at various key points throughout the year rather than in extremely lengthy periods just at the beginning of the school year. During testing time, the role of the assessor(s) would be to assist with test scoring and curricular placement decisions and to administer individual tests to learners who were absent during group testing or whose performance during group testing was suspect.

The Developed Assessment Techniques Should Be Usable with Other Learners After the Collaborative Consultation Relationship Has Terminated

If the assessment techniques and tools are so specialized that they are designed for use only with particular individual learners, the long-term benefits to the classroom teacher are negligible. The same can be said of testing procedures that are too elaborate or complicated. The key is to develop assessment tools that are based on classroom curricula so that they may be used repeatedly by teachers. A more difficult, but possible, task is to develop testing procedures that are valid and reliable as well as practical.

Collaborators Must Be Willing to Share Assessment Tools and Techniques with Other Teachers Who Are Using a Similar Curriculum

A common negative reaction to the use of curricular or classroom assessment is that too much time is required to develop the testing materials. Willingness to share assessment materials is a simple solution to this problem. In many schools and school districts, the majority of classroom curricula have been standardized, at least within grade levels. Certain collaborators can thus serve as advocates and facilitators by bringing together groups of teachers who use identical or similar curricula. These groups of individuals can quickly develop two alternate forms of a CBA and thus have an assessment instrument that will be useful for several years (development of two forms would also permit use of a pretest/posttest evaluation system). Such an effort would also likely result in an improved assessment product.

COLLABORATIVE CONSULTATION TECHNIQUES FOR ASSESSMENT

Several specific techniques are available for facilitating classroom assessment. These techniques, which should be coupled with the assessment principles of Collaborative Consultation, pertain to the following areas:

- Observations in classrooms
- Appropriate use of standardized tests

- Normative sampling to establish performance criteria
- Use of general classroom curricula as the basis for assessment
- Portfolio assessment of learners' work samples
- Determination of the difference between acquisition and proficiency stages of learning
- Development of intermittent assessment systems
- Examination of learning environments

Standardized Tests

Although the primary mode of assessment advocated in this chapter is classroom-based, standardized tests have their place within the assessment process. Several important aspects of standardized tests must be considered by those concerned with the classroom education of learners with special needs. First, standardized tests are often the primary means of evaluating learner performance in classrooms. This is true whether the intent is to classify exceptional learners for special education services; to track academic progress of learners within school districts, states, or the nation; to determine competency levels for graduation; or to select more valid dependent measures for educational research and evaluation projects. Thus, there is a strong chance that any learner referred for collaborative consultation services will have a cumulative folder containing performance data on various standardized tests. Such tests may be concerned with intelligence or achievement, or they may be perceptual tests designed for either individual or group use. They normally include both norm-referenced and criterion-referenced tests. One task of a collaborative consultation group is to determine what the various test scores mean in relation to classroom performance.

Test Validity. Collaborators may be interested in monitoring learner progress on various tests administered at different points in time. If this option is chosen, content validity of the test in relationship to the curriculum used must be considered. Also, the validity of learner performance on the test must be considered. Finally, monitoring of learner performance on standardized tests should not be the only means of evaluating program effectiveness, as stipulated by P.L. 94-142 guidelines.

Content validity of tests in relationship to curricula is a problem that is often overlooked by teachers and teacher educators alike. Research evidence suggests that there is no consistent and predictable relationship between learner performance and standardized achievement tests in various reading curricula (Armbruster, Stevens, & Rosenshine, 1977; Jenkins & Pany, 1978a, 1978b). At the very least, collaborators should examine standardized tests for their actual content and compare that content to the goals and objectives of the curriculum being used with learners.

Teachers must also seriously consider the validity of a learner's performance on a test. Many learners who have learning and/or behavior problems guess at or randomly select answer items on tests. This behavior is especially prevalent when group tests are administered. Many problem learners also exhibit unpredictable and variable test performance behavior. Because of this, teachers should be somewhat wary of single-instance testing where decisions are based on a learner's performance during a single testing situation. Thus, when testing in the classroom, it is recommended that measurement of learner performance be obtained on several occasions.

White and Liberty (1976) offered an excellent example of the dangers of basing decisions on single instances of testing: Figure 5.1 represents pretest-

FIGURE 5.1. Pretest-posttest data reflecting effects of four different tactics for teaching math facts.

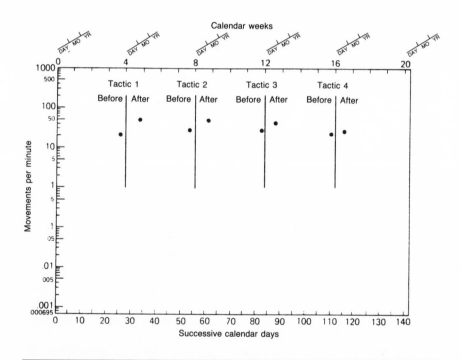

posttest data for four tactics for teaching math facts. If one were to rank order the four tactics in order of effectiveness, most persons would agree that Tactic 1 is the most effective, Tactic 2 the second most effective, Tactic 3 the third most, and Tactic 4 the least effective. Now, compare these data with those in Figure 5.2, where continuous measurement is taken over 10 consecutive days, 5 days prior to using the tactic (baseline measurement) and 5 days after using the tactic. The last data point in each phase (i.e., the data points before and after the change) are the same data points as those shown in Figure 5.1. Again, if one were to rank order the four tactics for effectiveness, the results would be strikingly different from those for the pretest-posttest data. Note that the solid trend lines prior to and during the initiation of the tactic indicate the average rate of progress, whereas the broken lines represent what the predicted rate of progress would have been if the baseline condi-

FIGURE 5.2. Continuous data reflecting effects of four different tactics for teaching math facts.

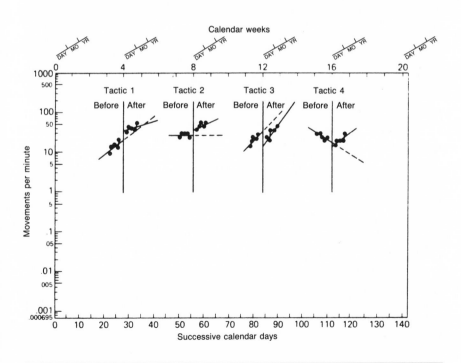

Note. From *Teaching Special Children* (p. 41) by N. G. Haring and R. L. Schiefelbusch (Eds.), 1976, New York: McGraw-Hill Book Company. Copyright 1976 by McGraw-Hill Book Company. Reprinted by permission.

tions had been continued. For Tactics 1 and 3, pupil performance was improving prior to implementing the tactics. With Tactic 2, no progress was being made prior to implementing the tactic, and with Tactic 4, performance was deteriorating prior to using the tactic. Thus, the interpretation of order of effectiveness of strategies is the reverse of those results depicted in Figure 5.1.

Cautions.   The example offered by White and Liberty (1976) is an illustration of the difficulties that collaborators can expect to encounter when programming decisions are based on single instances of measurement. By developing ways of monitoring learner progress on a more continuous basis, collaborators are afforded the opportunity to select interventions or tactics only when they are truly necessary. Continuous measurement systems also provide collaborators and learners with immediate performance feedback.

Given the problems that can arise due to a lack of agreement between standardized tests and curricula, variable learner performance, and single-instance testing, teachers should be wary of using a single standardized pretest and posttest process as means of evaluating learner progress and program effectiveness. As one alternative, teachers might consider monitoring progress by readministering on an annual basis different forms of previously administered, standardized tests. The resulting information would be useful in testing the relationship between the progress a learner might make in class compared to progress made on a given achievement test. If there were discrepancies, they could be used in formulating recommendations to local school agencies, indicating which standardized tests are unrelated to the goals and objectives of classroom teachers.

Observations in Classrooms

Careful observations in classrooms have long been recognized as an integral part of the information-gathering process in the school consultation process. When implementing the Collaborative Consultation Model, a critical key is for these classroom observations to be conducted collaboratively, and not viewed as an outside consultant coming to the classroom to assess the classroom teacher.

Collaborators must establish times and procedures for classroom observations. The specific role of the person conducting the observations must be specified in advance. This observer could be the classroom teacher, while another collaborator teaches the students; or it might be a member of the collaborative team, while the classroom teacher is teaching. Regardless, this should be a collaborative decision and determined in advance of the observation.

Observers should only observe (not interact or teach), so they can learn maximally from the observation experience with the major purpose to understand better how teachers, learners, and curriculum are interacting. Collaborators should also determine in advance what the purpose of the observation will be. It might be to determine either positive or negative occurrences concerning the classroom learning or management environment, teacher-learner interactions, materials, teaching/learning procedures, learners' responses or behaviors, and so on. Whatever the purpose, all collaborators should be clear on what it is and expect that information relevant to that purpose will be collected.

Collaborators also determine how the observational data will be collected and how those data will be utilized. They may decide to share in observations to determine that the observations are truly reliable. After the information is gathered, collaborators should meet, first to clarify the gathered information and then to make decisions regarding the meaning behind the information gathered. After all, the major purpose of gathering such information is to clarify the collaborative team's perspective on the problem to be solved.

The second case study in Chapter 9 provides an example of how a consulting teacher and a high school home economics teacher used classroom observations as a means of clarifying the problem of disruptive students in an inclusive classroom. Other case studies of classroom teachers and resource/consulting teachers using classroom observations can be found in Idol (1993). Specific training opportunities on techniques for classroom observation can be found in West, Idol, and Cannon (1989, Module 28) and in Idol and West (1993, Module 5).

Normative Sampling

A normative sample of average learner performance in the skill area in which a learner is having difficulty can be obtained by measuring performances of other learners in the classroom. As Idol (1993) pointed out:

> A normative sample can be used to (a) give teachers a specific, behavioral description of how an average student performs a skill, (b) give teachers a clear idea of whether average students are meeting teacher expectations, (c) determine any discrepancy between how a low-achieving student performs and how the teacher(s) would like the student to perform, or (d) give teachers a guide for setting goals, objectives, and criterial performance levels for students. (pp. 150–151)

Point d is a particularly useful way of employing a normative sampling procedure.

A normative sample provides a measure of how socially valid a goal, an objective, or a criterion level might be. Kazdin (1977) described two methods of social validation: social comparison and subjective evaluation. Epstein and

Cullinan (1979) defined a social comparison method as one by which the "target behavior of the individual selected for treatment is compared to the same behavior of another person, who is similar to the selected individual but not in need of treatment" (pp. 93–94). Epstein and Cullinan pointed out that the social comparison method can be based on the performance of several individuals to obtain useful behavioral criteria. In their study, they showed how social comparison data can be used to formulate instructional objectives. First, they collected social-comparison arithmetic data from fourth-, fifth-, and sixth-grade students; then instructional objectives were written, based on the comparative data, and matched to appropriate grade levels.

Walker and Hops (1976); Walker, Shinn, O'Neill, and Ramsey (1987); and Walker, Steiber, Ramsey, and O'Neill (1991) have demonstrated how the effectiveness of a training program designed to teach appropriate classroom behavior can be tested by obtaining normative data on classroom peer behavior. Other examples of how social comparison data can be used for classroom consultation can be found in Idol (1993); in this source the procedure is referred to as normative sampling.

In contrast, a subjective evaluation method is one in which "persons who either interact with the selected individuals or possess particular expertise with respect to the target behavior are asked to provide value judgements about the importance of the actual improvements in the target behavior" (Epstein & Cullinan, 1979, p. 94). The subjective evaluation method could be particularly useful in assessing the impact of remedial instruction on overall classroom performance.

Collaborators will find that a wealth of information can be gleaned from the classroom environment. In particular, important information can be gathered by observing behaviors and performances of other learners in the classroom or by eliciting judgments of acceptable behavior from other persons. This information can then be used to formulate realistic performance criteria, goals, and objectives that are specific to the environment to which a special needs learner is expected to adapt, yet are attainable goals for that learner.

Curriculum-Based Assessment

One method of assessing student performance in the classroom is to use a curriculum-based assessment (CBA) (Blankenship & Lilly, 1981: Gickling & Havertape, n.d.; Idol, 1993; Idol-Maestas, Ritter, & Lloyd, 1983). Over the past 10 years many professionals have written about the use of curriculum-based assessment (CBA), although the initial work was developed in the 1970s by scholars such as Stan Deno, Edward Gickling, Ed Havertape, Joseph Jenkins, Tom Lovitt, and Phyllis Mirkin. In recent years, general information and CBA models have been further refined and developed by several researchers (Auerbach, 1986; Blankenship & Lilly, 1981; Gickling & Thompson, 1985; Howell

& Morehead, 1987; Idol, 1993; Idol, Nevin, & Paolucci-Whitcomb, 1986; Marston & Magnusson, 1985; Peterson, Heistad, Peterson, & Reynolds, 1985; Rosenfield & Rubinson, 1985; Tucker, 1985).

A CBA is a type of informal inventory in which test items are taken from or are similar to items from the curriculum used in the classroom. Gickling and Havertape (n.d.) defined curriculum-based assessment as a procedure for determining the instructional needs of a learner based on the learner's ongoing performance in existing course content. A CBA includes (a) direct observation of the learning environment, (b) analysis of the process used by the student in approaching tasks, (c) examination of the tasks completed, and (d) control and arrangement of tasks for the learner. A CBA can be used to measure performance in any type of academic subject. Sometimes the curriculum, which forms the base for the CBA, is sequenced, such as in curricula for math, reading, and spelling. At other times, the curriculum is one that is teacher-developed, as in creative writing, language arts, study skills, reading comprehension, dictionary skills, and so on. Sometimes the curriculum is not established prior to consultation but is rather a subject area that needs to be taught.

How the CBA is constructed depends on the type of curricula being used, for example, developmental curricula (reading and spelling), spiraling curricula (mathematics), or unestablished curricula (dictionary skills, study skills, following directions). The supplementary materials to this textbook on curriculum-based assessment (Idol et al., 1986) contain sample CBAs for each of these subjects, together with procedures for administering them. In addition, a preparatory module for educators learning to use CBAs can be found in Idol and West (1993, Module 4).

Portfolio Assessment

According to Idol and West (1993),

> a *portfolio* is a collection of selected examples of the types and quality of work that a student has produced in any given subject area. This collection serves as an exhibit of work that reflects that particular student's skills at either a single point in time or at various points in time. Portfolios are used in many different fields of endeavor for the same general purpose: To provide a display or evidence of what a particular individual can produce. (p. 26)

More specifically, Paulson, Paulson, and Meyer (1991) defined a portfolio as

> a purposeful collection of a student's work that exhibits the student's efforts, progress, and achievements in one or more areas. The collection must include:

1. student participation in selecting contents;

2. the criteria for selection;

3. the criteria for judging merit;

4. evidence of student reflection. (p. 60)

Within the collaborative consultation framework, portfolio assessment becomes a means to achieve three important assessment purposes: (a) to gather systematically samples of learners' work to determine their current level of functioning in the learning environment, (b) to compare a learner's portfolio performance to those of classmates, (c) to monitor any learner's progress in the classroom over time, (d) to use a classroom assessment system that can be used with all learners in the classroom, without drawing unnecessary attention or teacher time to the learner with special needs, and (e) to provide parents and other decision makers with concrete evidence of the learner's classroom productions.

For more specific details on recommended guidelines and suggested contents, the reader is referred to Idol and West (1993), Paulson et al. (1991), and Wolf (1989). A specific preparatory module for educators learning how to develop and use student portfolios, with particular emphasis placed on special needs learners, can be found in Idol and West (1993, Module 3).

Assessment of Stages of Learning

When assessing the skill levels of learners, teachers can observe three different patterns of responses. The first pattern indicates that the learner is in the *acquisition* stage of learning, that is, the learner is in the process of acquiring, or has not yet acquired, the skill (Haring, Lovitt, Eaton, & Hansen, 1978; Idol, 1989, 1993; Smith, 1981). The characteristic pattern of a learner ready to enter the acquisition stage is one in which the learner never responds correctly, no matter how many times he or she is tested. For this pattern, instruction should center on offering direct instruction, followed by practice in the skill area.

The second pattern is one in which the learner is in the process of acquisition. Here, the learner performance is erratic and inconsistent; sometimes the responses are incorrect and sometimes they are correct. Idol (1993) refers to this as the *reversion* stage of learning, in which sometimes the learner reverts back to the entry level of the acquisition stage, at times exhibiting incorrect responses, but at other times exhibiting correct responses, indicting that the learner has had some instruction in the skill area. The instruction here would center on reinforcing the correct response and either ignoring the incorrect or pinpointing the error pattern in the incorrect response.

A third type of pattern that might be exhibited by a learner during the assessment process occurs when the learner is in the *proficiency* stage. At this stage, the learner responds correctly, but the rate of response is slow and arduous (Idol, 1993). When this pattern occurs, instruction should center on providing reinforcement for faster rates of responding. For example, teachers could use a changing criterion design; that is, once the learner is reinforced and begins to perform at a consistently higher rate compared to baseline conditions, the criterion is increased slightly with contingent reinforcement. This process is repeated again and again until the rate of response is at an acceptable level.

Thus, an awareness of the stages of learning during the assessment process can result in a more efficient type of assessment and avoidance of unnecessary instructional time. For instance, a learner who is in the proficiency stage may appear not to know how to work math problems, whereas the real problem may be that the learner works too slowly to complete an assessment test in an allotted amount of time. If collaborators were to decide erroneously that the learner did not possess the skills, precious time would be wasted by offering direct instruction in the skill areas. In contrast, if a proper assessment were made initially, an instructional method using time practice and contingent reinforcement would produce improvement more quickly. This example should not be interpreted to mean that reinforcement is always preferable to direct instruction. The important point is that collaborators should be skilled in determining which instructional method is the better one for the type of problem being exhibited and based on a differential assessment of the stages of learning.

Intermittent Assessment

As noted earlier, standardized tests could be administered periodically to assess learner progress. Periodic assessment using CBAs or informal testing could also be used, and no doubt would provide more detailed and specific information than most standardized tests. A major reason for periodic CBA administration would be to assess at higher curricular levels than those tested during initial CBA administration. For example, if a learner were assessed in a spiraling curriculum for mathematics, the initial assessment might have been on only a few concepts. After the learner mastered those concepts, a new assessment might be conducted on a second set of more difficult concepts. This process could be repeated throughout the school year.

Another situation in which intermittent assessment would be appropriate is one in which reading levels are reestablished for poor readers who are progressing rapidly. Once a poor reader begins direct and daily practice of reading, it is not unusual for rapid advances to occur (Idol-Maestas, Lloyd, & Lilly, 1981; Idol-Maestas, Ritter, & Lloyd, 1983). In short, there are two reasons for conducting reassessment: one is that the learner might have advanced sufficiently to warrant a higher placement in the curriculum. The other is that, once a learner becomes accustomed to and can master oral reading of materials, improved performance might occur on the CBA, again warranting a higher placement in the curriculum.

Thus, collaborators are advised to assess periodically the skills of learners. Once assessment materials are constructed, teaching schedules can be designed that incorporate frequent assessment of learners. Related to the idea of intermittent assessment is the concept of *continuously* monitoring progress of learners.

Assessment of Learning Environments

Problems within the classroom environment may stimulate some consultation referrals. These problems might include (a) attention problems, (b) problems of peer pressure, (c) motivation problems, (d) problems relating to lack of the learner's ability to work independently, and (e) problems of classroom management. Frequently, collaborators find that problems stem from some combination of these, coupled with poor academic skills of learners. In this section, we first describe a system for examining the classroom environment to determine the reasons for the above type of learner problems that are unrelated to academic skills. We then delineate an appropriate classroom assessment system.

Attention Problems.   A common source of achievement deficits and classroom behavior problems is related to the attention problems of learners. For example, learners labeled as having learning disabilities are generally rated less favorably on measures of personal and social adjustment. Such learners have been found to spend less time on task-oriented behavior than comparison learners (Bryan & Wheeler, 1972). They have been reported as being less attentive than normally achieving learners in a variety of school subjects, and they are more likely to be ignored by teachers (Bryan, 1974). They are also reported to be more distractible and inattentive, showing less persistence and effort (Forman & McKinney, 1975). However, very few studies have undertaken an observational analysis of learners with learning disabilities or other mainstreamed learners' classroom behavior.

One such study, conducted in second- and fourth-grade classrooms, compared task-oriented, social, and affective behavior patterns of learners with learning disabilities to other learners in the classes (McKinney, McClure, & Feagans, 1982). All of the learners were paired and then observed. The pairs performed similar activities in the classrooms, but the learners with learning disabilities were instructed more often in small groups than as individuals or in large groups. The learners with learning disabilities were found to be more distractible, but a further interesting finding also emerged. Grade-level effects accounted for more variance in classroom behavior patterns than did group differences, meaning that, as learners progressed through the grades, they were less likely to be distractible, regardless of whether or not they had learning disabilities. Two other important variables found to affect classroom behavior were the size of the groups during instruction and teacher presence or absence, with the smaller groups and teacher presence producing better results. The researchers concluded that distractibility characteristics could not be attributed just to learning disabilities without considering the environmental context in which they occurred.

Some of the results of the McKinney et al. (1982) study are similar to the findings of Moore, Haskins, and McKinney (1980), who studied reflective and impulsive learners. These researchers found no group differences in 13 categories of task-oriented and social behavior summed across individual, small-group, and large-group settings. For all learners (reflective and impulsive), less off-task behavior was found when the learners were instructed individually, as opposed to being taught in small-group settings.

Both of these studies lend support to the premise that the environmental context in which a problem occurs should be considered when searching for causality.

Peer Pressure Problems.   Another factor to be considered when examining the classroom environment is the pressure exerted on learners by their peers. This pressure may be either covertly or overtly applied by the peers themselves, or it could be merely perceived as such by the target learner. One of the more impressive and consistent findings reported in the child management literature is that on-task behavior of disruptive learners can be controlled by reinforcing classroom peers who are on task while differentially ignoring disruptive behavior. It has been shown that disruptive classroom behavior can be reduced by forming peer groups in which the entire group must collectively behave to earn classroom rewards (Harris & Sherman, 1973). Clearly, collaborators must examine the context in which behavior occurs, looking for possible antecedent initiations or consequential reinforcement from peers as sources of continuing disruptive classroom behavior.

Motivation Problems.   It is wise to separate problems due to academic deficits from those due simply to lack of motivation. Motivational problems seem to be particularly pervasive as learners with special needs grow older. By the time such learners reach the upper grades, they have experienced many years of dismal classroom failure. By this time, they may not be motivated to learn, sometimes even erroneously believing that they cannot learn or that they have mental retardation or are simply weird.

Motivational problems have to be identified primarily on a trial-and-error basis. One method is to talk with the targeted learners, examining how they feel about themselves and what they want to accomplish in school. This should be combined with observation of the amount of time the learners actually spend working on classroom assignments, determining when lack of productivity is due to lack of skill and when it is due to lack of motivation. Another way to identify motivational problems is to provide a source of motivation that is reinforcing to the learners, and then look for increased work productivity. However, a characteristic problem with this method is that it is sometimes difficult to find the right reinforcer for a particular learner. Personal talks with learners, their parents, and other teachers and the use of reinforcer surveys (see Chapter 7) are ways to solve this problem.

As collaborators examine learner problems related to motivation, it is important to assess the degree of commitment the learner has to the plan to intervene and how involved personally the learner is in that plan. Brophy (1987) constructed an equation to use as learners are involved in the planning of their educational programs. Brophy described this as an equation consisting of two parts: Expectancy and Value. The two parts are:

Part 1: The degree to which learners *expect* to be able to perform the task, if they apply themselves.

Part 2: The degree to which learners *value* participation in the task itself or the benefits or reward that successful task completion will bring to them.

Of course, use of this equation is directly related to helping learners discover what motivates them to learn. The reader is referred to Ames and Ames (1991) for a recent review of research on motivation of learners and effective teaching.

Deficient Independent Work Skills.   Some learners may possess the academic skills to complete work assignments; but they may not know how to work independently, or the work materials may not be designed to facilitate independent learning. For learners who do not possess independent work skills, teachers should design strategies to teach them to work by themselves. The reader is reminded that many learners with special needs spend a portion of their school day receiving very intense, teacher-directed instruction via special service programs. Less often, we see special service teachers teaching those learners to first master the skill and then execute the skill independently prior to transfer from special to general classroom programs. Certainly, this type of transfer training should take place (see Idol, 1993, for examples of transfer programs developed for learners with special needs).

Learners in general classrooms can be taught to work independently. This can be done by starting with short and easy independent tasks, then gradually increasing the level of difficulty. It has been demonstrated that learners with disabilities can be taught to self-monitor their performance on work activities as a means of improving attention to required school tasks (Hallahan, Marshall, & Lloyd, 1981).

Poor independent work completion can also be due to difficult or confusing work materials. Moyer (1979) examined 10 commonly used basal reading series. She compared the readability (Fry Graph) of the basal readers to the accompanying workbooks. The reading level of the workbooks was consistently more difficult than that of the readers, even though the workbooks were to be used for independent work and the readers for teacher-directed instruction.

Osborn (1984) spent considerable time examining the workbook activities themselves from several widely used basal series. She identified a number of problem areas that teachers could modify in workbook materials (her recommendations can be found in Osborn, 1984, or Idol, 1993). If learners are identified who have seemingly mastered the skill area but still fail to complete assignments, collaborators should examine the independent activities themselves, looking for problems associated with the type of response required, clarity of directions, readability of materials, relevancy of tasks, vocabulary, language and concept level, page layout, and sufficient practice opportunity (Osborn, 1984).

Classroom Management Problems. The most important factor that may be affecting learner behavior adversely is the structure or lack of structure of the classroom management system. Classroom management structure includes (a) the pattern of teacher attention, (b) the classroom rules, (c) the delivery of consequences, and (d) the monitoring system being used.

The pattern of teacher attention refers to the manner in which the classroom teacher responds to the learners. It is the responsibility of the collaborators to decide whether to attend to negative learner behavior, subsequently reinforcing unwanted behavior, or whether to attend to desired classroom behavior, as demonstrated early in the applied behavior analysis literature (Becker et al., 1967; Broden, Bruce, Mitchell, Carter, & Hall, 1970; Broden, Hall, Dunlap, & Clark, 1970; Hall, Lund, & Jackson, 1968; Thomas et al., 1968).

Classroom rules refer to the system the classroom teacher has developed for signaling learners about desired classroom behavior. Here are some guidelines for formulating classroom rules. The rules:

- should be clearly stated

- should be posted in the classroom, using large print displayed on posterboard

- should be based on input from learners, indicating what they think the rules should be

- should be stated positively

- should be revised, when necessary, to fit more appropriately the general welfare of the class group and teacher

- should be consistently enforced by the teacher

These guidelines can serve as criteria for deciding whether the rules used in the classroom are sufficient to meet the rigors of effective class management.

Assessment of a classroom management system should include an analysis of the types of consequences delivered to learners for negative and positive behavior. These consequences might include positive reinforcement as well as negative reinforcement or punishment. It may be that there are no consequences for the classroom behavior, that the consequences are too negative, or that the consequences are not consistently delivered. Idol (1993) cited several examples of how consistent and positive reinforcement has been used in consultation projects in classroom and school settings. There are also several sources that the reader may find useful for developing classroom management strategies (e.g., Canter & Canter, 1976; Charles, 1981; Kauffman, 1993; Kerr & Nelson, 1983; Smith, 1981).

An important area in effective classroom management that is sometimes overlooked is the *monitoring system* that is used by teachers. A monitoring system refers to the way in which a teacher decides whether a behavior is acceptable (performance criteria), as well as to the way in which the classroom teacher measures the occurrence or rate of the behavior. In some cases, a classroom teacher may have classroom rules, but the system for determining whether the rules have been followed may not be explicit or easy to operationalize.

All of these components—pattern of teacher attention, classroom rules, delivery of consequences, and monitoring system—must be included in an effective classroom management system. It is the task of the collaborators to assess the occurrence and quality of each of these components, and then to design a more effective system based on improving or adding to each of them.

METHODOLOGY FOR ASSESSMENT OF LEARNING ENVIRONMENTS

The methodology for assessment of classroom environments has four major parts: (1) defining target behaviors, (2) obtaining baseline observations, (3) collecting frequent data, (4) making instructional decisions.

The target behavior is the behavior that the collaborators are trying to change. In most instances, and certainly during initial consultation, this will be a learner's behavior; occasionally, and usually later in time, it will be a teacher behavior. Defining the target behavior is one of the most important steps in the collaborative consultation process. Often the initial behavior, the problem that initiated the consultation, will become more clearly specified as it is transformed into a target behavior. The role of the collaborators during this process is to listen actively to one another and to ask questions to specify the behavior.

It is not unusual for the first-defined target behavior to be transformed into a different target behavior as a result of consultation and classroom observation. The reason for this is that it may take collaborators a while to identify specific troublesome behaviors. The initial impression of the person most directly involved with the learner may be that there is a general problem (e.g., disruptiveness, hyperactivity, inattention, talkativeness, being rude). Then, during the observation and collaborative consultation processes, the general problem is transformed into specific behaviors (e.g., walking around the room, dropping books, gazing out the window, talking without teacher permission, not saying "please"). Refer to the appendix to this chapter for examples of recording forms for use while observing classroom behavior.

Once the target behavior(s) have been defined, the collaborating group must decide when and how they are going to observe the behavior. The period of observation is known as the baseline condition. The intent is to gain a clear idea of the environmental conditions that are present when the behavior occurs. It is recommended that the length of the baseline observation phase be approximately 5 days, unless the behavior is improving during that period. If improvement is observed, it is recommended that no intervention be implemented until the data stabilize or until it becomes evident that the intervention is not necessary. It is possible that the behavior will improve on its own, as a result of having implemented a system for data collection or observation.

Measurement Techniques

A behavior can be measured in many ways. Jenkins and Pany (1974) adapted six standard ways of measuring behavior that seem most suited to consultation problems in the classroom (Hall, 1975). The six measurement techniques are (a) event recording, (b) interval recording, (c) duration recording, (d) planned activity check, (e) direct measurement of permanent products, and (f) time sampling.

Event Recording. An observer using event-recording procedures makes a cumulative record of discrete events, that is, a frequency count of the events as they occur. For example, a teacher may record the number of times a learner gets out of the chair without permission. One way to do this is to tally the number of times with a pencil on a note pad. Or a parent may use a wrist golf-counter to tally how many times a son or daughter cries during the day. An advantage of event recording is that it is a simple procedure that does not significantly interfere with ongoing tasks. Event recording also produces a numerical output.

Interval Recording. Each observation session is divided into equal time periods to make an interval recording. The observer then records the occurrence of behavior during those intervals. For example, in the illustration below, an observer has recorded whether or not a learner has physically assaulted either another learner or property during ½-hour intervals of a school day.

8:30	9:00	9:30	10:00	10:30	11:00	11:30	12:30	1:00	1:30	2:00	2:30
A	N	N	A	A	A	N	A	N	N	A	N

A = Assault   N = No Assault

In this example, the learner exhibited assaults during six (50%) of the twelve ½-hour intervals.

Duration Recording. Duration recording is used if it is important to know how long a particular behavior lasts. The elapsed time of a specific behavior is recorded during a specific observation period. A stopwatch is the most efficient tool for making duration recordings. However, clocks and conventional watches can be used in situations in which less-precise measures are sufficient.

Problematic behaviors for which duration recording may be appropriate are: time spent out of seat, lateness for class, time taken to begin work, long tantrums, sleeping or sitting with head down, and staring out the window.

Planned Activity Check. A recording technique called a planned activity check (PLA-check) has been proved to be suitable for use by teachers and parents working with groups (Risley, 1972). The PLA-check is similar in some respects to time sampling, but it includes other features:

- The behavior (planned activity) the observer wishes to record in a group of learners is scientifically defined.

- At given intervals (e.g., every 10 minutes), the observer counts as quickly as possible how many individuals are engaged in the behavior and then records the total.

- The observer then counts and records as quickly as possible how many individuals are present in the area of the activity.

- The number of learners present can then be divided into the number of pupils engaged in the behavior. By multiplying the result by 100, the observer finds the percentage of those engaged in the behavior at that particular time.

To illustrate the technique, suppose a shop teacher wanted to check on what portion of a class was working on an assigned woodworking project during a 50-minute period. Every 10 minutes the teacher would quickly count how many were working on the project, and would then count the number of learners present. Let us assume that, during the first part of the period, the teacher found that 10 of 20 and 15 of 20 learners were working. During the second part of the period, 10 boys who had been excused to work on another project returned to the class. The teacher then found 15 of 30, 30 of 30, and

20 of 30 of those present working on the assigned project. That is, at various times, 50%, 75%, 50%, 100%, and 67% were working. This results in an average of 68% who worked on the assigned project during the class period.

Direct Measurement of Permanent Products. The behaviors of learners sometimes result in permanent products, that is, tangible things that can be observed and counted. For example, when a learner completes assignments, writes answers to math problems, stacks blocks, or strings beads, direct measures can be obtained from the products of such behaviors. The direct measurement of products has several advantages, including (a) precise records, (b) permanent records that are usually translatable into numerical terms, and (c) products that are often the end result of important academic behaviors.

Time Sampling. Time sampling is similar to interval recording, except that it does not require continuous observation. The observation sessions are divided into equal intervals, but the behavior is recorded only at the end of each interval. In the example below, a 60-minute math class is divided into a series of unequal intervals that average 5 minutes. In this situation, a kitchen timer or calculator with an alarm buzzer can be used by the mediator. When the alarm sounds, the adult looks at the learner to see whether the behavior (in this case, out of seat) is occurring at that instant. The adult then records the behavior on a sheet. A plus sign (+) indicates the presence of out-of-seat behavior, and a minus sign (–) indicates that the learner was in the seat. In this example, as can be seen, the learner was out of the seat on 8 of 12 occasions, or 67% of the time.

1	2	3	4	5	6	7	8	9	10	11	12
+	–	–	+	+	+	–	+	+	–	+	+

After recording the presence or absence of the behavior, the adult resets the timer. It is wise to vary the length of the timer setting so that the learner cannot anticipate the observation. A time-sampling procedure is appropriate for behaviors that either are very frequent or have long durations. Collaborators can adopt any of these techniques to enable learners to monitor their own behaviors.

Rules and Guidelines

Collaborators might use any one or a combination of the above six ways of measuring behavior; refer to Alberto and Troutman (1986) for elaborations on how these techniques can be applied in the classroom. Collaborators must be certain to select and recommend measurement systems that are simple and easy to administer in classroom settings. The collaborators should work together to select or design the recording system that will be used.

Once the collaborators have agreed on a recording system, they should practice using it to make certain they are observing the same behavior. Then they must decide who will collect the primary data and who will collect the secondary (reliability) data. Some teachers question the importance of collecting reliability data, but a single experience of obtaining discrepant data will convince most skeptics of the value and importance of reliability procedures. It is thus recommended that reliability data can be collected at least one or two times in each phase (baseline and the various intervention and maintenance phases).

The following are some rules for classroom observers suggested by Marcia Broden (in Hall, 1975). These are simple guidelines for observers to follow regardless of whether the observer is collecting primary data or reliability data. In each case, the guideline has been adapted for use in Collaborative Consultation.

- If possible, enter the classroom at a normal break in classroom routine.

- Sit where you can see, usually at the side or rear of the classroom.

- Have your chair placed in the observation site in advance.

- If it is necessary to move about, have other chairs or stools near places the students may go.

- Avoid all contact with teachers or students. Avoid eye contact; look away if the observed student looks at you; put the student "on extinction." If the student persists, say, "I'm busy," then avoid the student.

- Vary your glances; appear to be looking around.

- If possible, make observations at the same time each day. This is less disturbing and reduces the possibility of error. An exception would be if the collaborators have agreed to observe at specific times throughout the day.

- If it is necessary for adaptation or to establish reliability, make several prerecording observations.

- Avoid chewing gum, eating candy, and wearing distracting clothes.

- Keep all scheduled observation appointments.

- Review with the teacher what you have observed.

Once the baseline data have been collected, the collaborators should meet to discuss the results and decide if the data offer an accurate picture of the situation. If they do not, new target behaviors, times of observation, measurement systems, and so on, must be determined. In this case, a second baseline should be collected. If, on the other hand, the data provide an accurate representation of the situation, the collaborators will be more convinced that the data can continue to be collected in the same manner. If the recording system is too complicated, the collaborators can (a) devise a simpler system, (b) collect a few more days of baseline data, (c) meet to design an intervention program, (d) implement the program, and (e) continue to collect daily learner progress data. The collaborators should meet periodically to examine the data, discuss the impact of the program, and decide whether to continue the intervention, implement a program change, or move to a maintenance phase. Examples of data depicting these various phases, together with discussion of applicable decision-making rules, can be found in Alberto and Troutman (1986) and Blankenship and Lilly (1981). Training modules on classroom observation techniques can be found in Idol and West (1993) and West et al. (1989).

Summary of Assessment Techniques

The theoretical position espoused in this section is one that favors direct assessment of skill levels as a means of determining appropriate instructional environments and programs for learners with special needs. We believe that, for many of these learners, the general classroom is the most appropriate, as well as the most educationally enhancing educational domain. The assignment of labels to learners, describing the type of supportive special education they might be eligible to receive, does not provide concrete information concerning how to teach those learners.

The first step in facilitating the learning of students is to conduct a systematic and precise examination of the level of functioning of the learners in their natural classroom environment. The assessment procedure might include (a) appropriate use of standardized tests, (b) observations in classrooms, (c) use of normative sampling as a means of establishing social validity and performance criteria, (d) assessment of the learners using classroom curricula, (e) portfolio assessment of learners' work samples, (f) determination for each skill area the stage of learning the learners might be in, (g) implementation of an intermittent assessment system that is used throughout the school year, and (h) examination of the classroom environment to determine the effects of antecedent and consequential stimuli on learner response. The implementation of appropriate assessment strategies in each of these areas should be coupled with instructional and evaluation strategies presented in Chapters 6, 7, and 8.

The assessment techniques we have examined are best implemented by teachers in the classroom setting. In this context, collaborators should practice behaviors that facilitate the effective assessment of learners with special needs. To this end, collaborators should be guided by the assessment principles we have discussed, each of which is designed to enhance a truly collaborative effort to evaluate efficiently student performance in the classroom.

SETTING GOALS AND OBJECTIVES FOR LEARNERS

Goals are abstract statements concerning long-term educational intentions. They are usually based on an educational philosophy and reflect the ideal purposes of education. Instructional objectives are specific, short-term descriptions of educational outcomes that can be directly and immediately observed (Wheeler & Fox, 1972).

Larsen and Poplin (1980) once noted the differences in annual goals and short-term instructional objectives:

> Annual goals constitute those goals appropriate for the child's immediate education and projected to be accomplished within the present school year. In addition to guiding instructional personnel in developing activities and materials, appropriate development of short-term instructional objectives provides a structure for continuous monitoring of pupil progress. (p. 306)

Goals are important in providing landmarks for learner progress. We believe learners should be eligible for special services until they have demonstrated all of the maximum skills and knowledge identified as being necessary to have a reasonable chance for success in their communities and future lives. Goals and objectives for learners who qualify for special education services must comply with IEP rules and regulations as described in Chapter 3.

Functional enabling objectives include the components of conditions, behavior, and criteria. Under the conditions component, the person responsible for instruction is identified (teacher, aide, parent or peer, etc.) as well as the material necessary for the specified task (reading, math, or physical materials, etc.). Under the behavior component, the type of required response is described (verbal, written, or physical). Finally, under the criteria component the accuracy and time expectations are clarified (e.g. 90% to 100% correct within 20 minutes). All of these components help to ensure that collaborators understand what is expected and will be able to recognize the relevant demonstrations of skills and knowledge when they occur.

Following is a sample set of goals and objectives that meet the above criteria:

1. *Goal:* Upon graduation from school, learners will have acquired academic knowledge and social skills that will enable them to lead productive and satisfying lives.

2. *Annual goal:* Given grade-level materials and instruction provided by classroom teachers, learners will demonstrate mastery of reading comprehension by completing by the end of each academic year the 10 grade-level comprehension tests (one test per month for each of the 10 months of the school year) at 90% to 100% accuracy.

3. *Instructional objective:* Given total class, small-group, and individualized instruction from the reading materials provided by the classroom teacher, learners will demonstrate by the last day of September mastery of reading comprehension skills for Test 1 at 90% to 100% accuracy.

Additional examples of instruction objectives are listed in Table 5.1. Another source regarding content for goals and objectives is Lovitt (1991), who broadened the definitions of IEP goals to include an enormous variety: study skills,

TABLE 5.1. Examples of Instructional Objectives

Conditions	Behaviors	Criteria
Elementary Level Reading Comprehension Objective		
Given individualized instruction in the third-grade basal reading series provided by the classroom teacher,	the learners will complete workbook assignments in writing . . .	at 90% to 100% accuracy on a daily basis.
Middle School Level Reading Comprehension Objective		
Given small-group instruction in various eighth-grade reading material, provided by the classroom teacher,	the learners will act out the main ideas . . .	at 90% to 100% accuracy at least once a month. The teacher and the rest of the class will judge the accuracy of matching the main ideas delineated in the reading materials with those observed through the skit.
High School Level Reading Comprehension Objective		
Given total class instruction related to research topics discussed by the classroom teacher,	the learners will complete a written critique, on the basis of which they will give an oral presentation to the class . . .	at 90% to 100% accuracy at least four times a year. The critique must include a summary of key ideas, a comparison of at least 10 different sources, and an evaluation of the material from the learners' point of view. The critique will be judged by the teacher and at least one other independent reader.

social behaviors, attendance, motivation, health, basic skills, compliance, self-concept, attitude, generating personal goals (e.g., contracts, completing long-term assignments, setting priorities), and participation (e.g., self-monitoring participation in class discussions, "looking alive," answering questions by rephrasing questions, and alternative ways to ask questions).

Both long-range goals and short-term instructional objectives are important. Long-range goals help remind collaborators of their responsibility to facilitate long-range growth and development, whereas short-term instructional objectives provide small progress indicators toward that overall goal.

It is relatively easy to focus on cognitive skills, since they are the ones most commonly associated with schooling. However, Bloom, Engelhart, Furst, Hill, and Krathwohl (1956) long ago set a standard indicating that there are at least three major domains that educators should address in their efforts to facilitate school improvement: the cognitive, the affective, and the psychomotor. The *cognitive domain* includes those objectives that deal with the recall or recognition of knowledge and the development of intellectual abilities and skills. The *affective domain* includes objectives that describe changes in interest, attitudes, and values. The *psychomotor domain* includes objectives that deal with manipulative or motor skills. Clearly, all three domains are important and should be included in educational programs.

Joyce, Hersh, and McKibbin (1983) have a slightly different focus in defining the three domains of learning. They refer to the personal, social, and academic domains. Their definition of the *academic domain* is similar to the cognitive domain defined by Bloom et al. (1956) over 35 years ago, in that it relates to academic subjects, such as mathematics and English. However, their description of the *personal domain* is somewhat different, in that it refers to personal capabilities, such as intelligence, creativity, and motivation. Their definition of the *social domain* is also different, since it focuses on interactive social and economic skills.

As collaborators continue to work together to develop both the technology and the art of identifying goals and specifying instructional objectives, it is hoped that those goals and objectives will be expanded. Our ultimate hope is that all learners will have opportunities to learn in individualized, small-group, and large-group situations and that they will have opportunities to demonstrate their skills and knowledge through reading, writing, and a variety of physical activities. To this end, learners need opportunities to learn in their own classrooms, communities, and states. They need to travel and learn from and with others at various ages, religions, and races. Learning through a variety of activities, places, and people should become the rule, rather than the exception, for all learners (Villa & Thousand, 1992).

In support of these ideas, Eisner (1991) wrote of the need for broadening our perspectives of understanding the missions of schooling. In particular, he called for going beyond the "merely measurable to a consideration of more profound purposes" (p. 10). Six "aims that count in schools" (p. 11) include:

(a) teaching learners that the "exploration of ideas is sometimes difficult, often exciting, and occasionally fun" (p. 11); (b) helping learners "learn how to formulate their own problems and how to design the tactics and strategies to solve them" (p. 14); (c) developing in all learners "multiple forms of literacy" (p. 14); (d) teaching learners the "importance of wonder" (p. 15), such as daydreaming, imagining, or questioning; (e) helping learners "realize that they are part of a caring community" (p. 16); and (f) teaching learners that "they have a unique and important personal significance" (p. 16). Eisner believes that formulating and achieving goals such as these will require attention "to the ways in which we organize our workplaces, to the scope of the programs that we provide, to the quality of our teaching, and to the means through which we assess what really matters" (p. 17).

A major task of collaborators is to demonstrate that, given appropriate conditions, all learners can learn, and that all teachers can learn the appropriate skills and necessary attitudes to facilitate their learners' progress. Blanchard and Johnson (1982) and Blanchard and Lorber (1984) suggested a similar positive attitude in business settings; they noted that everyone is a potential winner, even if he or she is sometimes cited as a loser. They suggested that leaders should not be fooled by appearances but should rather focus on the conditions that facilitate winners. One of the essential conditions of goal setting is to have positive expectations. Collaborators must encourage one another to believe that all of their learners are winners who can learn and that their beliefs are based on their own positive experiences in facilitating that learning.

Finally, collaborative consultants must continually strive to facilitate growth and change among each other, as well as in the learners with special needs. Blanchard and Johnson (1982) offered helpful suggestions for facilitating such human growth and development. They noted that people who feel good about themselves usually produce good results. Collaborators can work to ensure that they as well as their learners receive positive feedback about what they are doing well so that they can face their areas of need with confidence and willingness to improve. Blanchard and Johnson (1982) indicated that one of the best ways to help people reach their full potential is to catch them doing something right. Finally, they noted that goals only initiate the behaviors, consequences are needed to maintain them. (Consequences for maintaining learner behavior are more fully described in Chapter 7.)

FACTORS THAT INFLUENCE THE FORMULATION OF GOALS

Many factors influence the formulation of goals and objectives. National and state mandates as well as local school district expectations act as major facilitators or barriers to the specification of educational goals and instructional objectives. For years there was considerable controversy over the need, importance, even the appropriateness of educational objectives, and apparently this continues to be a debated issue (Stainback & Stainback, 1992). Since the passage of P.L. 94-142, however, goals and objectives have become the rule rather than the exception.

The attitudes and skills of administrators and teachers play a major part in influencing the formulation of goals and objectives. Educators who believe in the importance of goals and objectives are more willing to take the time required to learn how to write them. Beyond that, educators who not only believe in the importance of goals and objectives but have also been taught how to specify them are more apt to use them as part of their normal teaching/learning processes.

The consequences of specifying objectives or not specifying them play a major role in determining whether or not the behaviors of writing and using instructional objectives are initiated and maintained. It is thus important that representatives of the community, as well as the student body, work with teachers and administrators in identifying the important goals and objectives for their school systems. Schools are only as good as their communities expect and allow them to be (Edmonds, 1979; Joyce et al., 1983). Therefore, community citizens need to play a major role in defining their school's educational goals.

Instructional objectives are usually specified by the teachers and specialists who are responsible for the learners' achievement of those objectives. Successful completion of all of the instructional objectives should increase the probability that learners will ultimately achieve the educational goals of their schools. Joyce et al. (1983) concluded that

> the improvement of schools takes place in a social context that both impels innovations and complicates the process. We open with the current theoretical and empirical bases for establishing a process of school improvement as a part of the regular business of educational life. Our strategy depends on the development of an organization that we will call the Responsible Parties to scrutinize the health of each school and oversee its improvement. The Responsible Parties examine the program of the school and make decisions about how to refine it to make it more effective, renovate particular curriculum areas, and eventually, redesign the entire educational program. (p. 1)

Joyce and his colleagues emphasized the importance of responsible parties or community citizens to help ensure the improvement of their schools. Community citizens can have positive effects on their schools when they expect excellence and provide consequences that reinforce excellence. Here, however, community citizens may need to learn from business (Hersey & Blanchard, 1988; Peters & Waterman, 1982); they must be careful not to punish personnel who have positive attitudes and skills to facilitate excellence. Educational excellence starts with goals and objectives. Brookover et al. (1982) noted that the school staff should communicate clearly and simply to parents its needs for support and involvement that can facilitate high student achievement. The staff should initiate this communication by designing a school plan for parent support and involvement that coordinates the efforts of school and home to improve achievement. The plan should establish a norm for parent behavior that will facilitate and promote student success in school. (p. 270)

Thus, national, state, and local mandates, the attitudes and skills of educators, and the positive participation of concerned citizens all influence the identification of educational goals and the specification of instructional objectives.

COLLABORATIVE CONSULTATION TECHNIQUES FOR SETTING GOALS AND OBJECTIVES

Four specific techniques can be used to encourage collaborators to become more interested and skilled in developing goals and objectives: (a) discussing, (b) reviewing, (c) specifying, and (d) reinforcing.

Discussing the Importance of Goals and Objectives

Collaborators should discuss the importance of goals and objectives for learners with one another. They must explain the importance of having educational goals reflect the purposes of education as defined by their particular community. Finally, they must help one another learn about the differences between goals and objectives so that they will be able to specify the conditions, behavior, and criteria for instructional objectives in four areas: (a) self-help and basic living skills, (b) academic skills, (c) vocational and career skills, and (d) sociobehavioral skills (Larsen & Poplin, 1980).

Collaborators should talk about the need to design instructional objectives that are directly related to the general classroom curriculum. Without such objectives, learners could not be expected to acquire grade-level skills. Further, since instructional objectives help define the focus for classroom observation, instruction, evaluation, and redesign, it is imperative that all collaborators are in agreement about what should be taught. Minimum instructional objectives help define the essential skills and knowledge that all learners need.

Time-on-task has been directly correlated with higher learner achievement (Denham & Lieberman, 1980). Time-on-task is often related specifically to the criteria section of well-written instructional objectives. The very process of task analysis (breaking down complex skills or behavioral chains into their component parts) requires and facilitates opportunities for collaborators to work together on behalf of learners with special needs in general classrooms. Such learners can typically function in the curriculum but often need the academic tasks broken down into smaller steps than those in the tasks of their classmates. They may also need more time to complete assignments or have new skills modeled for them. Instructional objectives that specify these necessary conditions, behavior, and criteria will help ensure the educational progress of the learners for whom they were developed.

Reviewing Instructional Objectives

Collaborators must take the time to review instructional objectives. The review process provides collaborators who are inexperienced in writing objectives with the opportunity to see some helpful models. For those with more experience, it provides an opportunity to compare and contrast their objectives with those that have been written by others in their own school, district, and state. The review process may help identify information that indicates that collaborators are expecting too much, or too little, of their learners. It can also provide new ideas, reveal inappropriate expectations, and indicate how well they have developed and maintained their willingness and ability to specify the educational goals toward which they expect their learners to strive. All of this information is, in turn, helpful to the collaborators in determining how and when to work with each other on behalf of their students.

Specifying Objectives

Collaborators should also guide one another in how to specify and write objectives. They should provide opportunities to review and discuss a variety of objectives and their component parts. Consensus should be reached regarding the critical information that should be in each of the three components: conditions, behavior, and criteria.

Wheeler and Fox (1972) provided one of the easiest models for specifying instructional objectives that include these three components. They suggested that teachers follow a complete model for the first few times they try to write instructional objectives. After they successfully follow a complete model, they should try writing one section of the objectives on their own. After successfully completing that section, they should try writing two sections on their own, and then, finally, all three sections. The writing should be in a group situation so that collaborators can get immediate feedback, both from matching their responses with model responses and from discussing their progress and problems with team members.

Reinforcing the Specification of Objectives

After specifying objectives, it is important to reinforce the practice of writing and using the objectives. This can be done in a variety of ways. In any

case, it is most helpful when collaborators brainstorm a list of potential reinforcers. Reinforcement needs and interests may vary from day to day.

Figure 5.3 shows a modification of Maslow's (1954) hierarchy of needs
matched to potential reinforcers for educators. In our own experience, educators have confirmed the usefulness of these reinforcers. At the initial (phys-
iological) level, they have requested the opportunity to work for workshop
or course credit as they attempted to learn new knowledge and skills. As they
earned additional credits, they also earned increased salaries. At the second,
(safety) level, the educators seemed thankful just to have the assistance of
and positive interactions with collaborators as they worked together to provide effective and appropriate educational services for learners with special
needs, who had been mainstreamed into their general classrooms. At the third
(social) level, educators appeared to enjoy the acceptance of their peers and
the recognition provided by other teachers, administrators, parents, and
learners as they became advocates for all learners and especially skilled at
providing special education in their general classroom settings. At the fourth
(esteem) level, educators seemed to be reinforced most by sharing their skills
and knowledge through local, state, and national presentations and publications. Finally, at the fifth (self-actualization) level, they seemed to become
intrinsically reinforced largely by their increased skills and responsibilities.
Some even sought more role changes, such as moving along a continuum
from classroom teaching, to consulting, to coordinating special education,
to directing all learner personnel services, and finally to functioning as a super-
intendent. Although each of these roles moved educators further and further

FIGURE 5.3.   Maslow's Hierarchy of Needs adapted to match potential
reinforcers for educators who collaborate.

Need	Definition	Reinforcers for collaborators
1. *Physiological*	Basic needs: food, shelter, clothing	Academic credit, scholarships, increased salary
2. *Safety*	Freedom from fear of loss of basic needs	Help with learners with special needs
3. *Social*	Need to be accepted by groups	Acceptance and recognition by administrators, peers, parents, and learners
4. *Esteem*	Recognition from others	Presentations, publications
5. *Self-Actualization*	Maximization of one's potential	Increased skills, responsibilities, and more challenging work

away from direct contact with learners, the roles also provided them with role changes, which included more responsibilities for larger numbers of learners.

In adapting and responding to Maslow's Hierarchy of Needs, Kunc (1992) presented the idea that learners actually experience an inversion of Maslow's hierarchy: "Educators often work from the premise that achievement and mastery rather than belonging are the primary if not sole precursors for self-esteem" (p. 31). Collaborators need to develop schools as caring communities for *all* learners so that acceptance is a given condition, *not* one that needs to be earned. After all, the challenge of learning academic content requirements alone is a full-time task for even the most able learners.

Summary of Goals and Objectives

Goals and objectives provide the direction for instruction and, ultimately, for the implementation of effective collaboration. They also set the expectations for growth and improvement. Further, goals and objectives provide the basis for an essential accountability system. For all these reasons, they are of vital importance. Successful collaborators keep in mind the rationale for developing goals and objectives and the factors that influence their formulation as described in this chapter. Goals and objectives provide important indicators of effectiveness as we strive to facilitate educational excellence for all learners.

SUMMARY

In this chapter we have defined problem identification as a consensual process in which collaborators engage. Collaborators expect they will be combining a myriad of resources, skills, and assessment information to build the clearest and most accurate description of the problem. They share in the gathering of this information and in the building of a problem statement. They use that problem statement to form the base for developing a set of goals and objectives for targeted learners to achieve. The goals and objectives provide the direction for the next step in collaborative problem solving, which is for the team to explore a collection of possible strategies or ways to solve the problem (interventions). Interventions that we have found useful through the use of the Collaborative Consultation Model are described in Chapters 6 and 7.

STUDY QUESTIONS

1. What are the major limitations of traditional assessment systems for learners with special needs? Why does applying a collaborative consultation process to assessment result in better assessment?

2. Describe four of the assessment techniques you find most challenging to implement. Analyze the barriers and facilitators to help you implement them.

3. Compare and contrast two standardized tests with their curriculum-based assessment systems. Why is it important to use a general education curriculum as a comparison point for data-based decisions?

4. Discuss two methods of assessing the learning environment that you can use in your situation. What advantages does the planned activity check (PLA-check) have over other methods?

5. Discuss two of the five factors that influence goals and objectives that are important to your setting. Describe how your collaborative consultation team might develop goals and objectives that take those factors into consideration.

6. When ensuring broad goals and objectives that are also accountable to learners with special needs, how does the IEP process help a collaborative consultation team?

REFERENCES

Alberto, P. S., & Troutman, A. C. (1986). *Applied behavior analysis for teachers: Influencing student performance.* Columbus, OH: Merrill.

Ames, R., & Ames, C. (1991). Motivation and effective teaching. In L. Idol & B. F. Jones, *Educational values and cognitive instruction: Implications for reform* (pp. 247–272). Hillsdale, NJ: Erlbaum.

Armbruster, B. B., Stevens, R. S., & Rosenshine, B. (1977). *Analyzing content coverage and emphasis: A study of three curricula and two tests* (Technical Report No. 26). Urbana-Champaign: University of Illinois, Center for the Study of Reading.

Auerbach, S. (1986). Data based cooperative planning: A proposal for mainstreamed remediation of learning disabled students. *British Journal of Special Education, 10*(1), 37–47.

Becker, W. C., Madsen, C. H., Jr., Arnold, C. R., & Thomas, D. R. (1967). The contingent use of teacher attention and praise in reducing disruptive behavior in a classroom. *The Journal of Special Education, 1,* 287–301.

Blanchard, K., & Johnson, S. (1982). *The one-minute manager.* New York: Morrow.

Blanchard, K. & Lorber, R. (1984). *Putting the one-minute manager to work.* New York: Morrow.

Blankenship, C., & Lilly, M. S. (1981). *Mainstreaming students with learning and behavior problems.* New York: Holt, Rinehart & Winston.

Bloom, B. S., Englehart, M. D., Furst, E. J., Hill, W. H., & Krathwohl, D. R. (1956). *Taxonomy of educational objectives.* New York: MacKay.

Broden, M., Bruce, C., Mitchell, M. A., Carter, U., & Hall, V. (1970). Effects of teacher attention on attending behavior of two boys at adjacent desks. *Journal of Applied Behavior Analysis, 3,* 199–203.

Broden, M., Hall, R. V., Dunlap, A., & Clark, R. (1970). Effects of teacher attention and a token reinforcement system in a junior high school special education class. *Exceptional Children, 36,* 341–349.

Brookover, W., Beamer, L., Efthim, H., Hathaway, D., Lezotte, L. Miller, S., Passalacqua, J., & Tornatzky, L. (1982). *Creating effective schools: An inservice program for enhancing school learning climate and achievement.* Holmes Beach, FL: Learning Publications.

Brophy, J. (1987). Synthesis research on strategies for motivating students to learn. *Educational Leadership, 45*(2), 40–48.

Bryan, T. H., (1974). An observational analysis of the classroom behaviors of children with learning disabilities. *Journal of Learning Disabilities, 7,* 35–43.

Bryan, T., & Wheeler, R. (1972). Perception of learning disabled children: The eye of the observer. *Journal of Learning Disabilities, 5,* 484–488.

Canter, L., & Canter, M. (1976). *Assertive discipline.* Los Angeles: Lee Canter.

Charles, C. M. (1981). *Building classroom discipline: From models to practice.* New York: Longman.

Denham, C., & Lieberman, A. (1980). *Time to learn.* Washington, DC: National Institute of Education.

Edmonds, R. R. (1979). Effective schools for the urban poor. *Educational Leadership, 37*(1). 15–18, 20–24.

Eisner, E. (1991). What really counts in schools. *Educational Leadership, 48*(5), 10–17.

Epstein, M. H., & Cullinan, D. (1979). Social validation: Use of normative peer data to evaluate LD interventions. *Learning Disability Quarterly, 2*(4), 93–98.

Forman, B., & McKinney, J. D. (1975). Teacher perceptions of the classroom behavior of learning disabled and non-learning disabled children. *Proceedings of the National Association of School Psychologists, 2,* 285–286.

Foster, G. G., & Salvia, J. (1977). Teacher response to the label "learning disabled" as a function of demand characteristics. *Exceptional Children, 43,* 533–534.

Foster, G. G., Schmidt, C. R., & Sabatino, D. (1976). Teacher expectancies and the label "learning disabilities." *Journal of Learning Disabilities, 9,* 58–61.

Gickling, E. E., & Havertape, J. (n.d.). *Curriculum-based assessment (CB).* From nontest-based assessment module. Minneapolis: University of Minnesota, National School Psychology Inservice Training Network.

Gickling, E. E., & Thompson, V. P. (1985). A personal view of curriculum-based assessment. *Exceptional Children, 52*(3), 244–265.

Gillung, T. B., & Rucker, C. N. (1977). Labels and teacher expectations. *Exceptional Children, 43*(7), 464–465.

Graubard, P. S., Rosenberg, H., & Miller, M. B. (1971). Student applications of behavior modification to teachers and environments or ecological approaches to social deviancy. In E. A. Ramp & B. L. Hopkins (Eds), *A new direction for education: Behavior analysis* (pp. 80–101). Lawrence: University of Kansas.

Hall, R. V., Lund, D., & Jackson, D. (1968). Effects of teacher attention on study behavior. *Journal of Applied Behavior Analysis, 1,* 1–12.

Hall, R. V., Panyan, M., Rabon, D., & Broden, M. (1968). Instructing beginning teachers in reinforcement procedures which improve classroom control. *Journal of Applied Behavior Analysis, 1*(4), 315–327.

Hall, V. (1975). *Managing behavior: Part 1.* Austin, TX: PRO-ED.

Hallahan, D. P., Marshall, K. J., & Lloyd, J. W. (1981). Self-recording during group instruction: Effects on attention to task. *Learning Disability Quarterly, 4*(14), 407–413.

Haring, N. G., Lovitt, T. C., Eaton, M. D., & Hansen, C. L. (1978). *The fourth R: Research in the classroom.* Columbus, OH: Merrill.

Harris, V. W., & Sherman, J. A. (1973). Use and analysis of the "good behavior game" to reduce disruptive classroom behavior. *Journal of Applied Behavior Analysis, 6*(3), 405–417.

Hersey, P., & Blanchard, K. H. (1988). *Management of organizational behavior: Utilizing human resources.* Englewood Cliffs, NJ: Prentice-Hall.

Howell, K. W., & Morehead, M. K. (1987). *Curriculum-based evaluation in remedial and special education.* Columbus, OH: Merrill.

Idol, L. (1989). The resource/consulting teacher: An integrated model of service delivery. *Remedial and Special Education, 9*(6), 48–58.

Idol, L., (1993). *Special educator's consultation handbook* (2nd ed.). Austin, TX: PRO-ED.

Idol, L., Nevin, A., & Paolucci-Whitcomb, P. (1986). *Models of curriculum-based assessment.* Austin, TX: PRO-ED.

Idol, L., & West, J. F. (1993). *Effective instruction of difficult-to-teach students: An inservice and preservice professional development program for classroom, remedial, and special education teachers.* Austin, TX: PRO-ED.

Idol-Maestas, L., Ritter, S., & Lloyd, S. (1983). A model for direct, data-based reading instruction. *Journal of Special Education Technology, 6*(3), 61–78.

Jenkins, J. R., & Pany, D. (1974). *Some resources to help teachers manage classroom behavior problems.* Unpublished manuscript, University of Illinois at Urbana-Champaign, Department of Special Education.

Jenkins, J. R., & Pany, D. (1978a). Curriculum biases in reading achievement tests. *Journal of Reading Behavior, 10*(4), 345–357.

Jenkins, J. R., & Pany, D. (1978b). Standardized achievement tests: How useful for special education? *Exceptional Children, 44*(6) 448–453.

Joyce, B. R., Hersh, R. H., & McKibbin, M. (1983). *The structure of school improvement.* New York: Longman.

Kauffman, J. M. (1993). *Characteristics of children's behavior disorders* (5th ed.). Columbus, OH: Merrill.

Kazdin, A. E. (1977). Assessing the clinical or applied significance of behavior change through social validation. *Behavior Modification, 1*, 427–452.

Kerr, M. M., & Nelson, M. (1983). *Strategies for managing behavior problems in the classroom.* Columbus, OH: Merrill.

Kunc, N. (1992). The need to belong: Rediscovering Maslow's Hierarchy of Needs. In R. A. Villa, J. S. Thousand, W. Stainback, & S. Stainback (Eds.), *Restructuring for caring and effective education: An administrative guide to creating heterogeneous schools* (pp. 25–39). Baltimore: Brookes.

Larsen, S. C., & Poplin, M. S. (1980). *Methods for educating the handicapped: An individualized education program approach.* Boston: Allyn & Bacon.

Lovitt, T. (1991). *Preventing school dropouts: Tactics for at-risk, remedial, and mildly handicapped adolescents.* Austin, TX: PRO-ED.

Marston, D., & Magnusson, D. (1985). Implementing curriculum-based measurement in special and regular education settings. *Exceptional Children, 52*(3), 266–276.

Maslow, A. H. (1954) *Motivation and personality.* New York: Harper & Row.

McKinney, J. D., McClure, S., & Feagans, L. (1982). Classroom behavior of learning disabled children. *Learning Disability Quarterly, 5*(1) 45–52.

Moore, M. G., Haskins, R., & McKinney, J. D. (1980). Classroom behavior of reflective and impulsive children. *Journal of Applied Developmental Psychology, 1*(1), 59–75.

Moyer, S. B. (1979). Readability of basal readers and workbooks: A comparison. *Learning Disability Quarterly, 2,* 23–28.

Osborn, J. (1984). The purposes, uses and contents of workbooks and some guidelines for publishers. In R. C. Anderson, J. Osborn, & R. J. Tierney, *Learning to read in American schools: Basal readers and content text* (pp. 45–112). Hillsdale, NJ: Erlbaum.

Paulson, F. L., Paulson, P. R., & Meyer, C. A. (1991). What makes a portfolio a portfolio? *Educational Leadership, 48*(5), 60–63.

Peters, T. J., & Waterman, R. H. (1982). *In search of excellence: Lessons from America's best-run companies.* New York: Harper & Row.

Peterson, J., Heistad, D., Peterson, D., & Reynolds, M. (1985). Montevideo individualized prescriptive instructional management system. *Exceptional Children, 52*(3), 239–243.

Risley, T. R. (1972). Spontaneous language and the preschool. In J. C. Stanley (Ed.), *Preschool programs for the disadvantaged: Five experimental approaches to early childhood education.* Baltimore: Johns Hopkins University Press.

Rosenfield, S., & Rubinson, F. (1985). Introducing curriculum-based assessment through consultation. *Exceptional Children, 52*(3), 282–287.

Smith, D. D. (1981). *Teaching the learning disabled.* Englewood Cliffs, NJ: Prentice-Hall.

Stainback, W., & Stainback, S. (Eds.). (1992). *Controversial issues confronting special education: Divergent perspectives.* Boston: Allyn & Bacon.

Thomas, D. R., Becker, W. C., & Armstrong, M. (1968). Production and elimination of disruptive classroom behavior by systematically varying teacher's behavior. *Journal of Applied Behavior Analysis 1,* 35–45.

Thurlow, M. L., & Ysseldyke, J. E. (1979). Current assessment and decision-making practices in model LD programs. *Learning Disability Quarterly, 2,* 15–24.

Tucker, J. A. (1985). Curriculum-based assessment: An introduction. *Exceptional Children, 52*(3), 199–204.

Villa, R., & Thousand, J. (1992). Student collaboration: An essential for curriculum delivery in the 21st century. In S. Stainback & W. Stainback (Eds.), *Curriculum considerations in inclusive classrooms: Facilitating learning for all students* (pp. 117–142). Baltimore: Brookes.

Walker, H. M., & Hops, H. (1976). Use of normative peer data as standard for evaluating classroom treatment effects. *Journal of Applied Behavior Analysis, 9*(2), 159–168.

Walker, H. M., Shinn, M. R., O'Neill, R. E., & Ramsey, E. (1987). A longitudinal assessment of the development of antisocial behavior in boys: Rationale, methodology, and first-year results. *Remedial and Special Education, 8*(4), 7–16.

Walker, H. M., Steiber, Ramsey, E., & O'Neill, R. (1991). Longitudinal prediction of the social achievement, adjustment, and delinquency of antisocial versus at-risk boys. *Remedial and Special Education, 12*(4), 43–51.

West, J. F., Idol, L., & Cannon, G. (1989). *Collaboration in the schools: An inservice and preservice curriculum for teachers, support staff, and administrators.* Austin, TX: PRO-ED.

Wheeler, A., & Fox, W. (1972). *Managing behavior: A guide to writing instructional objectives.* Lawrence, KS: H & H.

White, O. R., & Liberty, K. A. (1976). Behavioral assessment and precise educational measurement. In N. G. Haring & R. L. Schiefelbusch (Eds.), *Teaching special children* (pp. 31–71). New York: McGraw-Hill.

Wolf, D. P. (1989). Portfolio assessment: Sampling student work. *Educational Leadership, 46*(7), 35–39.

Ysseldyke, J. E., Algozzine, B., Potter, M., & Regan, R. (1980). *Descriptive analysis of students enrolled in a program for severely learning disabled* (Research Report No. 45). Minneapolis: University of Minnesota, Institute for Research and Learning Disabilities.

Ysseldyke, J., Algozzine, B., Shinn, M., & McGue, M. (1982). Similarities and differences between low achievers and students classified as learning disabled. *The Journal of Special Education, 16,* 73–85.

APPENDIX 5

SAMPLES OF FORMS FOR RECORDING CLASSROOM BEHAVIOR

A CLASSROOM OBSERVATION SHEET

OBSERVATION NO. _____

Observer: _____ Date: _____

Time: from _____ to _____

Learner's Name: _____

Grade: _____ Activity: _____

Describe, in behavioral terms, the setting within which the activity takes place.

_____

_____

_____

_____

List all the behaviors displayed by the learner during a 10-minute period in which he or she is engaged (or is supposed to be engaged) in the chosen activity. If the same behavior occurs more than once, indicate this by making tallies in the frequency column.

Description of Behavior   Frequency

_____

_____

_____

_____

_____

_____

Description of Behavior	Frequency

RECORD OF FREQUENCY OF BEHAVIOR

Date: from _____ to _____

Name: _____

Observer: _____

Description of Behavior: _____

_____

Days	Tallies	Total
1	_____	_____
2	_____	_____
3	_____	_____
4	_____	_____
5	_____	_____

Average per day: _____

Name: _____ Date: _____

Observer: _____ Time: _____

Setting: _____

Incident:

CHAPTER 6

Learning Processes in the Inclusive Classroom

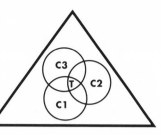

IN PREVIOUS CHAPTERS WE HAVE discussed the importance of (a) establishing contact and rapport among collaborators, (b) defining learner problem areas, (c) determining skill and behavioral levels of learners, and (d) projecting the type of learner progress that is desirable. Once these preliminary and prerequisite activities have occurred, the essence of Collaborative Consultation emerges as the implementation of programs of instruction that facilitate classroom performance of learners with special needs or who are at risk for school failure because of disruptive and other difficult-to-teach behaviors.

The next stage in collaborative problem solving is for collaborators to explore possible recommendations for solving the problem. When using the Collaborative Consultation Model, team members explore a variety of possible interventions to support and enhance school progress for learners with special needs. West, Idol, and Cannon (1989, Module 29) described a process where collaborators, using brainstorming techniques, explore the viable alternatives for solving the identified problem.

The contents of this chapter, as well as those of Chapter 7, reflect a collection of possible ways to solve learning and behavior problems of learners who are experiencing difficulty in classroom. In this chapter, the focus is on possible ways to alter how learning takes place in the inclusive classroom. In Chapter 7 is a collection of techniques for adapting instruction, management, and materials. Collaborators might use any one of these solutions (Chapters 6 and 7), or they might use another intervention brought to the team by one or more members. In line with our definition of the collaborative problem-solving process (see the Preface), when team members share their ideas and resources for possible interventions, the merging results in a richer collection of options, as well as in improved and enhanced individual options.

After the collaborators explore possible ways of solving the problem, they then evaluate each of the intervention alternatives (see West et al., 1989, Module 30). The collaborators anticipate the possible pros and cons of each suggested intervention, being careful at this point in the problem-solving process that all solutions belong to the entire team, rather than to the individual collaborators who might have suggested using them. This is very important to enable the team to explore collaboratively the possible options, rather than to make any team member feel that his or her "personal" ideas are being evaluated by the team. As demonstrated by West et al. (1989, Module 30), the collaborators gradually reduce the list of possible solutions to the problem in a prioritization process, until the collaborators reach consensus on a single and final solution to the problem. This reduction process is important because sometimes teams want to implement every single solution brought forward for discussion. This type of action results in chaos, with no single intervention being fully implemented. Instead, West et al. recommended that the team find the best solution to the problem. These authors offered a series of guidelines to assist collaborative teams in evaluating the various solutions and finding the best solution that is acceptable to all team members.

Persons interested in the Collaborative Consultative Model of service delivery often think of the essence of consultation as centering on the communicative process of consultation. It is true that the process of artful communication is essential, but the interactive process itself is not sufficient. In our experience, effective collaborators must also possess a body of knowledge about effective teaching and learning procedures that has been shown to be effective in teaching and managing learners with special needs. Special consideration must be given to being knowledgeable about and being skilled at adapting effective teaching (Chapter 7) and learning processes (this chapter) for use in general classroom and/or group instruction.

An essential theme that must be woven into the collaborative relationship is the belief that general classroom instruction can be modified and organized so that learners with special needs can learn in such settings without hardship or decreased learning for other classmates. Coupled with this is the belief that the inclusive classroom is, in fact, the least restrictive environment (LRE) for many learners with special education needs. Here, LRE is defined as an educational setting that offers such learners the best opportunities to develop and progress to the fullest extent possible. Within the inclusive classroom, development and growth includes cognitive, academic, social, linguistic, and behavioral domains. In contrast, consider these common beliefs:

- Learners in graded classes should all receive the same instruction at the same time.

- Learners in grade-level classes should be learning the exact and same body of knowledge because they are all of similar ages.

- The best way to teach any group of learners is to direct the instruction toward the "average" learners in the group.

- The professional teacher is usually the best person to teach the learners directly.

- The role of teachers is to teach learners, not to make them behave.

It is probable that these beliefs are myths, as they are stated. It is also probable that they may serve as obstacles to the effective integration of learners with special needs. Consider for a moment the following modifications of the five statements:

- Learners in graded classes could receive various forms and levels of instruction at various times.

- Learners in graded classes could be mastering different levels of a body of knowledge unrelated to chronological age.

- One way to teach any group of learners is to form flexible groups comprising learners with similar skills and to expect all group members to master each skill that is presented, reforming the groups if their members' mastery levels become too diverse.

- The professional teacher does not always have to be the person to teach learners directly. With careful programming and management by teachers, other learners can sometimes be the "best" teachers for other learners.

- The role of teaching includes using people management skills designed to get learners ready to learn prior to offering instruction.

The focus of this chapter is on the presentation and discussion of various teaching and learning procedures for educating learners who are difficult to teach or who have special learning needs. An underlying premise for these procedures is that the above five modified beliefs are possible to implement in large-group classroom settings. It is also implied that procedures that have been found to be effective in teaching such learners can also be used with a *variety* of problem learners commonly found in classrooms, including those who are low achievers, learners who are difficult to manage, or those who are at risk for school failure under normal instruction.

ROLES OF THE COLLABORATORS

The degree of involvement of each collaborator during implementation of the instructional program itself must be determined on an individual basis. Collaborators can use situational leadership to determine how each group member can be involved. In some cases, the leadership style (selling, telling, participating, or delegating) exhibited by collaborators during the previous stage of consultation (defining goals and objectives) will remain the same. In other cases, some collaborators will have shifted their preferred style. Collaborators must be particularly astute at discerning this type of shift to ensure that the appropriate leadership style is being used.

Once the leadership style has been identified, each collaborator should define his or her involvement in the program. If one collaborator needs a participating style, then other group members will probably suggest ways that the team can work together in the classroom to carry out the intervention program. Collaborators must be careful to determine gradual shifts in one another's needs, working toward more direct involvement in the actual teaching by supportive staff (other collaborators on the team). This reduction of direct involvement by outside collaborators should be gradual and determined by group consensus.

If the necessary style for an individual collaborator is selling, another collaborator may have to begin the actual intervention program, explaining all steps and procedures. It should be clear from the onset that this is a temporary state and that the classroom teacher will eventually carry out the program after receiving the necessary information and support. In this case, the collaborators must be sensitive to two conditions. The first is that the teaching and learning procedures must be designed so that the classroom teacher could implement them alone, even though initially other collaborators will be demonstrating how and/or helping to carry out the procedures. The second condition—the same as that for a participatory style—is that a collaborator must be sensitive to the appropriate time to make a shift in his or her direct involvement in the instructional program.

If the best leadership style for the classroom teacher to receive is a telling one, then other collaborators must design the instructional or management program and be careful to involve the classroom teacher in the planning. Under these circumstances collaborators are essentially writing a prescription to be fulfilled by one group member. Collaborators must be carefully tuned in to the individual needs of the classroom teacher, being ready to shift leadership styles when that person is ready.

The easiest role for collaborators to assume is that of a delegating style, where one group member wants others simply to confirm an instructional program for the targeted learner(s). In this case collaborators must provide a supporting role. Although this could be the easiest condition, requiring the least direct involvement on the part of other collaborators, an important problem could arise when a group member simply wants the authority to work with the target learner but the chosen methods are not effective. Then, collaborators must be diplomatic and supportive to help one another make changes in the intervention program by temporarily shifting to one of the other three leadership styles or adhering to the generic principles of Collaborative Consultation or both (see Chapter 2). It is especially important for collaborators to use the generic principles of ownership, appropriate confrontation skills, and giving and receiving feedback.

Finally, regardless of the preferred leadership style of collaborators, group members must always be ready and willing to shift leadership styles. This is important to this stage if the collaborators are to be successful in implementing a set of teaching and learning procedures that will be effective for all learners and useful in a large-group setting.

THE TEACHING AND LEARNING PROCESS

In this section we discuss the procedural principles of Collaborative Consultation and the very important influences of (a) academic learning time and (b) learners' perceptions of locus of control on the learning process.

Procedural Principles

The generic principles of Collaborative Consultation discussed in Chapter 2 are used to enhance the process of implementing the various teaching and learning procedures presented in this chapter. Supplementing these basic principles are six procedural principles, described below, that are likely to facilitate performance of difficult-to-teach learners in inclusive classrooms. Collaborators reach agreement on the importance and usefulness of these principles before beginning any classroom instructional project. A shared philosophy about these procedural principles, coupled with diligent application of the generic principles, will set the stage for successful instructional programs.

Procedural Principles Designed to Facilitate Teaching and Learning of Difficult-to-Teach Learners Must Be Easy to Implement in Inclusive Classroom Settings. If the teaching and learning procedures are complicated or require inordinate amounts of teacher time for individual learners, classroom teachers are unlikely to use them. It may be that such complicated and time-consuming techniques have been effectively used in one-to-one instruction in special instructional settings. If so, these procedures and strategies must be modified and redefined to fit within the context of inclusive classrooms. This will help ensure that the teachers actually use the techniques when other collaborators are not in the classroom.

Teaching and Learning Procedures Should Be Designed for Use with Any Student Who Is Achieving Poorly, Rather than for a Single Learner with Special Needs. When collaborators work together to design or select procedures that are generic in nature, several very important results might ensue. The classroom teacher tends to be more likely to use the procedures with other low-achieving learners, rather than just with the one for whom the procedures were designed. Another result is that when the procedures prove to be effective for other problem learners, the classroom teacher tends to implement an increased number of remedial programs in the classroom, as opposed to referring problem learners for special education instruction.

Teaching and Learning Procedures Need to Be Based on the Use of Classroom Curricula. When the design of remediation is based on the classroom curricula, a troublesome characteristic of many learners with special needs is alleviated. Learners with special needs are often poor at generalizing concepts and skills learned across situations, settings, and behaviors. If students are taught in curricula different from those generally used in the classroom, teachers can expect that the learners will still not have mastered the classroom curricula. An obvious way to bypass this problem is to offer instruction in the classroom curricula. This usually means modification in one of several ways: (a) placing the student in the same curriculum but at a lower level, (b) increasing the opportunities for practice on the materials, (c) rearranging the way the material is presented, or (d) modifying the way the learner responds.

Another point in favor of using classroom curricula, rather than special education curricula, is that the former is an example of mainstreamed education. If the general classroom is, in fact, the least restrictive environment for a particular learner, then effort should be made to teach the learner to master educational goals relevant to instruction in that classroom. This is not to imply that precisely the same goals should be set for each learner in the classroom, but the goal areas should be similar. For example, a classroom goal area might be to improve all learners' writing skills. For Learner A, the goal might be for the learner to write a three-paragraph paper containing an introduction, discussion of issues, and summary sections, with 95% of the words spelled correctly and 100% of the sentences formed correctly, and with legible, cursive handwriting. For Learner B, the goal might be to write mastered spelling words in complete sentences with 100% correct sentence formation and with legible, manuscript handwriting.

Classroom teachers may feel more comfortable and ready to accommodate special needs learners if the educational goals are relevant to the inclusive classroom. Some classroom teachers believe that learners with special needs are so difficult to teach that the instruction must be highly specialized, requiring a teacher who is a specialist in the area. The use of classroom curricula as the bases for forming teaching and learning procedures ensures that the focus is on teaching problem learners to survive in the classroom, not merely to coexist in the classroom.

Teaching and Learning Procedures Must Include Components That Teach Learners to Generalize.   Certainly, teaching learners in classroom curricula is a beginning step toward solving the generalization problem. It is also essential, however, to provide the learners with a type of instruction and practice that affords them the opportunity to generalize. The key is to develop responses in learners that are likely to occur in other appropriate settings and materials and at other appropriate times.

Teaching and Learning Procedures Need to Be Useful for Group Instruction.   Unless the procedures are developed for group use, the amount of actual implementation will be minimal. Classroom teachers, with 25 to 35 learners in their classes, have little time for one-to-one instruction. As

Stevens and Rosenshine (1981) pointed out, in a class of 20 students a teacher would have 3 minutes of individualized instruction per student in a 1-hour lesson. The important point here is to help teachers design ways of managing groups of students for instruction.

A second, and probably the most important, reason for developing teaching and learning procedures that are useful for group instruction is that classroom teachers tend to report that more-individualized types of instructional adaptations are not acceptable to them. For example, elementary teachers who were actually observed made few adaptations in their instructional procedures, and generally taught "by the book," using undifferentiated large-group instruction (Baker & Zigmond, 1990).

Also in support of this premise are the findings of Ysseldyke, Thurlow, Wotruba, and Nania (1990), who reported that classroom teachers seldom identify ways of adapting classroom instruction for special education learners in their classrooms. Over 40% of the surveyed teachers (elementary and secondary) indicated that their classrooms were structured, and 55% of those surveyed said that the classroom instructional procedures did not differ due to the presence of learners with disabilities.

Another group of researchers (Schumm & Vaughn, 1991) found that both elementary and high school teachers appear to be willing to include learners with special needs within whole-class activities. These teachers also reported that, in their opinions, making changes in instructional procedures or in the classroom learning environment was neither feasible nor desirable. These were *not* teachers who had worked together on collaborative teams to develop workable and feasible teaching and learning procedures.

Learners Must Be Directly Taught the Skill Areas They Are Required to Master. This final principle may seem obvious, but classroom observational studies have indicated that this is in fact an area of concern, at least for elementary classroom instruction (Duffy & Roehler, 1980; Durkin, 1977, 1978–1979; Mason & Osborn, 1982). In this discussion it is important to remember that mastery learning has been shown to be superior to conventional instruction (see review in Bloom, 1984). More precisely, about 90% of tutorial learners and 70% of mastery learning learners attained the level of summative achievement reached by only 20% of learners under conventional instructional conditions. For instance, Durkin's (1977) observational studies were designed to determine whether elementary school teachers provide reading comprehension instruction and, if so, the amount of time allotted for it. Based on substudies, including a total of 6,643 minutes observing reading instruction and 3,894 minutes for social studies instruction in 36 classes, Durkin reached the ominous conclusion that direct instruction on reading comprehension was not really taking place in these classrooms. It was assumed that, when teaching reading, teachers would follow a sequential pattern that would flow from instruction to practice to application. Instead, the teachers were found to be "mentioners," assignment-givers, checkers, and interrogators. Durkin also found that teachers of third- and fourth-grade classes, where reading comprehension should take precedence over decoding instruction, frequently did not use teachers' manuals for instruction. Instead, they used them merely for vocabulary reference and as a source of questions to ask after stories were read.

In support of Durkin's (1977) work, Mason and Osborn (1982) found that, although teachers report that they believe comprehension instruction ought to be taught, they actually spend little time teaching analysis, summarization, or interpretation of text information. Also, according to teacher self-reports, teachers provide some text-level comprehension for their highest achieving learners but next to nothing for low achievers. Duffy and Roehler (1980), who observed and worked closely with classroom teachers, redefined instruction as an ongoing interaction between teachers and learners, rather than as a prepared and directed lesson. For instance, Duffy (1981) noted that teachers often do not give a precise aim or purpose for lessons prior to instruction, do not model how to perform the task, or do not offer guided practice in how to do it. The underlying implication is that, given the apparent lack of direct instruction in teaching reading comprehension skills, learners who have difficulty with reading comprehension are doomed to continue to be poor comprehenders.

One can infer from these studies that, even though teachers may consider a skill to be important, they may not always offer direct instruction about the skill prior to requiring their learners to master it. Thus, two important areas for collaborators to work on are (a) identifying the important skill areas and (b) designing direct instruction programs for the skill areas.

Influences of Academic Learning Time

In a review of the relationship between classroom instruction and learner achievement gains, Rosenshine (1979) pointed out that the number of minutes learners were actively engaged in instruction was positively related to the achievement gains made by those same learners. The studies reviewed by Rosenshine were conducted in elementary classrooms with average learner gains reported. One must question what the implications of these findings are for those learners who have considerable difficulty with the learning process itself.

Academic learning time (ALT) is another way of referring to the number of minutes learners are engaged in learning activities. ALT has been found to be a predictor of academic achievement in effective schools (see review by Squires, Huitt, & Segars, 1983). In particular to learners with special education needs and ALT, Haynes and Jenkins (1986) conducted an observational study, comparing resource programs for students with learning disabilities with general classroom programs. Findings indicated that in schools where

ALT is high, one can expect to find the same high rates of ALT in the resource programs. Unfortunately, the negative counterpart was also found to be true. Schools with overall low rates of ALT also had low rates in the resource programs.

A primary consideration must be given to how much time is actually spent in instruction and learning in any classroom. This is especially important when there are learners in the class who are at risk for school failure. When considering inclusion of a learner with special needs, the collaborative team must determine how best to maintain ALT in classes where it is high for all learners in the class. If it is a class where ALT is low, then the efforts of the collaborative team could be centered in two areas: (a) first, how to increase overall ALT for all learners and (b) second, how to include the learner with special needs, determining appropriate ALT for that learner and not decreasing it for other learners in the class.

The Influences of Locus of Control and Sources of Motivation

An important part of including learners who are difficult to teach and/or who have learning and behavior problems in general classroom instruction is to consider how such learners are or are not motivated to learn. To facilitate the teaching and learning process, collaborators need to understand a problem learner's perception of locus of control of reinforcement and the impact that perception has on the learner's motivation to learn and to achieve.

What Locus of Control Is. Locus of control of reinforcement refers to an individual's belief about how reinforcers are determined—internally or externally (Rotter, 1966), a concept derived from social learning theory (Rotter, 1954). Locus of control refers to the way in which individuals perceive sources of control over events in their lives. Some persons perceive that reinforcers are contingent on certain aspects of their own behaviors, whereas others attribute the sources of control to fate, chance, or other outside forces beyond their control. These bi-directional differences are referred to as one having an *internal locus of control* in the first case and an *external locus of control* in the second.

Many researchers have studied the relationship of locus of control to academic achievement. Two reviews of literature have concluded that internality and academic achievement are positively related (Bar-Tal & Bar-Zohar, 1977; Findley & Cooper, 1983). Over the years, researchers (e.g., Bialar, 1961; Crandall, Katkovsky, & Crandall, 1965; Halpin & Ottinger, 1983; Lefcourt, 1976; Lifshitz, 1973; Nowicki & Duke, 1974; Nowicki & Strickland, 1973) have established that there is a developmental pattern in children in general in which the degree of internality increases with age.

Locus of Control and Low-Achieving Learners. These general patterns as described above have been consistently confounded by socioeconomic class, sex, intelligence quotients, and academic achievement over a considerable amount of time (Crandall et al., 1965; Crandall, Katkovsky, & Preston, 1962; Friend & Neale, 1972; Lefcourt, 1976; Lessing, 1969; McGhee & Crandall, 1968; Messer, 1972; Murray & Mednick, 1975). In general, however, these findings suggest that low achievers are more likely to have external locus of control. For example, in examining underachieving and control learners' beliefs about the causes of successes and failures (Pearl, Bryan, & Donahue, 1980), underachieving learners had weaker feelings of internal control over success than did the control learners. The underachieving learners believed lack of effort played less of a role in their failure than did control learners.

Locus of Control and Special Needs Learners. Even more specific to the problems of integrating learners with special needs into general classroom programs is that several researchers have found that children and adolescents with learning and behavior problems do not follow the typical developmental pattern described above. A series of studies have been made of learners with exceptionalities (both children and adolescents) to determine whether their locus of control and motivation to learn are, in fact, different from those of same-age peers. Most published studies have documented such differences. More recently, studies of learners with learning disabilities have shown that both children and adolescents are more likely to attribute successes and failures to external causes, which will be discussed as follows.

Studies also have described attribution differences in other groups of learners with exceptionalities. For instance, Baken (1978) found no differences in locus of control among three groups of home-bound learners with emotional disturbance, physical handicaps, and health impairments. Considerable evidence suggests that learners with learning problems tend to ascribe successes and failures to internally controlled causes less often than do learners without learning problems (Hallahan, Gajar, Cohen, & Tarver, 1978), especially in attributions for failures for children with learning disabilities who were not identified by the schools (Pearl et al., 1980) and for those who were school-identified (Pearl, 1982). Perna, Dunlap, and Dillard (1983) studied boys with mild emotional disturbances who attended special education and inclusive classes. They also reported a positive relationship between LOC and academic achievement that was unaffected by chronological age or IQ scores.

Aponik and Dembo (1983) compared adolescents' causal attributions of success and failure performances on various levels of task difficulty. The comparisons were between normally achieving learners and those with learning disabilities. They found learners' perceptions of task difficulty levels were a significant determinant of the two groups' differing causal attributions. However, locus of control alone was inadequate for explaining the differences in attribution ascribed by the two groups. The learners with learning disabilities had causal ascriptions for performance outcomes similar to those of learners classified as being failure oriented. High-achieving learners were different from the group with learning disabilities in many ways that are characteristic of the differences between success-oriented and failure-oriented (learned helplessness) learners. For example, the higher achieving learners attributed success more to their own ability than did those with learning disabilities, who perceived ability to be more influential in their failure than success. These special needs learners also ascribed success more often to luck (external factor) than did the learners without special needs.

In another study of older learners (Tollefson et al., 1982), general self-esteem and attributions of junior high school learners (some were normally achieving and some had learning disabilities) were compared. On a general measure of attribution, the learners with learning disabilities were internally oriented, but on task-specific measures they were externally oriented. This finding may help explain why some learners with learning difficulties may verbalize a desire to do well in school, but fail to expend the effort necessary to complete work and, consequently, appear to be poorly motivated.

When such learners do develop internality, it is internality for failure and not for success. Such learners appear to believe that any failure they encounter is a result of their own behavior, but the successes are still due to chance or to the actions of others. However, a very important instructional implication concerning locus of control measurement is that teachers have been found to perceive in their learners with learning disabilities significantly more internally oriented success experiences than the learners perceive in themselves (Lewis & Lawrence-Patterson, 1989).

Sources of Motivation. Another way to think about locus of control is to consider whether learners in any classroom are motivated to learn intrinsically or extrinsically. Deci's (1975) broad psychological definition of intrinsic motivation is: Intrinsically motivated behaviors are behaviors in which a person engages to feel competent and self-determining. They are of two general kinds: (a) seeking of stimulation and (b) the conquering of challenges or reducing incongruity/dissonance. A basic assumption of intrinsic motivation is the learner's innate need for feeling competent and self-determining, yet this basic conceptual development might be different for learners who have learning difficulties (Adelman, 1978). Adelman and Taylor (1982) described something they call inferred motivation to learn and suggested that it is related to a learner's degree of learning ability and misbehavior.

One set of results of studying learners with learning disabilities (Kleinhammer-Tramill, Tramill, Schrepel, & Davis, 1983) suggested that these children may acquire learned helplessness as a result of instructional interventions involving the use of noncontingent rewards. Another example is that adolescents with learning disabilities learned more in spelling when externally motivated (Bendell, Tollefson, & Fine, 1980). Difficulty is encountered in attempting to change learners' attributions, at least when using an indirect approach (Pflaum & Pascarella, 1982). Such an indirect approach included gradual shifts from teacher determination of learner errors and teacher exhortations to learners to try harder.

It appears that a more promising approach is to use direct training as a means of changing learners' attributions. Thomas and Pashley (1982) did so with 162 children with severe learning disabilities, training 36 of their teachers. The training involved teacher modeling, learner rehearsal of self-statements and effort attributions, and teacher reinforcement for learner self-statements. Prior to training, these special learners had lower persistence, lower perceptions of their own ability, and a helpless learning style as rated by parents and teachers. Experimental group training produced significant increases in task persistence but no changes in achievement attributions (attitudes).

Particularly germane to this discussion are the cognitive-motivational theories where motivation is thought to be determined by what one expects to get and the likelihood of actually getting it (discussed in Weiner, 1982). This line of thinking and research has important implications for collaborators interested in why certain learners do not perform well in the classroom. In practical terms Brophy (1987) described an expectancy-value formula that he says must be in place for learners, particularly adolescents, to learn new strategies. This expectancy-value has two parts that instructional decision makers must determine: (a) the degree to which learners *expect* to be able to perform the task, if they apply themselves, and (b) the degree to which learners *value* participation in the task itself or the benefits or reward that successful task completion will bring to them.

If collaborators are to support learners who experience learning and behavior difficulties in the classroom, they must first be aware of (a) whether or not learners, especially older ones, perceive themselves as being in control of their learning environment and (b) what their achievement motivation actually is. Second, when engaged in problem identification, collaborators must include the gathering of information related to a learner's locus of control of reinforcement and how that learner, if at all, is motivated to learn. Certainly, emphasis should be placed on supporting learners with special needs to be more intrinsically motivated and to learn to grasp control over their own accomplishments and achievements.

THE STRUCTURE AND MANAGEMENT OF THE LEARNING PROCESS

In this section we discuss the learning process from the point of view of (a) cooperative learning, (b) behavior management, and (c) tutored instruction.

Cooperative Learning

Teachers can structure groups to promote improved group responses by teaching group members to work either cooperatively or competitively. A meta-analysis of studies that examined the effects of various types of goal structuring on groups has yielded results that strongly favor the use of cooperative learning in groups (Johnson & Johnson, 1987). Compared are the relative effects on achievement and productivity of (a) a cooperative social situation, (b) cooperation with intergroup competition, (c) interpersonal competition, and (d) individualistic goal structures. A *cooperative* social situation was defined as one in which a group member seeks an outcome that is beneficial for all group members. A *competitive* social situation, as defined by Deutsch (1949), is one in which the goals of the individual participants are so linked that there is a negative correlation among goal attainments. Under purely competitive conditions, persons can attain their goals if—and only if—other group members fail to achieve theirs. An *individualistic* situation is one in which there is no correlation among the goal attainments of the individual group members.

The results strongly favored cooperative over competitive learning. Specifically, cooperation was found to be considerably more effective than either interpersonal competition or individualistic efforts toward achievement and productivity. Cooperation with intergroup competition was also found to be superior to interpersonal competition and individualistic efforts. Finally, no significant differences were found between interpersonal competitive and individualistic efforts in effecting achievement and productivity.

More pertinent to the intent of this chapter, four major reviews on cooperative learning have indicated the same basic findings. Cooperative learning can be expected to be an effective means of increasing learner achievement, but only when group goals and individual accountability are incorporated in the cooperative methods (Johnson, Johnson, & Maruyama, 1983; Newmann & Thompson, 1987; Slavin, in press). Other factors are thought to mediate the effectiveness of cooperative learning methods as well, such as the subject area taught in the cooperative group (Sharan, 1980), the composition of the group (Laughlin, 1978; Webb, 1982), and the form of academic and social exchange in the group (Webb, 1980a, 1980b, 1982).

A team of researchers and a classroom teacher collaborated in implementing heterogeneous cooperative learning groups to facilitate the social integration of a first-grade learner with severely challenging needs (Wilcox, Sbardellati, & Nevin, 1987). They selected a cooperative learning approach for several reasons: (a) A research review indicated that children eligible for special education interact less often or more negatively with peers, compared with normal children (Gresham, 1982); (b) research indicates that increased contact between special education students and general education classmates does not necessarily lead to increased social acceptance (Iano, Ayers, Heller, McGettigan, & Walker, 1974); (c) research has established that social acceptance can be increased for learners with special needs when the learning environment is carefully structured. The latter finding has been empirically demonstrated for learners with learning disabilities during swimming (Martino & Johnson, 1979), for academic lessons (Nevin, Johnson, & Johnson, 1982), for children labeled mentally retarded in social studies classes (Ballard, Corman, Gottlieb, & Kaufman, 1977), and for adolescents labeled moderately retarded in a community bowling center (Rynders, Johnson, Johnson, & Schmidt, 1980).

Cooperative learning may benefit some groups of children, such as low achievers (DeVries, Mescon, & Shackman, 1975; Edwards, DeVries, & Snyder, 1972) or minorities (Lucker, Rosenfield, Sikes, & Aronson, 1976; Slavin, 1978) more than others. It has been found to improve the social performance of learners with behavior problems and labeled as emotionally disturbed, but not their academic achievement (Janke, 1978; Slavin, 1977, 1983). In mainstreamed classrooms of a total of 183 third, fourth, and sixth graders, including 40 learners with academic handicaps, the effects of cooperative groups on classmates' acceptance of learners with academic handicaps was tested (Madden & Slavin, 1983). Responses to questionnaires indicated that classmates in cooperative groups were less likely than control learners to reject the learners with academic handicaps, but were not more likely than controls to choose such learners for friends. Both groups of learners made academic gains, although the gains of the learners with special needs were the only statistically significant ones.

In a study (Wilcox et al. 1981) designed to test cooperative learning and special education integration, the teacher followed eight steps for structuring cooperative learning environments, as advocated by Johnson and Johnson (1987):

- *Step 1: Select the objectives.* The teacher specified the instructional objectives. In each of nine activities scheduled to occur on separate days, the [learners] were to complete the task cooperatively. The activities included block building, coloring designs on the blackboard, completing puzzles, making a collage, using pegboard designs, covering paper, lacing boards, using colored cube designs, and dialing the telephone.

- *Step 2: Assign [learners] to groups.* The teacher specified the size of the group as four [learners] per group.

- *Step 3: Arrange the classroom.* The teacher organized the assignment of [learners] to groups. A schedule was set so that there were two groups, each with four members, meeting each morning. The groups were different each day, with one group always including a [learner with handicapping conditions], Debbie. Thus, during the 9-day cycle of lessons, each child in the class participated in a group at least three times and, in at least one lesson, participated in a group with Debbie.

- *Step 4: Provide the appropriate materials.* The teacher arranged for each group to have appropriate materials. Depending on the activities planned for the lesson, the teacher saw to it that each group had access to one necessary item (e.g., one pegboard, one set of colored blocks, one telephone to practice dialing, one puzzle, etc.) to ensure the need for sharing materials within the group.

- *Step 5: Set the task and goal structure.* The teacher set the academic task and cooperative goal structure. The academic task was to complete the activity in such a way that each [learner] helped and shared with the others. Members of each group were to focus on giving positive reinforcement to each other. The teacher stressed that the groups were for fun; everyone could "win" if they worked together and helped each other; the group was not racing with other groups. When the group members did a good job, they were told so.

- *Step 6: Monitor the [learner-learner] interaction.* The teacher monitored the groups by listening to and observing the [learners] as they completed the activities. The teacher encouraged and publicly praised the group members who were sharing or helping, giving response-specific reinforcement, for example, "I like the way Debbie showed you how to find the right color."

- *Step 7: Intervene to solve problems and teach skills.* The teacher intervened when a group was having trouble in completing or understanding the activity or when the group was having trouble in solving interpersonal problems. The teacher did this by providing direct instruction, for example, "What does taking turns mean? It means each goes one at a time." When a [learner] behaved inappropriately, the teacher instituted an already established classroom discipline system, saying, "_____, This is a warning. If you can behave correctly, you may stay with the group. If not, you'll have to sit over here on the side." The teacher was specific about which behaviors were appropriate and which were inappropriate behaviors. The other [learners] who were behaving correctly were praised. After a few minutes of the "time-out," the misbehaving [learner] was invited into the group again.

- *Step 8: Evaluate outcomes.* The teacher evaluated the groups' performances. When the groups had completed their tasks, or after approximately 15 minutes, the teacher asked and commented on such questions as: "Did you enjoy your groups?" "What did you like best?" "What was the hardest/easiest part of the task?" "Did anyone help another person?" "How does it make you feel when you help someone?" "How does it feel when someone helps you?" "How do you think your group could work better together?" At the conclusion of the evaluation process, the teacher gave stars to the members of each group who had successfully completed their task. The children placed the stars on the class chart. When all of the [learners] had accumulated three stars, a class game time was provided. At that time, the teacher or aide led the class in a variety of "new games" to further reinforce the concepts of cooperative learning. (Fluegelman, 1976)

Results from this study were encouraging. Debbie and her classmates all demonstrated significant improvement in initiating interactions. The frequency of positive interactions and children interacting with Debbie increased, and Debbie's classmates' attitudes toward her also improved.

Research findings on the effectiveness of using cooperative learning to promote learner progress and achievement, combined with the positive results from experiments designed to promote integration of the learners with special needs, are encouraging. The structuring of learning situations that promote cooperation rather than competition is an alternative that collaborators should strongly consider when searching for effective teaching procedures for use in inclusive classrooms. Readers are referred to Idol and West (1993) for staff development opportunities in preparing to use cooperative learning in integrated classrooms with learners with special needs as well as those who are difficult to teach. See also Nevin, Thousand, and Villa (1994) for cooperative group lesson plans at the preschool, primary, upper elementary, middle school, high school, college, and adult levels that feature modifications to meet the unique needs of learners with varying abilities (e.g., severe disabilities, gifted and talented, emotional challenges, and mild-moderate special education needs) in curriculum areas such as science, mathematics, language arts, career and vocation, oral expression, and art.

Behavior Management

For many groups, systematic structuring of the lesson is not sufficient to keep learners on task. Attentional problems, lack of motivation, and previous reinforcement of disruptive group behavior may impede the progress of the group. In such instances, collaborators need to consider how to manage individual and group behavior. Specifically, collaborators will need to design a behavior management program to accompany the group lesson.

The design and implementation of a behavior management program should encompass the following steps:

- *Step 1.* Define the problem areas. Then convert these areas into directly observable and measurable behaviors.

- *Step 2.* Obtain baseline measurement (see Chapter 5 on assessment procedures). This should be at least for 5 days unless the behavior is out of control.

- *Step 3.* Determine whether the behaviors being measured are sufficiently disturbing to warrant an intervention program. Determine if the behaviors being measured are the ones that are causing difficulty in the group situation. If there is a discrepancy, redefine the target behaviors and obtain a new baseline measurement.

- *Step 4.* Select antecedent events and/or contingencies that will be used to reinforce appropriate behavior.

- *Step 5.* Instruct the learners as to the contents of the new management program.

- *Step 6.* Implement the new program, continuing to measure the same target behaviors that provide the baseline measurement. The program should continue for at least 5 days before making additional changes.

- *Step 7.* Evaluate the effects of the behavior management program by daily examination of the target behaviors and the academic progress made by the learners as a result of the group instruction.

- *Step 8.* Decide whether (a) the program should be continued as is, (b) alterations should be made to make the management less cumbersome or to make the reinforcement less tangible or frequent, or (c) the program should be systematically faded out.

Examples of how collaborators have implemented behavior management systems in classroom settings can be found in Chapter 8 of Idol (1993). One particularly useful technique for managing groups of learners is the "good behavior game" (Barrish, Saunders, & Wolf, 1969; Harris & Sherman, 1973b). This game can be used with either small or large groups of learners. Procedures for implementing the good behavior game are shown in Figure 6.1. Lovitt (1991) also described tactics for improving the classroom behavior of learners who are at risk for school failure, as well as other adolescents who have mild learning handicaps or who are enrolled in remedial programs. The reader is also referred to Idol and West (1993) for preparatory lessons for teachers on how to develop, implement, and assess effective classroom programs for disciplining and managing groups of learners in integrated classrooms.

A second type of group management program was reported by Smith, Schumaker, Schaeffer, and Sherman (1982). In this program, participation and quality of discussion were improved in a seventh-grade social studies class. Specifically, it was found that an increased number of learners participated in discussions when rules were stated for the discussions, when learners were praised for their contributions, when the teacher restated or paraphrased learners' contributions aloud or on the blackboard, when the teacher planned an outline of discussion questions, when learners' contributions to discussions were recorded and used to determine part of the learners' grades for the class, and when discussion grades were publicly posted. To improve the quality of discussion, learners were taught to participate by providing reasons for their statements, comparisons between points they made, or examples supporting their statements.

Here are three major guidelines for teaching and managing groups of learners:

1. Teachers should provide structure for the group in the form of standard procedures and rules.

FIGURE 6.1. Procedure for implementing the good behavior game.

A. Goal: Reduce disruptive classroom behavior through a game involving competition for privileges natural to the classroom setting other than teacher attention.
B. Procedure:
   1. Select target behavior—define in observable, measurable terms (like out-of-seat or talk-outs without permission).
   2. Collect baseline data.
   3. Determine criterion performance level (a minimal acceptable number of demerits for winning).
   4. Select potential reinforcers—preferably privileges or events natural to the classroom or school setting (extra recess or free time, early dismissal, victory badges to wear).
   5. Divide class into teams.
   6. Implementation:
      a. Define target behaviors in specific terms to the class.
      b. Record a demerit for a team each time *any* member of the team talks out or is out-of-seat.
      c. At the end of the defined period tally the demerits for each team. The team with the fewer number of marks is the winning team. If neither team exceeds the set limit (e.g., 5 marks), then both teams are winners.
   7. Modify as needed. As behavior or levels stabilize, *gradually* lower criterion number of points or extend period during which behavior is measured.
C. Variations:
   1. One team (whole class)
   2. Give teams points at beginning of period. Erase points each time a target behavior is exhibited.
D. Problems and Solutions:
   1. If certain individuals try to "beat the system" by purposely causing demerits for their team:
      a. Place those individuals on own separate team.
      b. Have individual or group consequence of detention or extra homework assignments for teams that lose.
      c. Remove individual from setting or exclude from participation in game.
      d. Individual who causes team to lose for 2 consecutive days subject to expulsion from team by vote of team members.

Note. Adapted from *Journal of Applied Behavior Analysis, 2,* pp. 119–124. Copyright 1969 by Society for the Experiental Analysis of Behavior, Inc.; and "Some Resources to Help Teachers Manage Classroom Behavior Problems," unpublished manuscript by J. R. Jenkins and D. Pany, University of Illinois at Urbana-Champaign.

2. Teachers should directly instruct learners in deficient skill areas, rather than assume that, by merely providing the stimuli and setting, the desired learner behavior will result.

3. Teachers should provide learners with sufficient opportunity to practice skills to master them.

Tutor Instruction

One of the best ways to supplement teacher-directed instruction is to use a cross-age or peer tutoring program (Berliner, 1990; Jenkins & Jenkins, 1981; Lovitt, 1991; Maheady, Sacca, & Harper, 1988; Pierce, Stahlbrand, & Armstrong, 1984). This kind of program allows more time for direct instruction for more learners. In its implementation, a peer tutor follows a carefully designed instructional program and imparts the relevant information to another learner or tutee. An important characteristic of this type of program is that the tutor does not "teach," in the sense of making instructional decisions, but rather carries out a program designed by the teacher. An adult (collaborative consultation group member, paraprofessional aide, parent volunteer, building principal, student teacher) should be available for tutoring sessions to monitor the tutored lessons. The function of this adult is to check with each tutor-tutee pair on a daily basis to ensure that the tutoring procedures are being carefully followed.

Basic Components.   For several years, resource/consulting teachers from the University of Illinois under the direction of the first author experimented with cross-age and same-age tutor programs. The following were the basic components of a tutor program that they used.

- *Tutor selection orientation.* The selection of tutors is usually based on willingness to participate, but most teachers insist that tutors keep classroom assignments up-to-date and completed. In effect, the opportunity to tutor is treated as an honor or an earned reward. Once the tutors are selected, the collaborators must carefully describe the job purpose, give a description of the tutees, describe tutor responsibilities, and obtain parental permission for tutor participation.

- *Tutor training.* Tutors must be carefully trained prior to program implementation. The basic intent of the training program should be to teach the tutor to follow precisely an entire tutoring sequence. This will normally include all of the components of an instructional format sheet, that is: (a) how to get the tutee ready to learn, (b) how to present antecedent or stimulus items, (c) how to correct tutee errors, (d) how to measure daily progress, (e) how to chart daily progress, and most important, (f) how to reinforce the tutee positively. It is recommended that each component of the instructional program be taught separately and that the tutee be given an opportunity to practice each component until it is mastered. If mastery is not demonstrated, problems will arise in the future and the tutor will eventually have to be retrained. Jenkins and Jenkins (1981) is an excellent source for ways to implement tutor programs.

• *Tutor supervision.* Once the tutors have been trained, they must be carefully monitored to ensure that the teaching/learning procedures are being precisely followed. This is the key to a truly successful program, in that the monitoring ensures that the tutors are carrying out or replicating a teacher's lesson format. There are several excellent sources for information on how to monitor peer tutor behavior (e.g., Howell & Kaplan, 1978; Jenkins & Jenkins, 1981; Leary, 1987; Lovitt, 1991). Some general guidelines are (a) always supervise and monitor, (b) use a checklist or recording form to check off important behaviors to monitor, (c) deliver positive reinforcement to the tutor first, then give suggestions for improvement, and (d) give the tutor daily feedback.

Problems. Several problems may arise in a tutoring program. If a cross-age tutor program is being used, with older learners coming from other classrooms to serve as tutors, extra effort must be made to match the teachers' schedules. Also, in cross-age tutor programs, the tutors sometimes go on field trips with their own classes or are absent. For these reasons, it is recommended that substitute tutors be trained for use in emergencies. Even better, one can alternate tutoring assignments, so that some tutors are working while others are not. This may also help to alleviate problems when the tutors get tired of tutoring and need a vacation.

Another problem is that some parts of the instruction or the charting of progress data may require a complicated procedure or a difficult math formula. In such situations, it is useful to post a chart listing the steps of the procedure or the formula for calculating learner progress in the classroom or to list this information inside the first page of the tutor's work folder.

It is very important to reinforce tutors periodically for their hard work. To do this, the teachers may give tutor parties, set up tutor bulletin boards, distribute tutor newspapers, give tutor awards on awards day at the end of the year, send memos to teachers of cross-age tutors, tell the building principal about the tutors (using the tutors' report cards), select a "Tutor of the Week" for excellent performance, give occasional tutor vacations, and so on.

If same-age tutors in the same classroom are used, the teachers can reinforce the learners for doing reciprocal tutoring in tutor-tutee pairs. In this type of tutoring, the learners alternately take the role of tutor and tutee. Reciprocal tutoring can be used for tutoring in a single subject (e.g., learners drilling each other on math facts). It can also be used for tutoring learners based on skill expertise. For example, a learner skilled in math but poor in English might give math tutoring to a learner who is poor in math but good in English. Then, reciprocal tutoring in English could be offered the first learner by the second learner.

The Research and Evaluation Base. Tutor programs have been demonstrated to be an effective way of teaching a variety of learners with special needs, with both older and younger learners. For example, with elementary schoolchildren tutor programs have been used to teach arithmetic (Harris & Sherman, 1973a; Johnson & Bailey, 1974), spelling and word recognition (Jenkins, Mayhall, Peschka, & Jenkins, 1974), and reading using student athletes as tutors (Juel, 1991). Others have used it to improve Chapter 1 learners' performance in math, spelling, and vocabulary (Delquadri, Greenwood, Stretton, & Hall, 1983: Greenwood et al., 1987), to teach writing to learners in middle school with learning disabilities (Whitt, Paul, & Reynolds, 1988), and to improve low-achieving minority learners' weekly spelling test grades (Maheady & Harper, 1987). Tutoring programs have also been used as an alternative instructional strategy for learners with autism and other developmental disabilities (Whorton, 1988) and to improve social responses of socially withdrawn children (Lancioni, 1982).

A number of successful reports are available regarding how tutor programs have been used within an entire general classroom of adolescents. Such a classwide peer tutoring program developed at the Juniper Gardens Children's Project in Kansas City, Kansas, was designed to improve the basic skills performance of learners who were low achieving, socioeconomically disadvantaged, and/or with mild learning handicaps and from minority groups (Delquadri, Greenwood, Whorton, Carta, & Hall, 1986). In this project, a classroom teacher used classwide peer tutoring to improve the basic skills performance of such learners in three social studies classes of 10th graders containing a number of learners with mild handicaps in each of the classes.

Others who have independently evaluated this classwide peer tutoring system are Cooke, Heron, and Heward (1983); Maheady and Harper (1987); Nielson, Buechin, Slaughter, and Westling (1984); and Whorton et al. (in press). Whorton et al. (in press) used classwide peer tutoring to improve reading performance of learners with mild handicaps.

Using classwide learner tutoring teams, Maheady, Sacca, and Harper (1989) provided review instruction to 10th-grade learners in a general classroom; 14 had mild handicaps and 36 were normally achieving learners. The results were that no learners received grades below C after receiving tutoring. Peer tutoring has also been found to be socially acceptable by both teachers and learners (Greenwood et al., 1987; Maheady & Harper, 1987).

Tutoring programs should be well planned in advance, well supervised by competent adults, and used to reinforce previously taught material. They should not be used as a means of teaching new information. These types of tutoring programs can provide collaborators with an innovative and effective means of expanding opportunities for individualized review and practice in classrooms with large groups of learners, and certainly in those classrooms that include learners with special needs.

SUMMARY

In this chapter we have presented an alternative perspective on including learners with special needs (handicapping conditions or at risk for school failure) in inclusive classroom instruction. In the exploration of that altered perspective, professional educators collaborate with one another to determine how to best facilitate equal educational opportunities for the learning and achievement of all learners in their classrooms.

Regardless of the level of the classroom (preschool, primary or intermediate elementary, middle school or junior high school, or high school), a basic teaching and learning process is applicable. This teaching and learning process includes application of the generic principles of collaboration (discussed in Chapter 2 of this book) among the members of the problem-solving team, coupled with the six procedural principles presented in this chapter, which should be adhered to as collaborators develop effective integrated programs for general classrooms.

In addition to these procedural principles, we have found two very important influences that impact heavily on the success of collaborative programs. These are (a) the amount of time learners are actually engaged in instruction and (b) how those learners perceive themselves in the learning environment, particularly in terms of learners' locus of control and how motivated they are to achieve.

Such a teaching and learning process is also heavily influenced by how the actual learning environment in the classroom is structured and managed. In this chapter, three specific learner management structures are described and discussed: cooperative learning, behavior management, and tutor instruction in the classroom. These educational structures contribute to the approaches a collaborating team might use to create a more structured and effective learning environment for learners who are difficult to teach and manage. They also provide classroom teachers with more opportunities for their learners. A final benefit is that these management structures enable learners to learn academic content while concurrently learning and practicing important social skills.

Coupled with these principles, influences, and structures used to define a teaching and learning process are many instructional and management techniques that can be used to facilitate a myriad of diverse learning opportunities in a classroom. In the chapter that follows is a compilation of those techniques we have found to be most effective in the implementation of collaboratively developed educational programs.

STUDY QUESTIONS

1. How can the procedural principles used to facilitate learning processes for individuals be applied to the collaborative consultation team itself?

2. What advantages accrue to the special education teacher who team teaches with a classroom teacher to facilitate various learning processes for small and large groups of integrated learners?

3. Why is the concept "locus of control" important for a collaborative consultation team to consider?

4. How does knowing how to use peer tutoring, cooperative learning, or behavior management systems help a collaborative consultation team? What other best practices are important to consider?

5. Why is the concept "academic learning time" (ALT) important for educators? Discuss three ideas that increase engaged learning time for learners with special needs that can be easily practiced in a general education classroom.

REFERENCES

Adelman, H. S. (1978). The concept of intrinsic motivation: Implications for practice and research with the learning disabled. *Learning Disability Quarterly, 1*(2), 43–54.

Adelman, H. S., & Taylor, L. (1982). Enhancing the motivation and skills needed to overcome interpersonal problems. *Learning Disability Quarterly, 5*(4), 438–446.

Aponik, D., & Dembo, M. (1983). LD and normal adolescents' causal attributions of success and failure at different levels of task difficulty. *Learning Disability Quarterly, 6*(1), 31–39.

Baken, W. B. (1978). Locus of control: Characteristics of a homebound population. *Exceptional Children, 45*, 208–210.

Baker, J. M., & Zigmond, N. (1990). Are regular classes equipped to accommodate students with learning disabilities? *Exceptional Children, 56*(6), 515–526.

Ballard, M., Corman, L., Gottlieb, J., & Kaufman, M. J. (1977). Improving the social status of mainstreamed retarded children. *Journal of Educational Psychology, 69*, 605–611.

Barrish, H., Saunders, M., & Wolf, M. (1969). The good behavior game: Effects of individual contingencies for group consequences on disruptive behavior in a classroom. *Journal of Applied Behavior Analysis, 2*, 119–124.

Bar-Tal, D., & Bar-Zohar, Y. (1977). The relationship between perception of locus of control and academic achievement. *Contemporary Educational Psychology, 2*, 181–191.

Bendell, D., Tollefson, N., & Fine, M. (1980). Interaction of locus of control orientation and the performance of learning disabled adolescents. *Journal of Learning Disabilities, 13*, 32–35.

Berliner, D. (1990). The case for peer tutoring. *Instructor, 99*(8), 16–17.

Bialar, I. (1961). Conceptualization of success and failure in mentally retarded and normal children. *Journal of Personality, 29*, 303–320.

Bloom, B. J. (1984, May). The search for methods of group instruction as effective as one-to-one tutoring. *Educational Leadership*, pp. 4–17.

Brophy, J. (1987). Synthesis research on strategies for motivating students to learn. *Educational Leadership, 45*(2), 40–48.

Cooke, N. L., Heron, T. E., & Heward, W. L. (1983). *Peer tutoring: Implementing classwide programs in primary grades.* Columbus, OH: Special Press.

Crandall, V. C., Katkovsky, W., & Crandall, V. J. (1965). Children's belief in their own control of reinforcement in intellectual-academic achievement situations. *Child Development, 43,* 91–109.

Crandall, V. J., Katkovsky, W., & Preston, A. (1962). Motivational and ability determinants of young children's intellectual achievement behaviors. *Child Development, 33,* 643–661.

Deci, E. L. (1975). *Intrinsic motivation.* New York: Plenum.

Delquadri, J., Greenwood, C. R., Stretton, K., & Hall, R. V. (1983). The peer tutoring game: A classroom procedure for increasing opportunity to respond and spelling performance. *Education and Treatment of Children, 6,* 225–239.

Delquadri, J., Greenwood, C. R., Whorton, D., Carta, J. J., & Hall, R. V. (1986). Classwide peer tutoring. *Exceptional Children, 52,* 535–542.

Deutsch, M. (1949). A theory of cooperation and competition. *Human Relations, 2,* 129–152.

DeVries, D., Mescon, I., & Shackman, S. (1975). *Teams-games-tournaments (TGT) effects on reading skills in the elementary grades* (Rep. No. 200). Baltimore: Johns Hopkins University, Center for Social Organization in Schools.

Duffy, G. (1981). Teacher effectiveness research: Implications for the reading profession. In *Directions in reading research and instruction. Thirtieth Yearbook of the National Reading Conference* (pp. 113–136). Washington, DC: National Reading Conference.

Duffy, G., & Roehler, L. (1980). *Classroom teaching is more than opportunity to learn.* Unpublished manuscript, Michigan State University, East Lansing.

Durkin, D. (1977). *Comprehension instruction—Where are you?* (Reading Ed. Rep. No. 1). Urbana: University of Illinois, Center for the Study of Reading. (ERIC Document Reproduction Service No. ED 146 566)

Durkin, D. (1978–79). What classroom observations reveal about reading comprehension. *Reading Research Quarterly, 14,* 481–533.

Edwards, K., DeVries, D., & Snyder, J. (1972). Games and teams: A winning combination. *Simulation and Games, 3,* 247–269.

Findley, M. J., & Cooper, H. M. (1983). Locus of control and academic achievement: A literature review. *Journal of Personality and Social Psychology, 44,* 419–427.

Fluegelman, A. (Ed.). (1976). *The new games book.* Garden City, NJ: Doubleday.

Friend, R. N., & Neale, J. M. (1972). Children's belief about the causes of success and failure in school settings. *Journal of Educational Psychology, 72,* 186–196.

Greenwood, C. R., Dinwiddie, G., Bailey, V., Carta, J. J., Dersey, D., Kohler, F., Nelson, C., Rothholz, D., & Schulte, D. (1987). Field replication of classwide peer tutoring. *Journal of Applied Behavior Analysis, 17,* 521–538.

Gresham, F. (1982). Misguided mainstreaming: The case for social skills training with handicapped children. *Exceptional Children, 48,* 422–433.

Hallahan, D. P., Gajar, A. M., Cohen, A. B., & Tarver, S. G. (1978). Selective attention and locus of control in learning disabled and normal children. *Journal of Learning Disabilities, 4,* 47–52.

Halpin, B., & Ottinger, D. (1983). Children's locus-of-control scales: A reappraisal of reliability characteristics. *Child Development, 54,* 484–487.

Harris, V. W., & Sherman, J. A. (1973a). Effects of peer tutoring and consequences on the math performance of elementary classroom students. *Journal of Applied Behavior Analysis, 6,* 587–597.

Harris, V. W., & Sherman, J. A. (1973b). Use and analysis of the "good behavior game" to reduce disruptive classroom behavior. *Journal of Applied Behavior Analysis, 6*(3), 405–417.

Haynes, M. C., & Jenkins, J. R. (1986). Reading instruction in special education resource rooms. *American Educational Research Journal, 23*(2), 161–190.

Howell, K. W., & Kaplan, J. S. (1978). Monitoring peer tutor behavior. *Exceptional Children, 45*(2), 135–137.

Iano, R. P., Ayers, D., Heller, H. B., McGettigan, J. F., & Walker, V. S. (1974). Sociometric status of retarded children in an integrative program. *Exceptional Children, 40,* 267–271.

Idol, L. (1993). *The special educator's consultation handbook* (2nd ed.). Austin, TX: PRO-ED.

Idol, L., & West, J. F. (1993). *Effective instruction of difficult-to-teach students: An inservice and preservice professional development program for classroom, remedial, and special education teachers.* Austin, TX: PRO-ED.

Janke, R. (1978). *The Teams-Games-Tournament (TGT) method and the behavioral adjustment and academic achievement of emotionally disturbed adolescents.* Paper presented at the annual convention of the American Educational Research Association, Toronto.

Jenkins, J. R., & Jenkins, L. M. (1981). *Cross age and peer tutoring: Help for children with learning problems.* Reston, VA: Council for Exceptional Children.

Jenkins, J. R., Mayhall, W. F., Peschka, C. M., & Jenkins, L. M. (1974). Comparing small group and tutorial instruction in resource rooms. *Exceptional Children, 40*(4), 245–250.

Johnson, D. W., & Johnson, R. T. (1987). *Learning together and alone: Cooperation, competition, and individualization.* Englewood Cliffs, NJ: Prentice-Hall.

Johnson, D. W., Johnson, R. T., & Maruyama, G. (1983). Interdependence and interpersonal attraction among heterogeneous and homogeneous individuals: A theoretical formulation and a meta-analysis of the research. *Review of Educational Research, 53,* 5–54.

Johnson, M., & Bailey, J. S. (1974). Cross-age tutoring: First graders as arithmetic tutors for kindergarten children. *Journal of Applied Behavior Analysis, 7*(2), 223–231.

Juel, C. (1991). Cross-age tutoring between student athletes and at-risk children. *Reading Teacher, 45*(3), 178–187.

Kleinhammer-Tramill, P. J., Tramill, J. L., Schrepel, S. N., & Davis, S. F. (1983). Learned helplessness in learning disabled adolescents as a function of non-contingent rewards. *Learning Disability Quarterly, 6*(1), 61–66.

Lancioni, G. E. (1982). Normal children as tutors to teach social responses to withdrawn mentally retarded schoolmates: Training, maintenance, and generalization. *Journal of Applied Behavior Analysis, 15*(1), 17–40.

Laughlin, P. (1978). Ability and group problem solving. *Journal of Research and Development in Education, 12,* 114–120.

Leary, B. B. (1987). Interaction place maps: A tool for tutor training. *Journal of Developmental Education, 10*(3), 8–12.

Lefcourt, H. M. (1976). *Locus of control: Current trends in theory and research.* Hillsdale, NJ: Erlbaum.

Lessing, E. E. (1969). Racial differences in indices of ego functioning relevant to academic achievement. *Journal of Genetic Psychology, 115,* 153–167.

Lewis, S. K., & Lawrence-Patterson, E. (1989). Locus of control of children with learning disabilities and perceived locus of control by significant others. *Journal of Learning Disabilities, 22,* 255–257.

Lifshitz, M. (1973). Internal-external locus-of-control dimension as a function of age and the socialization milieu. *Child Development, 44*, 538–546.

Lovitt, T. C. (1991). *Preventing school dropouts: Tactics for at-risk, remedial, and mildly handicapped students.* Austin, TX: PRO-ED.

Lucker, G., Rosenfield, D., Sikes, J., & Aronson, E. (1976). Performance in the interdependent classroom: A field study. *American Educational Research Journal, 13*, 115–123.

Madden, N., & Slavin, R. (1983). Effects of cooperative learning on the social acceptance of mainstreamed academically handicapped students. *The Journal of Special Education, 17*, 171–182.

Maheady, L., & Harper, G. E. (1987). A class-wide peer tutoring program to improve the spelling test performance of low income, third- and fourth-grade students. *Education and Treatment of Children, 10*, 120–133.

Maheady, L., Harper, G. F., & Sacca, M. K. (1988). Peer-mediated instruction: A promising approach to meeting the diverse needs of LD adolescents. *Learning Disability Quarterly, 11*(2), 108–113.

Maheady, L., Sacca, M. K., & Harper, G. F. (1989). Class-wide peer tutoring with mildly handicapped high school students. *Exceptional Children, 55*, 52–59.

Martino, L., & Johnston, D. W. (1979). The effects of cooperative vs. individualistic instruction between normal progress and learning disabled students. *Journal of Social Psychology, 107*, 105.

Mason, J., & Osborn, J. (1982). *When do children begin "reading to learn?" A survey of classroom reading instruction practices in grades two through five.* Urbana: University of Illinois, Center for the Study of Reading.

McGhee, P. E., & Crandall, V. C. (1968). Beliefs of internal-external control of reinforcement and academic performance. *Child Development, 39*, 91–102.

Messer, S. B. (1972). The relation of internal-external control to academic performance. *Child Development, 43*, 1456–1462.

Murray, S. R., & Mednick, M. T. X. (1975). Perceiving the causes of success and failure in achievement: Sex, race and motivational comparisons. *Journal of Consulting and Clinical Psychology, 43*, 881–885.

Nevin, A., Johnson, R., & Johnson, D. (1982). The effects of individual vs. group contingencies on the academic and social behaviors of handicapped students in regular classrooms. *Journal of Social Psychology, 116*, 41–59.

Nevin, A., Thousand, J., & Villa, R. (1994). Creative cooperative group lesson plans. In J. Thousand, R. Villa, & A. Nevin (Eds.), *Creativity and collaborative learning: A practical guide to empowering students and teachers.* Baltimore: Brookes.

Newmann, F. M., & Thompson, J. (1987). *Effects of cooperative learning on achievement in secondary schools: A summary of research.* Madison: University of Wisconsin, National Center on Effective Secondary Schools.

Nielson, C., Buechin, N., Slaughter, R., & Westling, K. (1984, May). *The successful use of behavioral learning packages with school and parents served by a special education cooperative (LADSE): Factors which achieve use and adoption.* Paper presented at the Tenth Annual Applied Behavior Analysis Convention, Nashville.

Nowicki, S., & Duke, M. (1974). Preschool and primary internal-external control scale. *Developmental Psychology, 10*, 874–880.

Nowicki, S., & Strickland, B. (1973). A locus of control scale for children. *Journal of Consulting and Clinical Psychology, 40*, 148–154.

Pearl, R. (1982). LD children's attributions for success and failure: A replication with a labeled LD sample. *Learning Disability Quarterly, 5*(2), 173–176.

Pearl, R., Bryan, T., & Donahue, M. (1980). Learning disabled children's attributions for success and failure. *Learning Disability Quarterly, 3*(1), 3–9.

Perna, S. J., Jr., Dunlap, W. R., & Dillard, J. W. (1983). The relationship of internal locus of control, academic achievement, and IQ in emotionally disturbed boys. *Behavior Disorders, 9*(1), 36–42.

Pflaum, S. W., & Pascarella, E. T. (1982). Attribution retraining for learning disabled students: Some thoughts on the practical implications of the evidence. *Learning Disability Quarterly, 5*(4), 422–426.

Pierce, M. M., Stahlbrand, K., & Armstrong, S. B. (1984). *Increasing student productivity through peer tutoring programs.* Austin, TX: PRO-ED.

Rosenshine, B. V. (1979). Content, time, and direct instruction. In P. L. Peterson & H. J. Walberg (Eds.), *Research on teaching: Concepts, findings, and implications* (pp. 28–56). Berkeley, CA: McCutchan.

Rotter, J. (1954). *Social learning and clinical psychology.* Englewood Cliffs, NJ: Prentice-Hall.

Rotter, J. B. (1966). Generalized expectancies for internal vs. external control of reinforcement. *Psychological Monographs, 80* (Report No. 609).

Rynders, J., Johnson, R., Johnson, D., & Schmidt, B. (1980). Producing positive interactions among Downs syndrome and nonhandicapped teenagers through cooperative goal structuring. *American Journal of Mental Deficiency, 85,* 268–273.

Schumm, J. S., & Vaughn, S. (1991). Making adaptations for mainstreamed students: General classroom teachers' perceptions. *Remedial and Special Education, 12*(4), 18–27.

Sharan, S. (1980). Cooperative learning in small groups: Recent methods and effects of achievement attitudes, and ethnic relations. *Review of Educational Research, 50,* 241–271.

Slavin, R. E. (1977). A student team approach to teaching adolescents with special emotional and behavioral needs. *Psychology in the Schools, 14*(1), 77–84.

Slavin, R. E. (1978). Student teams and achievement divisions. *Journal of Research and Development in Education, 12,* 39–49.

Slavin, R. E. (1980). *Cooperative learning.* New York: Longman.

Slavin, R. E. (1983). When does cooperative learning increase student achievement? *Psychological Bulletin, 94,* 429–445.

Slavin, R. E. (in press). *Cooperative learning: Theory, research, and practice.* Englewood Cliffs, NJ: Prentice-Hall.

Smith, B. M., Schumaker, J. B., Schaeffer, J., & Sherman, J. A. (1982). Increasing participation and improving the quality of discussions in seventh-grade social studies classes. *Journal of Applied Behavior Analysis, 15*(1), 97–110.

Squires, D. A., Huitt, W. G., & Segars, J. K. (1983). *Effective schools and classrooms: A research-based perspective.* Alexandria, VA: Association for Supervision and Curriculum Development.

Stevens, R., & Rosenshine, B. (1981). Advances in research on teaching. *Exceptional Education Quarterly, 2*(1), 1–9.

Thomas, A., & Pashley, B. (1982). Effects of classroom training on LD students' task persistence and attributions. *Learning Disability Quarterly, 5*(2), 133–144.

Tollefson, N., Tracy, D., Johnson, E., Buenning, M., Farmer, A., & Barke, C. (1982). Attribution patterns of learning disabled adolescents. *Learning Disability Quarterly, 5*(1), 14–20.

Webb, N. (1980a). Group process: The key to learning in groups. *New Directions for Methodology of Social and Behavioral Science, 6,* 77–87.

Webb, N. (1980b). A process-outcome analysis of learning in groups and individual settings. *Educational Psychologist, 15,* 69–83.

Webb, N. (1982). Peer interaction and learning in cooperative small groups. *Journal of Educational Psychology, 74,* 642–655.

Weiner, B. (1982). History of motivational research in education. *Journal of Educational Psychology, 82*(4), 616–622.

West, J. F., Idol, L., & Cannon, G. (1989). *Collaboration in the schools: An inservice and preservice curriculum for teachers, support staff, and administrators.* Austin, TX: PRO-ED.

Whitt, J., Paul, P., & Reynolds, C. J. (1988). Motivate reluctant learning disabled writers. *Teaching Exceptional Children, 20*(3), 37–39.

Whorton, D. (1988). *Alternative instructional strategies for students with autism and other developmental disabilities: Peer tutoring and group teaching procedures.* Austin, TX: PRO-ED.

Whorton, D., Sasso, G., Elliot, M., Hughes, V., Critchlow, W., Terry, B., Standley, S. O., Greenwood, C. R., & Delquadri, J. (in press). Teaching formats that maximize the opportunity to learn: Parent and peer tutoring programs. *Education and Treatment of Children.*

Wilcox, J., Sbardellati, E., & Nevin, A. (1981). Cooperative learning aids integration. *Teaching Exceptional Children, 20*(1), 61–63.

Ysseldyke, J. E., Thurlow, M. L., Wotruba, J. W., & Nania, P. A. (1990). Instructional arrangements: Perceptions from general education. *Teaching Exceptional Children, 22*(4), 4–8.

CHAPTER 7

Classroom Adaptations

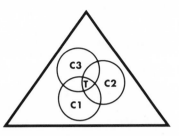

IN THIS CHAPTER WE DESCRIBE various adaptations for facilitating the teaching and learning process that focus on making technical adaptations in instruction, management, and materials. The solutions to problems described in this chapter could be coupled with those in Chapter 6 when collaborative consultation teams consider possible and viable solutions to problems related to learning and behavior in inclusive classrooms. These adaptations are organized in nine categories: (a) cognitive instruction, (b) scheduling and managing learners, (c) elements of group instruction, (d) applied behavior analysis, (e) effects of antecedent events, (f) the power of consequences, (g) teacher presentation styles and feedback, (h) shaping learning behavior, and (i) materials modification.

COGNITIVE INSTRUCTION

A major innovation in the past 5 years in education has been the focus on teaching learners how to think and solve problems as they are learning. *Cognitive instruction* refers to any effort by teachers or the design of instructional materials to help learners process information in meaningful ways and to become independent learners (Resnick, 1987). With cognitive instruction, the overall goals are (a) to teach for understanding in all subject areas and (b) to help students learn how to learn (Novak & Gowin, 1984).

The effective learner uses a repertoire of specific thinking and study strategies to interact with the instructional materials before, during, and after reading or problem solving (e.g., Anderson, 1984; Derry, 1990; O'Flahaven & Tierney, 1991; Schoenfeld, 1985). Novice learners and poor readers apparently do not develop this repertoire spontaneously (Derry, 1990; Feuerstein, Rand, Hoffman, Egozi, & Shachar-Segev, 1991; Pearson & Raphael, 1990). Also, low-achieving learners are hampered by strongly held misconceptions (Anderson & Smith, 1987; Larkin, 1983; Roth, 1990), lack of flexibility (Bransford, Vye, Kinzer, & Risko, 1990; Brown, 1980), failures in error detection (Maria & McGinitie, 1982), and ineffective problem-solving strategies (Larkin, 1983).

According to Idol, Jones, and Mayer (1991), cognitive instruction needs to (a) build on the learner's existing knowledge base, (b) extend the learner's repertoire of cognitive and metacognitive strategies, and (c) correct specific learning problems. In describing metacognition and academic learning, Paris and Winograd (1990) maintained that learners can enhance their learning by becoming aware of their own thinking as they read, write, and solve problems in school. For example, research on metacognitive learning indicates that a major component of effective learning involves planning, comprehension monitoring, and selecting appropriate strategies, as well as effective management of stress and time (Borkowski, Carr, Rellinger, & Pressley, 1990; Paris & Winograd, 1990; Weinstein & Mayer, 1986).

Gradually, these innovations are beginning to appear in curricular materials and guides for general classroom instruction, as well as in more advanced teacher preparation programs. The implications of teaching learners how to think strategically and to be aware of how they are thinking are vast indeed for the learner with special learning needs in the inclusive classroom. Some important resources for teachers challenged to use cognitive instruction in their classrooms include:

1. Methods for using cognitive instruction in the content areas (Bransford et al., 1990; Cook, 1989b; Jones, Palincsar, Ogle, & Carr, 1987)

2. Methods for teaching thinking skills in English and language arts classes (Cook, 1989a; Jones, Tinzmann, Friedman, & Walker, 1987)

3. Methods of teaching learners to combine thinking skills and reading comprehension skills (e.g., Adams, 1990; Anderson, Hiebert, Scott, & Wilkinson, 1985; Anderson, Osborn, & Tierney, 1984; Pearson & Raphael, 1990)

4. Methods for teaching learners to combine thinking and writing skills (Florio-Ruane, 1991; Hayes, 1990; O'Flahaven & Tierney, 1991)

5. Development of meaningful conceptual understanding in science (Roth, 1990; Tweney & Walker, 1990)

6. Understanding of mathematical and scientific problem solving (Secada, 1991; Silver & Marshall, 1990)

7. Surveys and critiques of programs designed for teaching thinking skills (Chance, 1986; Idol et al., 1991; Nickerson, Perkins, & Smith, 1985)

The majority of the above citations are chapters in Idol and Jones (1991) and Jones and Idol (1990). In addition, there is a staff development program for teaching difficult-to-teach learners in inclusive classrooms that has a training module focusing specifically on cognitive and strategic instruction (Idol & West, 1993). A related source is a methods textbook for teaching students with learning disabilities using a cognitive approach (Reid, 1988). Also, in terms of teaching thinking skills to learners with divergent cultural and ethnic experiences, the reader will find a helpful discussion in Secada (1991).

SCHEDULING AND MANAGING LEARNERS

A second important area in the successful teaching of various types of learners in classroom settings is that of general classroom scheduling and management. A common reaction of classroom teachers to support teachers is: "You have time for this type of instruction in the resource room, but it isn't possible for me to give learners this much individual attention. I have so many other learners in my classroom!" In this situation, a primary role of collaborator(s) should be to assist the classroom teacher in designing and implementing management plans that facilitate instruction to meet the acquisition levels of a variety of learners in the class.

The first task the collaborators have is to determine those instructional factors that are or are not present in the classroom that are likely to predict success or failure in the inclusion effort. Figure 7.1 contains a listing of some of these most critical factors, as described by Christenson, Ysseldyke, and Thurlow (1989).

Certainly, an equally important role of collaborator(s) is to design strategies that can be used in group settings; at this point, however, we are most concerned about exploring some ideas pertaining to scheduling and management. These ideas center around the use of lesson planning, flexible grouping, tutor

FIGURE 7.1. Instructional factors essential for learners with special needs.

- The degree to which classroom management is effective and efficient

- The degree to which there is a sense of "positiveness" in the school environment

- The degree to which there is an appropriate instructional match

- The degree to which teaching goals and teacher expectations for learner performance and success are clearly stated and understood by the learner

- The degree to which lessons are presented clearly and follow specific instructional procedures

- The degree to which instructional support is provided for the individual learner

- The degree to which sufficient time is allocated to academics and instructional activities are used efficiently

- The degree to which the learner's opportunity to respond is high

- The degree to which the teacher actively monitors learner progress and understanding

- The degree to which learner performance is evaluated appropriately and frequently

Note. From "Critical Instructional Factors for Students with Mild Handicaps" by S. L. Christenson, J. E. Ysseldyke, & M. L. Thurlow, 1989, *Remedial and Special Education, 10*(5), pp. 21–31.

instruction, structured independent work time, mastery learning, and data-based instruction. The following case study and discussion focus on some of these areas.

Scheduling Math Instruction

Math instruction typically poses problems because learners are usually at varying skill levels. The following case study demonstrates how group instruction in mathematics could be altered to meet the individual needs of learners.

Twenty-five fourth-grade learners had a single classroom teacher. Prior to working with a collaborator, the classroom teacher presented instruction to the entire group by putting examples on the chalkboard and calling on various learners to come forward to work sample problems. This was followed by all learners working on a seatwork assignment while the teacher sat at the teacher's desk, being available for learners who needed assistance or who needed completed assignments checked. The demonstration part of the lesson lasted about 20 minutes, and the seatwork activity lasted for 40 minutes. A class rule was that no more than three learners could be waiting at the teacher's desk for assistance. There were several residual problems, however: (a) The teacher had a tendency to ask more able learners to come forward to work the chalkboard examples; (b) all learners progressed to each subsequent lesson, regardless of performance on the learner's previous lesson; (c) several learners were kept waiting for teacher feedback; (d) several learners were off task and not completing the seatwork assignments; (e) some of the advanced learners finished the seatwork assignment before the time allotment had ended; and (f) the learners who failed to complete seatwork assignments had homework assignments; several of these learners failed to complete homework assignments as well.

In assessing the situation, the collaborative team decided to test all learners on the math skills required in the third-grade mathematics curriculum that was currently being used in the classroom. The team constructed a curriculum-based assessment (CBA) for math, following the guidelines presented in the materials on assessment found in Idol, Nevin, and Paolucci-Whitcomb (1986). They administered the majority of the testing strands to groups of learners, with the outside collaborator assuming responsibility for testing the learners who were absent on testing days and those whose performance during group testing was suspect. The two collaborators also reordered the sequence of the math book so that it reflected the same developmental order that they used with the math CBA. They then subdivided the class into three groups:

1. *Group A:* A basic skills group, consisting of learners who had not mastered basic addition and subtraction and related math facts and who were ready to begin studying place value, missing addends, and two-place addition.

2. *Group B:* An average group, consisting of learners who needed drill on multiplication facts and were ready to begin addition and subtraction programs with renaming (regrouping).

3. *Group C:* A fast-paced group, consisting of learners who would cover the following areas: missing factors, division with one-digit divisors, geometry, and beginning fractions.

The math period was extended from 60 to 75 minutes and was designed to include the following components:

• *Small-group instruction with the classroom teacher.* The teacher gave direct instruction and demonstration to a subgroup of learners. The basic instructional paradigm was based on model-lead-test, with the teacher modeling and then working sample problems with the learners. This was followed by a test situation in which the learners completed one or two problems under teacher supervision before returning to the large group.

• *Independent seatwork.* During independent seatwork, all learners were given an assignment with the same problem types as those taught during the demonstration lesson or in the lesson taught on the previous day. This time was essentially an extension of the test phase of the model-lead-test paradigm, but requiring the learner to perform with little supervision. The amount of time spent on this activity depended on the groups to which the learners were assigned, that is, the slower learners spent only 15 minutes at this task while the average and fast-paced group spent 30 minutes. Previously, all learners had spent 40 minutes engaged in seatwork activities.

• *Tutor instruction.* During this time, the learners were paired with other learners to drill on basic math facts. All learners in Groups A and B were engaged in this task. Tutor-tutee pairs were switched every week, so that the learners had the opportunity to work with many other individuals. All of the learners had been instructed by the collaborator in how to tutor. The rules for tutoring were posted on a large wall chart: (1) Each tutee had to bring the work packet to the tutor station; the work packet contained a set of cards showing math problems to be drilled, a pencil, and a chart for graphing progress. (2) Each tutor was responsible for (a) presenting the packet of cards (5 seconds per card), (b) using a model-lead-test procedure for correcting tutee errors, and (c) assisting the tutee in recording the correct number of facts mastered.

• *Word-problem solving.* The learners (by group) were given a small number of word problems to solve. In Groups A and B, the learners could work on these problems after tutoring was finished or after independent seatwork was completed. Group C gathered together as a group to discuss and solve word problems and tricky math problems; each day a different member of the group assumed the role of group leader.

- *Teacher feedback.* The teacher moved about the room, answering questions from learners in Groups A and B who were working on seatwork assignments. At the same time, the teacher served as an intermittent monitor of the learners in Group C as they worked on word problems and math puzzles.

- *Large-group proficiency drill.* At this point, the teacher administered one or two timed tests to the entire group; the worksheets differed depending on the skill area each group was working on. The time for testing for speed remained constant; the problems varied according to group.

- *Solutions to word-problem solving.* The learners were invited to offer solutions to word problems worked on during the day, with the entire group participating in the discussion.

Table 7.1 contains the scheduling plan for the entire math period, which lasted 75 minutes. Note that this represented an extension from 60 to 75 minutes. This plan was devised in an attempt to offer more individualized instruction and give the learners an opportunity to master each level of math

TABLE 7.1. A Scheduling Plan for Group Math Instruction

Group A	Group B	Group C
Tutor instruction: Drill math facts or word problem solving	Tutor instruction: Drill math facts or word problem solving	Small-group instruction with teacher
Independent seatwork based on previous day's mastered lesson	Small-group instruction with teacher	Independent seatwork
Small-group instruction with teacher	Independent seatwork	Independent seatwork
Independent seatwork[a]	Independent seatwork[a]	Word problem solving[a]
	Large-group proficiency drill Solutions to word problem solving	

[a]Teacher feedback available.

before proceeding to the next. Although this plan was designed for a fourth-grade classroom, its basic structure and underlying principles could be applied to any group, at any level of instruction.

Here are some general guidelines for scheduling and managing groups of learners:

- Assess the learners within the curriculum to determine appropriate levels of instruction.

- Design a grouping system that is flexible, in which groups can be constantly reformed depending on the skills of the group members.

- Design a time schedule that is constant and structured.

- Use a system that establishes a balance between offering direct, precise instruction and providing learners sufficient practice for skill mastery.

- Use a system that encourages independent learning and is carefully monitored and structured.

- Incorporate motivation programs within the system as a means of reinforcing learners for desired behavior.

- Be quick to "step back" and analyze environmental systems before making changes. Time spent on precise observation and situation analysis will result in improved management systems (see Chapter 5).

- Use systems that encourage learners to take responsibility for their own learning. For example, work assignments can be arranged in advance in work folders, leaving to the individual learners the responsibility for picking up folders and "getting ready to learn."

- Use systems that focus on using teachers as direct-instruction teachers and general management monitors. Teachers should not be placed in positions of doing busy work on low-level management activities and roles that can be taught to learners.

In summary, classroom organization is the key to creating successful learning environments. Learners, especially those who are more difficult to teach, must be taught how to attend and how to get ready to learn. The learning environment must be structured in such a way that learners can (a) work at the level that they are ready to master, (b) be given sufficient practice on tasks in order to master them, and (c) be active members of the classroom management team, in which they are responsible for helping the system work.

Planning the Lesson

To provide a basis for general organization and structure, the individual lessons should be organized in advance. Use of an instructional format sheet is one means of organizing and planning lessons. The format sheet shown in Figure 7.2 is designed for individual, tutorial, small-group, or large-group instruction. It can assist teachers in systematically planning instruction and provides a place for recording changes in the instructional plan. Use of this format sheet eliminates the writing of daily lesson plans; instead, the teacher can record the general instructional plan to be used and then record changes. It also provides a structure for others to follow when attempting to replicate an instructional program, especially when a substitute teacher is needed. Thus, it can be used as well by substitute teachers, cross-age tutors, paraprofessional aides, classroom assistants, and student teachers.

The instructional format sheet also contains the primary information for the instructional program section of a special education IEP. P.L. 94-142 requires that learners with special education needs must have IEPs (see relevant sections in Chapter 3). The IEPs of learners who receive a portion of their education in grade-level classrooms must be written and prepared by both classroom teachers and the special educators. Use of an instructional format sheet by a collaborator and a classroom teacher is a way to agree on what an educational program will consist of, as well as a means of providing the basis for the IEP.

Appendix 7.A contains a set of instructions for using an instructional format sheet. This sheet has been designed to accompany a progress chart for a learner's progress. The instructional format sheet can be used to determine the instruction being used at any point in time, as depicted on a progress chart. In Chapter 8 we discuss various ways of evaluating learner progress. Examples of corresponding instructional format sheets and charted learner progress data can also be found in Idol (1993, pp. 168–170).

ELEMENTS OF GROUP INSTRUCTION

The individual components of the instructional format sheet are essential to a well-planned and well-executed group lesson. Specifically, the instructional format sheet assists the collaborators in (a) defining the instructional tasks, (b) describing the conditions of the lesson, (c) setting the criterion or criteria to define lesson mastery, (d) determining the reinforcement and/or consequences to be delivered for lesson mastery, (e) defining how learner errors will be corrected, (f) planning for the time span of the lesson, and (g) deciding how learner progress will be measured.

Supplementing this basic structure of the lesson are some important elements of group instruction. These elements are (a) teaching procedures for groups, (b) behavior management for groups, and (c) tutor instruction with groups. In this context, the various teaching procedures we have discussed are pertinent to effective group instruction. Beyond that, certain specific procedures may be particularly useful in teaching groups. These have to do with physical proximity, teacher cueing, and learner responses.

FIGURE 7.2. An Instructional Format Sheet for designing group and individual lessons.

INSTRUCTIONAL FORMAT SHEET

Task	Instructional conditions	Criterion	Consequences	Error correction procedure	Time	Measure

Physical Proximity

The physical proximity of the classroom teacher to the group is important, whether the instruction is with a small or a large group. In small-group instruction, the teacher should be seated close enough to all learners to provide physical prompts, if necessary. The learners should be seated so that they all have equal opportunity to see the teacher. In some instances, it may be useful to seat problem learners closest to the teacher or between two other learners who attend well. Carnine and Silbert (1979) suggested that seating in a small semicircle, facing the teacher, is a good way to organize small-group seating. With larger groups, teachers can still exercise some control over physical proximity. By sitting behind desks and standing behind podiums, teachers create physical barriers between themselves and their learners. In contrast, by walking freely around the classroom, looking directly at individual learners, and moving among the group, teachers can create positive physical proximity.

Teacher Cueing

Teacher cueing, as discussed in a later section, is an important part of teaching systematically. It is a particularly useful device for getting learners ready to respond. Several of the cues developed within the DISTAR programs are excellent examples of how teacher cueing can be used.

Regardless of the type of cueing used, the teacher should establish a system that is consistent; even though the content of the lesson will change over time, the cueing system should remain constant. In this way, by sending them the same consistent message, the learners are prepared to behave or respond in certain ways. For example, a teacher may raise a hand in the air and drop it down to a midway stopping point as a signal to the group to respond chorally (Engelmann & Bruner, 1974).

Learner Response

Teachers who instruct systematically not only use cued instruction, they also define for their learners how they are expected to respond. Choral responding, an integral part of DISTAR instruction, is a useful way to form a group response before calling on individual learners. The teacher models the type of response that is expected from the learners. The teacher also defines the pace of the instruction so that all learners learn to respond quickly.

When teachers use individual responses rather than group responses, they must make certain that they systemically provide sufficient opportunity for all learners to respond. As Cazden (1981) observed, teachers sometimes fall into a pattern of calling on learners who show disruptive behaviors significantly more often as a means of controlling behavior. One way to avoid this is to define, in advance, a plan indicating which learners will be called. In general, the preferable pattern with younger learners is to begin with teacher modeling, then elicit group response, and finally test individual responses. With older learners, it may be preferable to model, obtain brief written responses, check individual responses, use a systematic error correction procedure, and then repeat the sequence.

An important requirement of small-group instruction is that it be fast-paced, fairly repetitious, and coupled with opportunity for individual responses. The teacher must ensure that all group members are responding correctly before assigning the group to an independent work activity. It is better to cover a small amount of material in a group lesson, with all group members firmly on the task prior to independent practice, than it is to cover more material lightly, resulting in more errors during independent work time.

For large-group instruction, teachers must carefully define (a) the goals of the instruction and (b) how individual progress will be mastered. Often, learners who are difficult to teach have to be taught how to learn in large-group settings. For instance, if the learners are expected to retain information given during a large-group lecture, some prerequisite skills might have to be mastered initially by certain learners. These might include lessons on how to take class notes, how to listen for the main idea, how to write outlines of major points of a lecture, how to ask questions about the lecture, and how to test oneself for understanding. The lecture lesson itself might include these five components:

1. *Getting ready to learn* (10 minutes). During this time, all learners get notebooks and texts ready. They scan their class notes from the day before and silently review the reading assignment for the forthcoming lecture. The teacher monitors during this time.

2. *Checking with your peers* (10 minutes). Learners then form small groups of two to four members in which they orally review major points from the previous lecture and readings. Again, the teacher monitors by moving from group to group.

3. *Previewing the lecture* (5 minutes). The large group forms and attempts to guess what may be covered in the forthcoming lecture. The teacher gives clues as to the general topic areas. The teacher then writes an outline on the chalkboard or provides a handout containing an outline of the lecture.

4. *Listening to the lecture* (25 minutes). The teacher delivers the lecture, following the outline and using a variety of media and methods for delivering the information.

5. *Perception checking* (10 minutes). The teacher and the learners review the major points of the lecture. During this time, the learners should be adding new information to their notes.

In summary, any group lesson, whether in a small or large group, should be designed not only to impart information, but to facilitate learning. A data collection system should accompany the lesson so that the teacher can be assured that mastery is occurring.

APPLIED BEHAVIOR ANALYSIS

For over 30 years, many teachers have used the principles of applied behavior analysis in their classrooms. In the first issue of the *Journal of Applied Behavior Analysis,* applied behavior analysis was defined as the "process of applying sometimes tentative principles of behavior to the improvement of specific behaviors, and simultaneously evaluating whether or not any changes noted are indeed attributable to the process of application" (Baer, Wolf, & Risley, 1968, p. 91). A later definition by Epstein and Cullinan (1979) placed emphasis on practicality: "Applied behavior analysis is defined as the application and experimental evaluation of procedures for changing important human behaviors within practical settings" (p. 93). In more generic terminology and in application to classroom problems, these definitions would seem to mean that teachers who are applied behavior analysts possess a body of knowledge pertaining to principles of managing behavior. Parts of this body of knowledge are delineated in subsequent sections on effects of antecedent events, effects of consequences, and shaping of learning behavior.

The conclusion that the principles of managing behavior may be known or tentatively known implies that the directions that teachers may choose to teach learners effectively have been established in the applied behavior analysis literature. Yet many of these principles have been tested only within limited domains of academic learning and the management of social behavior. In many cases, the testing may be limited to only certain types of individuals. Under these circumstances, teachers skilled in applied behavior analysis should accept tentatively the notion that the application of a given principle will work, but they should then test the effects of the principle on the problem before they conclude that the principle is effective.

Collaborators who use applied behavior analysis should note that there are several critical elements in applied behavior analysis:

- Careful definition of the observable behavior or products of behavior to be changed (specific behavior)

- Regular recording of specific behaviors throughout the project

- Systematic modification of certain aspects of the environment and recording of subsequent changes in the specific behavior

- Evaluation of the cause-effect relationship between environmental modifications and specific behavior changes through single-case experimental designs

Each of these critical elements should be included in the development of collaborative consultation programs. In this way, any remedial technique that is selected can be evaluated through applied behavior analysis.

EFFECTS OF ANTECEDENT EVENTS

In Chapter 5 the initial steps in planning systematic instructional programs were discussed. These steps center around the establishment of behavioral goals and objectives embracing four components (Alberto & Troutman, 1986, p. 64):

1. a statement identifying the learner(s)

2. a statement identifying the target behavior

3. a statement identifying the conditions under which the behavior is to be displayed

4. a statement identifying the criteria for acceptable performance

The third of these components, identifying the conditions or antecedent stimuli under which a behavior is expected to occur, is the focus of this section. The applied behavior analysis literature contains a body of knowledge on the effects of antecedent events on behavior. The relevant research centers around both the management and the instruction of individuals and groups of learners. In recent years, experimentation on the effects of antecedent stimuli has been conducted in classroom settings, focusing on accommodating exceptional individuals in mainstreamed settings (preschool through college-level classrooms).

In classroom settings, effective teachers carefully manage and control the conditions under which instruction is offered. This is especially important when teaching learners with special needs, those who are difficult to teach, and those at risk for school failure. Not only must collaborators identify and control the conditions, learners must also be made aware of the parameters of the conditions.

Identifying the Condition

Initial meetings between collaborators generally focus on defining the problem as it exists in the classroom. Once the target behaviors have been defined, the collaborators must decide which events or circumstances in the classroom environment preceded the occurrence of the behavior. A collaborator can aid in this process by using an interviewing strategy such as asking questions about classroom conditions. As information about when and where the behavior occurs is elicited, collaborators can clarify the communication process by reframing or reiterating, thereby checking to ensure identical perceptions of the antecedent conditions.

After the conditions have been defined, behavioral observation can be initiated. A frequently asked question by those training to be collaborators is: "Who should collect the observational data?" One important guide is that the system for collecting information be simple and easy to administer. If this guide is followed, it is more likely that the classroom teacher will be able to gather the information. However, the primary collector of information could be assisted by a second person collecting intermittent data to confirm reliability. [A training module on how collaborators can conduct classroom observations and gather classroom information can be found in West, Idol, and Cannon (1989, Module 28); also refer to Chapter 5.]

Once the observations or information-gathering processes have been completed, the collaborating team members should meet to discuss the findings. It is not unusual to find that the behavior is in fact not occurring under the defined conditions. This may require observing under different conditions and/or redefining the target behavior.

Altering the Condition

After the collaborators have sufficiently assessed the situation and have a thorough understanding of the conditions that precede and sometimes cause the behavior, remedial programming can be started. Usually, this means to make an alteration in the antecedent conditions. It may be an alteration of the way in which the behavior is managed. It may mean alteration of the teaching procedure materials, error-correction procedures, or performance criteria. It often means some combination of alterations. However, teachers are encouraged to make the least number of alterations possible at any given time. The reasoning behind this is that, if the team designs complicated remedial/intervention systems, it is less likely that they will actually be implemented or at least maintained when other collaborators are not present to assist. Another reason for controlling the number of program alterations is that it is impossible to assess the effects of a given change if a number of changes have been made simultaneously. The practical point here is that, if a single alteration will remediate the problem, there is little reason to implement a package of multiple procedures.

Enhancing Learner Awareness

After defining antecedent conditions and designing improved conditions, learners must be made aware of program changes. Some collaborators have discovered that, though they had clarified their plans with one another, the program failed because the learner did not understand the program.

Idol (1993) demonstrated creative ways that consulting teachers and classroom teachers have used to clarify program conditions. One very effective device is the contingency contract (Homme, 1970), in which the conditions are clearly written or displayed and all of the involved persons commit themselves to the program by signing the contract. Other ways to clarify altered antecedent conditions for learners are to display the rules or procedures on charts, in the front of notebooks, or on cards taped on desks.

Heron and Skinner (1981) recommended that delineation and implementation of certain observable and measurable variables would have tremendous impact on the learning of learners with disabilities in classroom settings. These variables are (a) maximizing opportunities to respond, (b) permitting teachers to interact proportionately with all learners in the classroom, and (c) fostering acceptable social relations between learners with and without handicapping conditions.

Improving Academic Learning

Investigations of the effect of structuring antecedent conditions to increase the academic performance of learners with special needs have consistently focused on increasing the opportunity to respond (Delquadri, Greenwood, & Hall, 1979; Hall, Delquadri, & Harris, 1977; Massad & Etzel, 1972). These studies have shown that there is an increase in learning when learners are given more opportunity to respond, and also that increasing response opportunities is more effective than increasing reinforcement. It is interesting to note that the direct-instruction programs that have proved to be most effective for teaching reading feature increased repetition and opportunities to respond (Becker, 1977). It has also been reported that increasing from 4.5 to 15.0 seconds the latency between the time a teacher asked a question and the time a learner responded increased the learner's hand-raising behavior (Broden, Copeland, Beasley, & Hall, 1977). Broden et al. also found that restating a question during discussion period (i.e., prompting) increased learner participation in the activity.

Beyond these very precise types of effective antecedent stimuli is an area that is more nebulous and less well-defined. This has to do with the relationship between teachers and learners. A positive correlation has been reported in the education literature between learner achievement and both teacher perception and teacher-learner interaction (Good, 1970; Morrison & McIntyre, 1969). Collaborators, thus, must examine carefully their perceptions of and attitudes toward learners with special needs. This is an especially important area for teachers to consider, since the research evidence suggests that teachers are likely to perceive learners negatively if a special education label has been assigned to them (Foster & Salvia, 1977; Foster, Schmidt, & Sabatino, 1976; Gillung & Rucker, 1977).

Improving Social Learning

The teacher also plays a critical role in preventing social rejection from being experienced by learners with special needs in classrooms. Gable, Strain, and Hendrickson (1979) posited seven antecedent strategies that have proven useful in teaching learners with special needs appropriate classroom behavior. The first is peer modeling, in which socially mature learners are paired with inappropriately behaving learners (O'Leary & O'Leary, 1977) and token reinforcers are given for good behavior (Csapo, 1972). Evidence shows that positive initiations from peers actually increases a learner's status in the classroom (Sulzer, Mayer, & Cody, 1968). The second type of antecedent stimulus is teacher modeling (Cooke & Apolloni, 1976), in which teachers model the type of behavior they expect from learners.

The third antecedent strategy is peer management. Solomon and Wahler (1973) demonstrated that normal learners can be taught to alter interactions of disruptive learners, causing substantial decreases in antisocial behavior. The key element here is to teach peers to attend to acceptable social behavior and to ignore antisocial behavior.

The fourth strategy is to teach the disruptive learners themselves to self-ignore and to self-reinforce. Graubard, Rosenberg, and Miller (1974) taught learners eligible for special education services due to their highly disruptive behaviors to initiate positive responses from peers and toward teachers. Specifically, the learners who had been disruptive were taught to request additional assignments, increase eye contact, and provide positive feedback to teachers regarding academic instruction.

The fifth strategy, verbal feedback, is probably the easiest to implement. Drabman and Lahey (1974) succeeded in reducing disruptive behavior of a 10-year-old girl by giving her verbal feedback about her behavior. Giving verbal feedback also resulted in increased positive comments from classroom peers toward the learner. Similar results have been reported by Drabman, Spitalnik, and Spitalnik (1974). Strain and Kerr (1979) used verbal feedback to shape the behavior of an entire group ($n = 11$) of boys with learning disabilities. In this case, the verbal feedback was paired with giving each boy a weekly goal to achieve that related to either a social or an academic behavior.

The sixth strategy is role playing (Barclay, 1967). Role playing is a particularly interesting way to offer learners practice in how to behave in classroom situations. It is a strategy that collaborators could use to prepare learners to be more successful in mainstreamed settings. The final strategy uses group contingencies as a means of managing individual behavior (Carlson, Arnold, Becker, & Madsen, 1968; Evans & Oswalt, 1968).

THE POWER OF CONSEQUENCES

Management of environmental consequences is another effective method of improving learner performance; its impact can in fact be just as powerful as that of controlling antecedent events. Controlling consequences for desired or undesired learner behavior can be used in both teaching and motivating learners who have been difficult to motivate. In this section various types of reinforcement and consequences for improving rates of responding are discussed.

Much of the research and intervention dealing with the effects of consequences on learner behavior revolves around the testing of the effects of various types of reinforcement and punishment. Appendix 7.B lists various terms used to describe different types of consequences (Alberto & Troutman, 1986). However, all of the terms refer to methods by which a stimulus is applied as a negative or positive consequence to a behavior, resulting in increases or decreases in the future probability of the occurrence of the behavior. Most researchers agree that effective teachers deliver corrections that (a) are positive in nature, (b) directly relate to learner responses, and (c) cue or prompt learners to self-correct rather than merely provide the correct answer (Brady & Taylor, 1989; Englert, 1983; Gable et al., 1979; Hendrickson, Roberts, & Shores, 1978; Larrivee, 1986; Rieth, Polsgrove, & Semmel, 1981).

Examples of how various stimuli have been used to manage behavior in classroom and school settings can be found in applied behavior analysis studies conducted in classroom settings. The power of a teacher's systematic delivery of consequences has been consistently demonstrated regarding the academic responding of learners who are typical (e.g., Greer & Poliestok, 1982) and exceptional (e.g., McEvoy & Brady, 1988).

One of the most interesting stimuli involves using the teacher to affect behavior. Contingent teacher attention (Broden, Bruce, Mitchell, Carter, & Hall, 1970) and contingent teacher attention paired with the ignoring of disruptive behaviors (Hall, Lund, & Jackson, 1968) are methods that have consistently been proven effective over a long period of time. These two methods also involve sources of reinforcement that are readily available and easy to administer. A more sophisticated version of teacher attention was described by Schutte and Hopkins (1970); in this early study, very precise teacher instructions were paired with teacher compliments for good behavior. Contingent teacher attention has been used to eliminate undesirable, off-task behaviors of a disruptive learner in a general education classroom, using a resource/consulting teacher model (Idol, 1993, Project 18).

Undesirable classroom behaviors have also been effectively remediated using a more tangible type of reinforcement in the form of token economy programs as developed by Ayllon and Azrin (1968); Breyer and Allen (1975); Kazdin (1977), and Wolf, Giles, and Hall (1968).

> Tokens are conditioned reinforcers such as poker chips, coins, tickets, stars, points, or checkmarks. Tokens are generalized reinforcers because they can be exchanged for a variety of reinforcing events referred to as back-up reinforcers. A reinforcement system based on tokens is referred to as a token economy. In a token economy, tokens function the same way money does in national economic systems. (Kazdin, 1975, p. 125)

Tests of social validity of token economy programs have demonstrated minimal negative or positive "side effects" on teacher popularity (Kistner, Hammer, Wolfe, Rothblum, & Drabman, 1982). The Kistner et al. social validation study was conducted in response to teacher concern about what would happen to the performance of learners in a class without a token economy if they were also attending a second class with a token economy.

Token reinforcement programs have been reconceptualized to use a type of token, contingent points, that is easier to deliver and keep a record of. Contingent points have been paired with a reinforcement menu (Kroth, 1975), which is a very effective way to allow learners to select what they want to earn and to accumulate points over time, thereby teaching the learners the concept of saving for improved long-term benefits. In one of the more interesting studies, conducted in a cafeteria setting, the points were paired with contingent recess and attention from the building principal as a means of controlling disruptive lunchroom behavior (Muller, Hasazi, Pierce, & Hasazi, 1975). Another interesting classroom study involved junior high school learners who willingly asked only for points, receiving nothing else as a reward for classroom performance (Sulzer-Azaroff & Mayer, 1977).

Classroom studies have also demonstrated the power of using free time (Long & William, 1973) and classroom privileges (Volrath & Clark, 1974) as a means of maintaining acceptable group behavior. The power of peer attention and peer approval has also been used to manage classroom behavior. Even contingent tutoring in academic subjects has been used to manage disruptive behavior (Robertson, DeReus, & Drabman, 1976). One of the more innovative uses of peer approval has been to use peer approval paired with earned group game playing, contingent on work completion by a learner with disruptive behavior (Tribble & Hall, 1971).

It is recommended that negative reinforcement and punishment programs be avoided, because effective results can usually be achieved using positive reinforcement programs. In addition, the application of punishment in human service programs continues to be controversial (Skiba & Deno, 1991). Concern of the application (or misapplication) of unpleasant or noxious stimuli has led to the suggestion that punishment and aversive procedures be abandoned in favor of less-aversive alternatives (Donnellan, Negri-Shoultz, Fassbendes, & La Vigna, 1988; Evans & Meyer, 1985; Guess, 1988). At least one major professional organization has renounced the use of intrusive procedures (The Association for Persons with Severe Handicaps, 1981). In addition, the legal problems that can arise when applying punishment in public schools without parental permission alone should serve as a major deterrent to using punishing consequences.

The implications of the differential impacts of positive reinforcement versus punishment and negative reinforcement programs on feelings of self-worth and positive self-identification are profound indeed. People love to feel good about themselves, so why not focus on positive reinforcement programs as a means of shaping immediate behavior problems, and also thereby indirectly teaching learners the tremendous power of feeling positive about oneself? It is also important to select reinforcers that learners prefer.

It is recommended that secondary reinforcers be given preference over primary reinforcers. Similarly, intangible reinforcement, such as praise and social approval, is preferred over token economy programs, because secondary and intangible reinforcers are more closely associated with existing reinforcers in our normal lives. In any case, regardless of the reinforcement program selected, it is recommended that the selected reinforcers always be paired with teacher or tutor praise. The primary reason for this is that, eventually, the more tangible reinforcer can be faded, thus teaching learners to perform well for social praise and approval alone. One effect that is difficult to measure but is often likely to occur is that the individuals who are praised may develop their own intrinsic systems of self-reinforcement and become less dependent on external praise and approval.

In summary, collaborators must be wary of two major problems that can occur when using contingency programs. First, adults can fall into the trap of selecting something they "think" is reinforcing for learners, even though the learners themselves would not select the same reinforcer. An effective way to avoid this trap is to use a reinforcer survey to find out what types of events and activities learners find to be personally reinforcing.

A second trap occurs when collaborators have a clear idea of what a management program will consist of but the learners themselves do not have a clear understanding of it. One solution here is to post rules that are explicitly and positively stated and are carefully reviewed with the learners prior to program implementation. Another solution is to use a contingency contract (e.g., Homme, 1970; Lovitt, 1991), stating explicitly the conditions of the management program and requiring the learner to treat the contract as a formal agreement among all parties involved in the program. White-Blackman, Semb, and Semb (1977) conducted an interesting general classroom study in which contingency contracting via a teacher-negotiated contract was used.

Kazdin (1975) pointed out several advantages to using contingency contracting that remain practical and useful:

• When people contribute, their performance may be better.

• Contingencies are not as likely to be rejected, since they are negotiated.

• Contracts are flexible and can be negotiated and revised.

• Contracts provide a way to make contingencies explicit.

• The use of contracts is one way to structure a relationship between individuals.

Figure 7.3 describes procedural steps in writing a contingency contract and shows a sample contract form.

A variety of approaches can be used to manage the behavior of learners consequentially in classroom settings. For studies in classroom settings that specifically involve collaboration, see Idol (1993). Also, a training module on student discipline and classroom management for inclusive classrooms can be found in Idol and West (1993, Module 10).

TEACHER PRESENTATION STYLES AND TEACHER FEEDBACK

A critical element of teaching is how teachers present information to be learned. This is often overlooked, with primary consideration given to organizing and

FIGURE 7.3. Procedural steps and sample form for writing a contingency contract.

A. Procedural Steps:
  1. Define the task (what must be done).
  2. Specify time period (when).
  3. Establish criteria (how it must be done).
  4. Reinforcer (what will be earned).
  5. Penalty clause (what happens if criteria is not met).
  6. Bonus clause (extra reinforcement for consistency).

B. Sample Form (can be adapted to social behaviors):

Task:	I will read one chapter of my history book and answer the questions at the end.
Time:	During history class.
Criteria:	Get at least 60% correct.
Reinforcer:	10 minutes of free time.
Penalty:	If less than 60% correct I must come in after school to make corrections.
Bonus:	60% for 5 consecutive days = no written assignment.

Signed: Learner _____

Teacher _____

Date: _____

Note. From "Some Resources to Help Teachers Manage Classroom Behavior Problems," unpublished manuscript by J. R. Jenkins and D. Pany, University of Illinois at Urbana–Champaign.

defining the body of information to be taught. Certainly, to impart a knowledge base (curricular and teacher-made materials) is the primary intent of instruction, but consideration must also be given to how the information will be presented, that is, how the teacher will cue learners to attend and get ready to learn.

A cue refers to initial information provided to a learner *before* an action is performed (Falvey, Brown, Lyon, Baumgart, & Schroeder, 1980). Falvey et al. defined six types of cued instruction that can be used to teach learners with severe handicaps: (a) primed (physical) cues, (b) modeled cues, (c) direct verbal cues, (d) indirect verbal cues, (e) gestural cues, and (f) pictorial cues.

Primed (Physical) Cues

Falvey et al. (1980) defined primed correction procedures as providing physical contact to assist or guide a learner through part or all of the performance of a desired action. This definition considers only one dimension of physical cuing, that is, the use of cueing as an instructional procedure. However, physical cuing can also be applied as a means of obtaining and directing learner attention.

Examples of physical cues to direct learner attention can be found in DISTAR (Engelmann & Bruner, 1974) programs for arithmetic, reading, and spelling. In these programs, teachers are instructed to use certain physical cues, which are repeated throughout the programs. For instance, teachers are instructed to point the index finger, to raise the hand while saying, "Get," and to bring the hand straight down half the distance of the initial hand raise while saying, "Ready." This results in a rapid, ascending-descending hand motion, paired with a verbal cue, to elicit learner attention. The rationale is that learners should always be given this cue to prompt them to get ready for learning, without using extensive teacher talk and teacher coaxing. This type of cuing or signaling is especially recommended for fast-paced group instruction (Carnine & Silbert, 1979; Silbert, Carnine, & Stein, 1981).

Another example of a physical cue occurs if the teacher were to say, "Say the name of this number when I point to the number." DISTAR programs are designed to eliminate explaining to the learners what they are to do when the teacher points to the stimulus item. Instead, the "get ready" hand signal is used, followed by the teacher pointing to the stimulus item. This eliminates excessive teacher talk and assists in presentation of a rapidly paced lesson.

As previously mentioned, physical or primed cuing can also be used to guide a learner through the acquisition of a skill. For example, a teacher might show a learner the distinction between the voiced and unvoiced *th* sounds while teaching sound-letter relations. The teacher could ask the learner to say the words *thick* and *the* while placing the learner's own hand on the teacher's throat. In this case, the teacher would be using a primed cue with the learner's own hand as a means of demonstrating that throat vibrations can be felt for the voiced but not the unvoiced *th* sound.

The use of the teacher as the source of the physical cue can be seen in the example of teaching a learner to form letters. The teacher takes the learner's hand in the teacher's hand while the learner is holding a pencil in the correct position for writing. The teacher then lifts the learner's hand from the shape of the letter several times in the air, removes the physical prompt, and directs the learner to initiate the hand motion.

In summary, primed or physical cues can be used to signal learners that it is time to begin attending or responding. They can also be used to guide learners in the formulation of some types of responses. Finally, they can be used in clarifying concepts. Primed cues are useful for both individual or group instruction. One interesting application results in rapidly paced lessons with physical teacher signals, thus eliminating excessive verbal directions.

Modeled Cues

Modeled cues provide learners with a demonstration of actions that are expected within a response (Falvey et al., 1980). Modeling is the first step in a teacher-model/learner-initiate teaching paradigm, where the learner is expected to initiate the actions performed by the teacher. This paradigm has been extended to include leading the learner to respond after modeling the desired action. Leading consists of the teacher and the learner responding together. The modeling and leading are then followed by testing, in which the learner is required to respond independently. Figure 7.4 illustrates how oral reading errors are corrected in a direct-reading instruction program used in the Resource/Consulting Teacher Program at the University of Illinois. Numerous examples of model-lead-test teaching paradigms can be found in DISTAR programs, in Carnine and Silbert (1979), and Engelmann and Carnine (1982).

Teacher modeling can be used in many ways to teach learners with mild learning and behavior problems. Modeling cues can be applied to many domains of instruction. Table 7.2 displays examples of modeling cues that can be used for teaching oral language, written language, spelling, and arithmetic. Notice that any of these examples could be extended to include a model-lead-test paradigm, with the teacher modeling the action, guiding the learner through the action, and then requiring the learner to perform alone.

Direct Verbal Cues

Falvey et al. (1980) defined direct verbal cues as verbal directions or commands that require specific actions. Of the six types of teaching cues presented here, verbal cuing is probably the one most commonly used by teachers. An important characteristic of verbal cuing is that it reduces excessive and sometimes distracting teacher verbiage, using instead a clear and concise direction on command. Compare the following transcripts containing verbal cues:

FIGURE 7.4. Error correction procedure used for oral reading instruction.

Teacher: "What word?"
A. If response is correct: Praise!
B. If response is incorrect and it is *not* a sound-out word:

- Teacher: say the word
- Teacher and Learner: say the word
- Learner: say the word

C. If response is incorrect *and* it is a sound-out word:

- Teacher: "Sound it out."

D. If response is incorrect:

- Teacher: "My turn."
  —say it slow   m-a-n
  —say it fast   man
- Teacher: "Our turn."
  —say it slow   m-a-n
  —say it fast   man
- Teacher: "Your turn."
  —say it slow   m-a-n
  —say it fast   man

Note. After the correction has been made, the learner always rereads the entire sentence containing the error word.

Transcript A: The teacher says: "Girls and boys, today we have a lot of work to do. I want you to be very good, come in the room quietly. . . . Jason, do you hear me? . . . Come in the room quietly, I said. Take your seats and get ready to work!"

Transcript B: The teacher says (calmly and quietly): "Walk in quietly. Sit down. No talking." (The teacher waits until all learners are seated, then tells them to take out a pencil and paper from their desks.)

Transcript A contains 46 words, with approximately 20 of them describing the desired actions. Compare this with Transcript B, which has 7 words, with the last 2 words reminders of the first 3. Possibly Transcript B could be further reduced to just 5 words: "Walk in quietly. Sit down."

Teachers should consider how much unnecessary talk they are using. Thoughtful consideration should be given to determining how many learners

TABLE 7.2. Examples of Teacher Modeling and Learner Response Across Several Instructional Domains

Domain	Task	Teacher Models	Learner Responds
Oral language	Learning to use past tense and irregular verbs correctly	Teacher says, "Today I sleep, yesterday I slept. Your turn."	Learner says, "Today I sleep, yesterday I slept."
Written language	Learning to form introductory paragraphs	Teacher writes a sample paragraph containing a lead-in sentence, a statement of the issue, and an example of the application of the issue. Teacher points out the three seaprate parts, then gives the learner a similar paragraph.	Learner finds the three separate parts of the second teacher-written paragraph.
Spelling	Learning to spell words correctly	Teacher says: "mmm-aaa-p" (sounding out); "m-a-p" (says letters); "map" (says word)	Learner says: "mmm-aaa-p, m-a-p, map."
Arithmetic	Learning to solve simple addition and word problems (Alan had nine marbles; he gave them all away to his three friends, giving each friend equal amounts. How many marbles did each friend receive?)	Teacher draws three persons on the blackboard and begins to distribute nine small circles (marbles) to the persons by drawing one circle by Person A, one circle by Person B, one by Person C, and then repeating the process two more times. Teacher says: "Each person has three marbles."	With a similar problem, the learner repeats the same process modeled by the teacher.

Note. With careful monitoring, these procedures can be implemented by trained cross-age or same-age tutors, volunteers, and other classroom teacher assistants.

in the classroom are distractible—as well as distracting. For these learners, clear and concise directions may be easier to attend to than a series of directions embedded in a set of distracting messages that are separate from the distinct verbal cues being given by the teacher. An added advantage of Transcript B over Transcript A is that the short, clear, and respectful directions set the stage for the teacher to be available to observe whether the desired actions are being carried out. An extra message might be signaled by posting the rule on the door, giving privileges to learners who comply, contributing toward a class privilege by complying, and so on. Based on observation for a few days, the teacher can decide if the extra message must be provided to get the learners to enter the classroom quietly and to sit down. In this case, the desired actions are also simple to observe.

Indirect Verbal Cues

Indirect verbal cues provide a learner with covert and implicit statements that require relatively specific actions (Falvey et al., 1980). Covert cues can be used positively, to the teacher's advantage, or they can be used negatively, creating added instructional and management problems. Indirect verbal cues can be used advantageously to shape learner responses and to teach learners to respond appropriately to implied messages. In some instances, the use of indirect cues is reflective of naturally occurring behaviors in natural environments.

Teachers can use indirect verbal cues as an effective means of managing classroom behavior. For instance, a teacher might attend to a learner who is working on an assignment by saying, "I like the way Charles is working," but the message is indirectly directed to Richard, who is not working on the assignment and who is disrupting other learners. Attention to on-task behavior and ignoring of undesired behavior has proven to be an effective means of managing disruptive learners (Hall et al., 1968).

Indirect verbal cues can also be used to influence academic instruction. They are especially useful in teaching learners to give the same response in a variety of settings, situations, or conditions. A good area to apply indirect verbal cues is in teaching learners to comprehend better by attending to implied meanings in texts. For instance, a teacher may want to teach learners to attend to the message conveyed by the author of a story, and the teacher cues the learners to look for this author message by asking, "What is the meaning of the story?" or, "What is the main idea of the story?"

Indirect verbal cues can be used inappropriately by teachers. This sometimes produces mixed messages or messages that are difficult to interpret, especially for learners who have attentional problems. For example, a teacher may say to a learner, "What do you think of this lesson?" The implied message is to reiterate important points made by the teacher. Some learners who are poor at interpreting social cues may think this means to tell the teacher exactly what they think of the lesson. For a disruptive learner who is prone to behaving inappropriately, the question may set the stage for undesirable behavior. One solution to this problem is to ask a more direct question: "What do I want to learn from this lesson?" A second solution is to teach the learners to respond appropriately to indirect cues. The latter approach is particularly useful when mainstreaming learners into content area classes. However, it requires observational time for the collaborator(s) to identify typical patterns and types of indirect cues used by the teacher. It then requires direct teaching time to teach the learner to respond appropriately. No doubt, the more expedient and efficient solution is for teachers to use direct verbal cues rather than indirect ones.

Use of indirect verbal cues can also cause difficulty with classroom management. For example, a teacher might say to a group of learners, "Well, it's time to go," when the desired message is, "Put your work away, sit quietly, and wait for the formal dismissal." The indirect cue could cause a rush to the classroom door, with paper and books left in disorderly array. Then the teacher is placed in the embarrassing position of appearing to rescind the original direction by requiring the learners to return to their desks, put materials away, and leave in an orderly manner. There is also the likelihood that at least one or two learners will leave the first time, and they will have learned that it is not always necessary to be orderly in the classroom.

Thus, teachers need to consider, in advance, whether they want to use a direct or an indirect verbal cue. They must decide whether they are looking for a generalized response, in which case an indirect cue could be valuable, or whether the use of an indirect cue would merely cause confusion and/or contribute to a problem.

Gestural Cues

According to Falvey et al. (1980), gestural cues are physical, nonverbal motions or movements that indicate that certain actions should be performed. Some teachers use nonverbal cues to manage learners masterfully, while reducing excessive verbal direction. For example, a teacher might motion for a learner to come forward for assistance or to work quietly without disturbing other learners in the group. Gestural cues can be powerful reinforcers for individual learners; they seem to connote a feeling of special and private communication between the learner and the teacher. For example, a teacher might wink at a learner or signal an approving hand motion (e.g., forming the index finger and thumb into a circle with remaining fingers extended upward) as a means of conveying approval.

Gestural cues can also be used to guide learner actions in a desired direction, for example, by using the fingers in a walking motion to indicate walking is preferred over running. Gestural cuing may be particularly useful in encouraging reluctant learners to respond and in guiding learners through difficult steps of a task.

Pictorial Cues

Pictorial cues provide representational, two-dimensional pictures, numbers, or other symbols to indicate that learners should perform specific actions (Falvey et al., 1980). In instructional settings, pictorial cues are usually paired with verbal and gestural cues. After verbal cues, pictorial cues are probably the most commonly used for instruction. Common examples are pictures on classroom bulletin boards, number and letter charts, symbol charts for chemicals studied in chemistry class, exercise positions for physical education classes, and pictures in reading materials designed to improve contextual understanding.

More recently, Mastropieri and Scruggs (e.g., Mastropieri & Scruggs, 1987, 1989, 1991; Scruggs & Mastropieri, 1992, in press) have developed a method of using pictorial cues to aid learners in studying and retaining material for content area instruction. These pictorial cues are used as mnemonic devices to aid learners in important concepts, ideas, dates, events, and so on. For example, Scruggs and Mastropieri (1992) used mnemonic pictures and teacher presentation to modify textbook-based science instruction for learners with learning disabilities and mild mental retardation and reported that learning nearly doubled. Similarly, pictorial-type cues have been used to improve reading comprehension in content area classes via predrawn story maps where the picture of the story map serves as a means of helping learners remember to look for certain salient pieces of information in the text they are reading (Idol, 1987a, 1987b; Idol & Croll, 1987). Of these various studies, one was conducted in an inclusive classroom (Idol, 1987a), where third and fourth graders, including some learners with special needs and some at risk for school failure, were taught to use story maps to increase comprehension of narrative stories.

In summary, teachers can exercise considerable control in teaching learners with diverse needs in a large group by utilizing several planned cues for presenting information to learners and for obtaining learner feedback. These cues can be modeled by the teacher; they can be direct or indirect; they can take a variety of sensory forms; but all are intended to increase learning involvement in an active learning process.

Aside from how teachers cue information for learners, a number of programming alternatives can be used to accommodate learners with special needs in inclusive classrooms. For example, Table 7.3 contains a listing of several types of instructional alternatives (Laurie, Buchwach, Silverman, & Zigmond, 1978). The categories are divided into five basic areas: classroom organization, classroom management, methods of presentation, methods of practice, and methods of testing. We have used Table 7.3 in two different ways in working with collaborative consultation teams in schools.

First, we have found that collaborators are prone to brainstorm spontaneously possible solutions to problems without considering the type of problem or category of alternatives that a particular solution might fit into. After collaborators identify the general categories of the interventions under

TABLE 7.3. Programming Alternatives for General Classroom Teachers with Learners with Special Needs

Classroom Organization	Classroom Management	Methods of Presentation	Methods of Practice	Methods of Testing
Vary grouping arrangements • large-group instruction • small-group instruction • individual instruction • peer tutoring • independent self-instructional activities • learning centers Vary methods of instruction • teacher-directed • student-directed	Vary grading systems • homework • tests • class discussion • special projects Vary reinforcement systems • praise • notes sent home • grades • free time • special activity • progress charts • tangibles Vary rules • differentiated for some learners • explicit/implicit	Vary content • amount to be learned • time to learn new information • conceptual level Vary general structure • advance organizers • previewing questions • cues, mnemonic devices • provide immediate feedback • involve learners actively Vary type • verbal-lecture, discussion • written texts, work sheets • demonstration • audiovisuals • tape recorders • filmstrips • movies • opaque projectors • trans-parencies	Vary general structure • amount to be practiced • time for practice • group/individual • teacher-directed/independent items ranging from easy to difficult Vary level of response • copying • recognition • recall with cues • recall without cues Vary type of materials • work sheets • texts • audiovisual equipment	Vary type • verbal • written • demonstra-tion Vary general structure • group/individual • amount to be tested • time for completion Vary level of recognition • recognition • recall with cues • recall

Note. From "Teaching Secondary Learning Disabled Students in the Mainstream" by L. Buchwach, R. Silverman, and N. Zigmond, Fall 1978, *Learning Disability Quarterly, 1,* p. 68.

consideration, collaborators narrow their search for solutions to the categories that have the highest relevancy to the identified problem. Therefore, we have used the five categories in Table 7.3 to help collaborators pinpoint more or less useful categories of intervention. Second, we have used Table 7.3 as a reference for novice collaborators so as to provide them with a partial listing of some standard solutions to classroom problems. Third, we have used Table 7.3 to stimulate team discussions of other potential solutions that are not contained in the table but fit within one of the categories.

SHAPING LEARNING BEHAVIOR

In this section we discuss the shaping of learning behavior as it relates to (a) coding of reinforceable behavior and (b) stages of learning.

Coding Reinforceable Behavior

As defined by Alberto and Troutman (1986), shaping a behavior is "the instructional procedure for teaching new behaviors through differential reinforcement of successive approximations to a specified target behavior" (p. 357). Essentially, the best response that a learner can produce is selected as the most reinforceable behavior. Engelmann and Carnine (1982, p. 255) offered the following procedure for shaping simple responses:

1. Take baseline data on the learners' performance.
2. Use the baseline sample to assign three groups of responses:
    a. Nonreinforceable responses; these are the worst three responses provided.
    b. Single-reinforceable responses; these are the middle three responses.
    c. Double-reinforceable responses; these are the best three responses.

Engelmann and Carnine (1982) regard nonreinforceable behaviors as those that would simply not be reinforced. Single-reinforceable responses would receive a single reinforcement, and double-reinforceable responses would receive twice the reinforcement given for single-reinforcement responses. Trials or stimulus items are then presented, using certain criteria, to decide when and how to deliver the reinforcement.

An example of an application of this procedure is a situation in which a teacher attempts to teach a learner to write legibly, using cursive handwriting. The teacher could collect three samples of the learner's handwriting by requesting the learner to copy three short paragraphs on three different occasions. Each of the words in the three paragraphs would then be rated by the teacher, using these criteria:

1. *Nonreinforceable responses.* These would be words that are not legible, in that all letters in the word are either poorly or incorrectly formed. An X would be drawn across these words.

2. *Single-reinforceable responses.* These would be words that contained some letters that were correctly formed. These words would be marked by drawing a rectangle around them.

3. *Double-reinforceable responses.* These would be words that were completely legible, with all letters correctly formed. These words would be identified by drawing a circle around them.

The baseline data in this example could be summarized in the following way, using the percentage of words within each of the three categories as the dependent measure.

	Single reinforceable	Double reinforceable
Day 1		
Day 2		
Day 3		

These data could then be plotted on a chart with multiple bands, recording percentage of words for each of the three categories. The shaping program would then be begun by continuing to require the learner to copy short paragraphs and by differentially reinforcing the various word formations. Upon completion of the writing, the learner would turn the paper in for correction. The grading procedure would require the teacher to evaluate the passage quickly, using the three marking codes: an X, a rectangle, and a circle. The marking would be done in the presence of the learner, with the teacher not commenting on nonreinforceable responses, saying "Good" for the single-reinforceable responses, and pairing verbal reinforcement with a tally point on the top of the paper for double-reinforceable responses. If it were impossible to give the learner direct feedback, verbal reinforcement could be replaced with a single tally point, with double-reinforceable responses earning 5 points. In either case, the tallied points could be translated later into grades, privileges, or reduced numbers of paragraph-copying assignments. It is important to remember that some learners will apparently work for points alone, not trading them for anything (Stanberry & Harris, 1974).

An effective way to use a shaping program is to change gradually the criteria for acceptable or reinforceable responses. In this way, what was initially a reinforceable behavior could eventually become a nonreinforceable behavior, as the behavior improves over time and practice trials. Shaping programs can be applied to a variety of types of learning and behavior management programs. They can be used with either individual learners or groups of learners. They provide a subtle way for a teacher to reinforce acceptable and desired responses without placing unnecessary attention on undesirable responses.

Stages of Learning

At a higher level, teachers are shaping behavior when they use stages of learning as a means of designing appropriate instructional programs for learners (see Chapter 5 for a discussion of using these stages for assessment purposes). In-depth explanations of the stages of learning can be found in various sources (Haring, Lovitt, Eaton, & Hansen, 1978; Idol, 1993; Smith, 1981). Six stages defined by Idol (1993, pp. 106–109) are:

1. *Acquisition.* The learner is in the processing of acquiring, but has not acquired the skill. The learner has no knowledge of how to perform the task accurately, and therefore never responds correctly, no matter how many times he or she is tested. In this stage, the teacher offers direct instruction, followed by practice in the skill area.

2. *Reversion.* The learner is in the process of acquiring the skill, responding erratically. The learner sometimes responds correctly, indicating some knowledge of how to perform accurately, but also responds incorrectly, showing reversion to the entry level of acquisition. The teacher reinforces correct responses and ignores incorrect responses or pinpoints the error pattern in the incorrect response.

3. *Proficiency.* The learner responds accurately but with insufficient speed. The learner performs accurately, indicating acquisition of the requisite information, but needs to perform the skill quickly enough as to be practically automatic, so that other skills may be built on this one, and not impeded by slow performance. The aim of instruction is for the teacher to reinforce the learner for faster *rates* of response.

4. *Maintenance.* The learner is expected to retain both accuracy and fluency with the skill. The learner may or may not continue to perform at a proficient level. Consequently, the teacher must periodically evaluate retention and again use direct instruction when necessary to maintain both accuracy and speed of response. The aim of instruction is *retention* of the skill.

5. *Generalization.* The learner is expected to transfer the skill to new situations or settings, regardless of the setting or response mode required. The teacher provides direct instruction in alternate settings and response modes when the learner fails to generalize. The teacher programs for generalization in different settings and modes, varying stimu-

lus conditions, telling learners which to attend to and which to ignore, and training other conditions in alternative settings to maintain similar procedures. The aim of instruction is *expansion* of the skill across situations, behaviors, and time.

6. *Adaptation.* The learner must be able to recognize how skills can be applied to entirely new situations. The learner should be able to capitalize on previous learning and extend knowledge and skills that have been previously acquired. New situations call for problem solving that draws on previous learning. The teacher should provide opportunities for application of old information to new problems and situations. Discovery learning may be appropriate at this stage. The aim of instruction is *extension* of knowledge and skills to new areas.

Readers can find a module offering in-depth training on stages of learning and how to apply them in inclusive classrooms with learners who are difficult to teach in Idol and West (1993, Module 4).

First, collaborators must decide the appropriate stages of learning; then they must select appropriate strategies to use, based on the stage of learning the learner is in. The primary distinction is whether the learner lacks a skill (acquisition stage) or whether the learner is just not fluent in using the skill (proficiency stage). The former requires direct instruction for skill mastery; the latter requires practice coupled with reinforcement. This distinction is very important because, if a learner does not possess a skill, reinforcement and practice strategies are useless; whereas, if a learner merely requires practice to gain fluency, then taking instructional time for skill instruction is an unnecessary waste of time. Smith (1981) cited teaching and management strategies that can be used in the various stages of learning; in-depth explanations and discussions of the strategies can be found in Chapters 4 and 5 of that book. More detailed ideas and suggestions for programming for the generalization stage can be found in Chapters 5 and 6 of Idol (1993).

MATERIALS MODIFICATION

Materials modification is an integral part of making adaptations in the inclusive classroom. A perusal of the literature on materials modification indicates that many authors confuse instructional adaptations with materials modification, often intermingling the two very different concepts. For our purposes, *materials modification* means to use the instructional materials currently being used in the general classroom and to make necessary modifications in those materials to facilitate academic progress of targeted learners with special needs or who are failing in school. *Instructional adaptation* means to make adjustments in how the actual instruction is offered in the classroom. The latter is discussed in various other sections of this chapter, as are training opportunities on instructional adaptations, which are available in Idol and West (1993, Module 8). Also, instructional adaptations are more likely to appear in most methods books on mainstreaming than are suggestions for materials modification.

When the collaborative team is faced with the decision of whether or not to modify materials, they must consider these key questions:

1. Will the materials modification make learning easier and more efficient for the targeted learner(s)?

2. Will the materials modification create an even larger discrepancy between what the targeted learner is expected to accomplish and what other learners in the same classroom are expected to accomplish?

3. Can the learner use the materials modification in a timely and independent manner in the classroom?

4. How much time will the collaborators need to devote to the preparation of the materials modification? Is there a collaborator who is willing to do it?

5. How much teacher time is required in teaching and monitoring the use of the modification?

The reader is also referred to Idol and West (1993, Module 2) for training opportunities in how to use a decision-making framework for adapting curriculum and instruction for learners with special needs.

Collaborative teams will find that in their collective knowledge base is a rich collection of ideas on how to make modifications in instructional materials. Our review of major methodology textbooks reveals that little is actually available on this topic, even though it is an integral part of including certain learners with special learning needs in general classrooms. As a means of stimulating discussion among collaborative teams when they pool their expertise on this topic, we have compiled a partial listing of some recommended methods of modifying instructional materials in Figure 7.5. Many of these methods rely on an experimental research base, as indicated by the reference citations. Training opportunities for making materials modifications can be found in Idol and West (1993, Module 7). Some other sources of methods books for teaching learners with special needs in general education that contain occasional references to materials modifications and many references to instructional adaptations are Glass, Christiansen, and Christiansen (1982); Gloeckler and Simpson (1988); Heron and Harris (1993); Lewis and Doorlag (1987); McCoy and Prehm (1987); Morsink (1984); and Turnbull and Schulz (1979).

SUMMARY

As with the learning processes discussed in Chapter 6, the classroom adaptations presented in this chapter are useful for individual, small-group, and large-

FIGURE 7.5. A partial listing of techniques for making materials modifications.

• Use highlighting to select certain passages for students to read.

• Use a magnifying glass, preferably on the size of a page of print, to enlarge the letters on a page.

• Prepare audiotapes of textbook material (e.g., Deshler & Graham, 1980).

• Prepare individual or audiotaped assessments (e.g., Salend, 1990, Chapter 8).

• Increase use of facilitative pictures or diagrams (e.g., Scruggs, Mastropieri, Levin, McLoone, & Morrison, 1987).

• Provide advanced organizers of the content to be read (see review by Lott, 1983).

• Provide chapter preview questions.

• Provide chapter study guides, which include vocabulary, content outline, cloze paragraphs, and chapter tests.

• Rewrite the chapter content at a lower readability and syntactic language level (Coleman, 1979).

• Use a work sheet to guide independent reading.

• Provide alternative assignments that don't require writing or reading.

• Provide reading materials on the same subject being presented in the standard textbook that are written at an easier level of difficulty.

• Use framed outlines coupled with precision teaching (e.g., Lovitt, Rudsit, Jenkins, Pious, & Benedetti, 1985, 1986).

• Use story maps or critical thinking maps to improve textbook comprehension (Idol, 1987a, 1987b; Idol & Croll, 1987).

• Place emphasis on activities-oriented approaches to teaching that deemphasize reading from textbooks, reduce vocabulary and terminology to a necessary minimum (Bay, Staver, Bryan, & Hale, in press; Scruggs & Mastropieri, 1993).

• Place main ideas of a chapter in an organizational diagram (Sprick, 1979).

• Provide extra work sheets that provide additional practice opportunities for concepts presented in the classroom textbook.

• Break the lessons and sublesson in the materials into smaller units.

• Vary the types of assignments using the classroom materials.

• Allow additional time for the completion of tasks defined in the materials.

• Vary the amount of work to be accomplished within varying time limits.

• Assign independent or small-group projects, using the materials cooperatively and with a signed contract specifying the required tasks.

---

group instruction. When coupled with the relevant principles of Collaborative Consultation, these adaptations should serve to facilitate collaborative work, to clarify and simplify communication among collaborators, and, in general, to enhance the academic and behavioral growth of all learners in inclusive classrooms.

Collaborative Problem Solving: Stages 3 and 4

Intervention Recommendations. In Stage 3 of the collaborative problem-solving process, Intervention Recommendations, collaborators engage in team decision making to determine which intervention or (combination of interventions) is best suited to solving the targeted problem and to reaching the specified goals and objectives for the learner with special needs. The collaborators explore possible solutions to the problem. In Chapters 6 and 7 we have described a broad collection of learning processes and classroom adaptations that might be considered as possible interventions. The collaborative team might rely on these chapters, coupled with their own knowledge bases, to select the best possible solution to the specified problem.

As the collaborators engage in this problem-solving process, they progress through the following steps:

1. Brainstorm the most-probable solutions to the problem.

2. Analyze and explore the possible positive and negative consequences and implications for using each of the possible solutions.

3. Based on the above analysis, prioritize the possible interventions with the express intent of reaching consensus on a final solution to the problem.

The consensus-building, decision-making process is further detailed in Modules 29 and 30 of West et al. (1989), with personnel development opportunities for preservice teachers and school staff to gain expertise in this type of decision making.

Implementation of Recommendations. Once the collaborators have successfully investigated and analyzed possible solutions to the problem and have reached consensus on a solution to be tried, their task is to implement the program. This is Stage 4 of the collaborative problem-solving process, Implementation of Recommendations. In this stage we recommend that collaborators develop a viable Plan of Action for carrying out the program, specifying what will be done, when it will be done, who will be responsible, and how the effect will be evaluated.

Figure 7.6 is an example of such a plan. It is an adaptation of a plan developed by a leadership team in Mt. Lebanon School District in Pittsburgh, Penn-

FIGURE 7.6. Collaborative Consultation Team Plan of Action.

Student Name: _____ Team Members: _____

Date: _____ _____

_____

Primary Goal(s):

Related Objectives:

Decision of the Team:

☐ Modify Interventions
☐ Continue Interventions to Maintain Progress

☐ Develop New Interventions Relevant to the New Goal(s)

☐ Refer for Multidisciplinary Team Evaluation

☐ Discontinue Intervention (Explain Below)

Date	Selected Intervention to be Implemented (Enumerate each substep necessary to carry out the plan)	Person(s) Responsible for Intervention	Target Date for Implementation	Review Date	Evaluation

sylvania. It is based on a model Plan of Action contained in the *Collaboration in the Schools* staff development program (West et al., 1989, Module 31) and is an example of what results when leadership teams have been given staff development opportunities in the collaborative problem-solving process.

Essentially, this Plan of Action is the map for how to implement the planned intervention, including steps necessary for implementation, delineating who will be responsible for each step, and how the team will know how to go to the next step. Once this plan has been developed, the collaborators move to the next stage of collaborative problem solving, Evaluation (Chapter 8). This chapter includes a collection of principles and techniques for deciding what and how to evaluate. It is followed by the final step in the collaborative problem-solving process, Follow-up, where guidance is offered in making evaluation decisions (also in Chapter 8).

STUDY QUESTIONS

1. Which of the various adaptations for facilitating the teaching and learning process are important to you? Why?

2. Describe your reactions to the authors' suggestions for scheduling and managing learners. How realistic are these suggestions? What barriers exist to implementing them? Choose one barrier and discuss how you would apply the information from Chapter 6 to overcome the barrier.

3. Why is it important to know about the process of shaping new behaviors for learners? How might a collaborative consultation team approach acquisition of new behaviors differently than maintenance of already taught behaviors?

4. What effect do presentation style and teacher feedback have on learning? Can a person change his or her presentation style and method of giving feedback, or are they functions of personality? Why?

5. Reexamine the nine teaching and learning adaptations described in this chapter. Rank them in order from least to most intrusive and intensive. Provide a rationale for your ranking.

REFERENCES

Adams, M. J. (1990). *Beginning to read: Thinking and learning about print.* Champaign: Center for the Study of Reading, University of Illinois.

Alberto, P. S., & Troutman, A. C. (1986). *Applied behavior analysis for teachers: Influencing student performance* (2nd ed.). Columbus, OH: Merrill.

Anderson, C. W., & Smith, L. (1987). Teaching science. In V. Richardson-Koehler (Ed.), *The educator's handbook: A research perspective* (pp. 84–112). New York: Longman.

Anderson, R. C.(1984). Role of the reader's schema in comprehension, learning and memory. In R. Anderson, J. Osborn, & R. Tierney (Eds.), *Learning to read in American schools: Basal readers and content texts* (pp. 243–257). Hillsdale, NJ: Erlbaum.

Anderson, R. C., Hiebert, E. H., Scott, J. A., & Wilkinson, I. A. G. (1985). *Becoming a nation of readers: The report of the commission on reading.* Washington, DC: The National Institute of Education.

Anderson, R. C., Osborn, J., & Tierney, R. J. (1984). *Learning to read in American schools: Basal readers and content texts.* Hillsdale, NJ: Erlbaum.

The Association for Persons with Severe Handicaps. (1981). Resolution on intrusive interventions. *TASH Newsletter, 7*(11), 1–2.

Ayllon, T., & Azrin, N. H. (1968). *The token economy: A motivational system for therapy and rehabilitation.* New York: Appleton-Century-Crofts.

Baer, D. M., Wolf, M. M., & Risley, T. R. (1968). Some current dimensions of applied behavior analysis. *Journal of Applied Behavior Analysis, 1*(1), 91–97.

Barclay, R. (1967). Effecting behavior change in the elementary classroom: An exploratory study. *Journal of Counseling Psychology, 14*, 240–247.

Bay, M., Staver, J. R., Bryan, T., & Hale, J. B. (in press). Science instruction for the mildly handicapped: Direct instruction versus discovery teaching. *Journal of Research in Science Teaching.*

Becker, W. C. (1977). Teaching reading and language to the disadvantaged—What we have learned from field research. *Harvard Educational Review, 47*, 518–543.

Borkowski, J. G., Carr, M., Rellinger, E., & Pressley, M. (1990). Self-regulated cognition: Interdependence of metacognition, attributions, and self-esteem. In B. F. Jones & L. Idol, *Dimensions of thinking and cognitive instruction* (pp. 53–92). Hillsdale, NJ: Erlbaum.

Brady, M. P., & Taylor, R. D. (1989). Instructional consequences in mainstreamed middle school classes: Reinforcement and corrections. *Remedial and Special Education, 10*(2), 31–36.

Bransford, J. D., Vye, N., Kinzer, C., & Risko, Y. (1990). Teaching thinking and content knowledge: Toward an integrated approach. In B. F. Jones & L. Idol, *Dimensions of thinking and cognitive instruction* (pp. 381–414). Hillsdale, NJ: Erlbaum.

Breyer, N. L., & Allen, G. J. (1975). Effects of implementing a token economy on teacher attending behavior. *Journal of Applied Behavior Analysis, 8*, 373–380.

Broden, M. C., Bruce, C., Mitchell, M., Carter, V., & Hall, R. V. (1970). Effects of teacher attention on attending behavior of two boys in adjacent desks. *Journal of Applied Behavior Analysis, 3*, 199–203.

Broden, M., Copeland, G., Beasley, A., & Hall, R. V. (1977). Altering student responses through changes in teacher verbal behavior. *Journal of Applied Behavior Analysis, 10*, 479–487.

Brown, A. L. (1980). Metacognitive development and reading. In R. J. Spiro, B. C. Bruce, & W. F. Brewer (Eds.), *Theoretical issues in reading comprehension* (pp. 453–483). Hillsdale, NJ: Erlbaum.

Carlson, C., Arnold, C., Becker, W., & Madsen, C. (1966). The elimination of tantrum behavior of a child in an elementary classroom. *Behavior Research and Therapy, 6*, 117–119.

Carnine, D., & Silbert, J. (1979). *Direct instruction reading.* Columbus, OH: Merrill.

Cazden, C. B. (1981). Social context of learning to read. In J. T. Guthrie (Ed.), *Comprehension and teaching: Research reviews* (pp. 118–139). Newark, DE: International Reading Association.

Chance, P. (1986). *Thinking in the classroom: A survey of programs.* New York: Teachers College Press.

Christenson, S. L., Ysseldyke, J. E., & Thurlow, M. L. (1989). Critical instructional factors for students with mild handicaps. *Remedial and Special Education, 10*(5), 21–31.

Coleman, L. J. (1979, October). Using readability data for adapting curriculum materials. *Education and Training of the Mentally Retarded, 14*, 163–169.

Cook, D. M. (1989a). *A guide to curriculum planning in reading.* Madison: Wisconsin Department of Public Instruction.

Cook, D. M. (1989b). *Strategic learning in the content areas.* Madison: Wisconsin Department of Public Instruction.

Cooke, T. P., & Apolloni, T. (1976). Developing positive social-emotional behaviors: A study of training and generalization effects. *Journal of Applied Behavior Analysis, 9*(1), 65–78.

Csapo, M. (1972). Peer models reverse the "one bad apple spoils the barrel" theory. *Teaching Exceptional Children, 5*(1), 20–24.

Delquadri, J., Greenwood, C. R., & Hall, R. V. (1979, June). *Opportunity to respond: An update.* Invited address presented at the fifth annual meeting of the Association for Behavior Analysis, Dearborn, MI.

Derry, S. J. (1990). Learning strategies for acquiring useful knowledge. In B. F. Jones & L. Idol, *Dimensions of thinking and cognitive instruction* (pp. 347–380). Hillsdale, NJ: Erlbaum.

Deshler, D., & Graham, S. (1980). Tape recording educational materials for secondary handicapped students. *Teaching Exceptional Children, 12*, 52–54.

Donnellan, A. M., Negri-Shoultz, N., Fassbendes, L., & LaVigna, G. (1988). *Progress without punishment: Effective approach for learners with behavior problems.* New York: Teachers College Press.

Drabman, R., & Lahey, B. (1974). Feedback in classroom behavior modification: Effects on the target and her peers. *Journal of Applied Behavior Analysis, 7*, 591–598.

Drabman, R., Spitalnik, R., & Spitalnik, K. (1974). Sociometric and disruptive behavior as a function of four types of token reinforcement programs. *Journal of Applied Behavior Analysis, 7*, 93–101.

Engelmann, S., & Bruner, E. (1974). *DISTAR reading level I.* Chicago, IL: Science Research Associates.

Engelmann, S., & Carnine, D. (1982). *Theory of instruction: Principles and applications.* New York: Irvington.

Englert, C. (1983). Measuring special education teacher effectiveness. *Exceptional Children, 50*, 247–254.

Epstein, M. H., & Cullinan, D. (1979). Social validation: Use of normative peer data to evaluate LD interventions. *Learning Disability Quarterly, 2*(4), 93–98.

Evans, G., & Oswalt, G. (1968). Acceleration of academic progress through the manipulation of peer influence. *Behavior Research and Therapy, 6*, 189–195.

Evans, I. M., & Meyer, L. H. (1985). *An educative approach to behavior problems: A practical decision model for interventions with severely handicapped learners.* Baltimore: Brookes.

Falvey, M., Brown, T., Lyon, S., Baumgart, D., & Schroeder, J. (1980). Strategies for using cues and correction procedures. In W. Sailor, B. Wilcox, & L. Brown (Eds.), *Methods of instruction for severely handicapped students* (pp. 109–134). Baltimore: Brookes.

Feuerstein, K., Rand, Y., Hoffman, M. B., Egozi, M., & Shachar-Segev, N. B. (1991). Intervention programs for retarded performers: Goals, means, and expected outcomes. In L. Idol & B. F. Jones (Eds.), *Educational values and cognitive instruction: Implications for reform* (pp. 139–178). Hillsdale, NJ: Erlbaum.

Florio-Ruane, S. (1991). Instructional conversations in learning to write and learning to teach. In L. Idol & B. F. Jones (Eds.), *Educational values and cognitive instruction: Implications for reform* (pp. 365–386). Hillsdale, NJ: Erlbaum.

Foster, G. G., & Salvia, J. (1977). Teacher response to the label "learning disabled" as a function of demand characteristics. *Exceptional Children, 43,* 533–534.

Foster, G. G., Schmidt, C. R., & Sabatino, D. (1976). Teacher expectancies and the label "learning disabilities." *Journal of Learning Disabilities, 9,* 58–61.

Gable, R. A., Strain, P. S., & Hendrickson, J. M. (1979). Strategies for improving the status of social behavior of learning disabled children. *Learning Disability Quarterly, 2*(3), 33–39.

Gillung, T. B., & Rucker, C. N. (1977). Labels and teacher expectations. *Exceptional Children, 43*(7), 464–465.

Glass, R. M., Christiansen, J., & Christiansen, J. L. (1982). *Teaching exceptional students in the regular classroom.* Boston: Little, Brown.

Gloeckler, T., & Simpson, C. (1988). *Exceptional students in regular classrooms: Challenges, services, and methods.* Mountain View, CA: Mayfield.

Good, T. (1970). Which pupils do teachers call on? *Elementary School Journal, 70,* 190–198.

Graubard, P., Rosenberg, H., & Miller, M. (1974). Student applications of behavior modification to teachers and environments, or ecological approaches to social deviancy. In R. Ulrich, T. Stachnik, & J. Mabry (Eds.), *Control of human behavior* (Vol. 3). Glenview, IL: Scott, Foresman.

Greer, R. D., & Poliestok, S. R. (1982). Collateral gains and short-term maintenance in reading and on task responses by some inner-city adolescents as a function of their use of social reinforcement while tutoring. *Journal of Applied Behavior Analysis, 15,* 123–139.

Guess, D. (1988). Problems and issues pertaining to the transmission of behavior management technologies from researchers to practitioners. In R. H. Horner (Ed.), *Behavior management and community integration for individuals with developmental disabilities and severe behavior problems.* Washington, DC: U. S. Office of Special Education and Rehabilitative Services.

Hall, R. V., Delquadri, J., & Harris, J. W. (1977, May). *Opportunity to respond: A new focus in the field of applied behavior analysis.* Invited address at the third annual convention of the Midwestern Association of Behavior Analysis. Chicago.

Hall, R. V., Lund, D., & Jackson, D. (1968). Effects of teacher attention on study behavior. *Journal of Applied Behavior Analysis, 1,* 1–12.

Haring, N. G., Lovitt, J. C., Eaton, M. D., & Hansen, C. L. (1978). *The fourth R: Research in the classroom.* Columbus, OH: Merrill.

Hayes, J. R. (1990). Individuals and environments in writing instruction. In B. F. Jones & L. Idol, *Dimensions of thinking and cognitive instruction* (pp. 241–263). Hillsdale, NJ: Erlbaum.

Hendrickson, J. M., Roberts, M., & Shores, R. E. (1978). Antecedent and contingent modeling procedures to teach reading to learning disabled children. *Journal of Learning Disabilities, 11,* 524–528.

Heron, T. E., & Harris, K. C. (1993). *The educational consultant: Helping professionals, parents, and mainstreamed students* (2nd ed.). Austin, TX: PRO-ED.

Heron, T. E., & Skinner, M. E. (1981). Criteria for defining the regular classroom as the least restrictive environment for LD students, *Learning Disability Quarterly, 4*(2), 115–120.

Homme, L. (1970). *How to use contingency contracting in the classroom.* Champaign, IL: Research Press.

Idol, L. (1987a). A critical thinking map to improve content area comprehension of poor readers. *Remedial and Special Education, 8*(4), 28–50.

Idol, L. (1987b). Group story mapping: A comprehension strategy for both skilled and unskilled readers. *Journal of Learning Disabilities, 20,* 196–205.

Idol, L. (1993). *The special educator's consultation handbook.* (2nd ed.). Austin, TX: PRO-ED.

Idol, L., & Croll, V. (1987). The effects of story mapping on poor comprehension. *Learning Disability Quarterly, 10*(3), 214–230.

Idol, L., & Jones, B. F. (Eds.). (1991). *Educational values and cognitive instruction: Implications for reform.* Hillsdale, NJ: Erlbaum.

Idol, L., Jones, B. F., & Mayer, R. (1991). Classroom instruction: The teaching of thinking. In L. Idol & B. F. Jones (Eds.), *Educational values and cognitive instruction: Implications for reform* (pp. 65–119). Hillsdale, NJ: Erlbaum.

Idol, L., Nevin, A., & Paolucci-Whitcomb, P. (1986). *Models of curriculum-based assessment.* Austin, TX: PRO-ED.

Idol, L., & West, J. F. (1993). *Effective instruction of difficult-to-teach students: An inservice and preservice development program for classroom, remedial, and special education teachers.* Austin, TX: PRO-ED.

Jones, B. F., & Idol, L. (Eds.). (1990). *Dimensions of thinking and cognitive instruction.* Hillsdale, NJ: Erlbaum.

Jones, B. F., Palincsar, A. S., Ogle, D. S., & Carr, E. G. (1987). *Strategic teaching and learning: Cognitive instruction in the content areas.* Alexandria, VA: Association for Supervision and Curriculum Development.

Jones, B. F., Tinzmann, M. B., Friedman, L. B., & Walker, B. B. (1987). *Teaching thinking skills: English/language arts.* Washington, DC: National Education Association.

Kazdin, A. (1975). *Behavior modification in applied settings.* Homewood, IL: Dorsey.

Kazdin, A. E. (1977). Assessing the clinical significance of behavior change through social validation. *Behavior Modification, 1,* 427–452.

Kistner, J., Hammer, D., Wolfe, D., Rothblum, E., & Drabman, S. (1982). Teacher popularity and contrast effects in a classroom token economy. *Journal of Applied Behavior Analysis, 15*(1), 85–96.

Kroth, R. L. (1975). *Communicating with parents of exceptional children.* Denver: Love.

Larkin, J. (1983). Research on science education. In A. M. Lesgold & F. Reif (Eds.), *Computers in education: Realizing the potential* (pp. 95–108) (Report of a research conference). Washington, DC: Office of the Assistant Secretary for Educational Research and Improvement.

Larrivee, B. (1986). Effective teaching for mainstreamed students is effective teaching for all students. *Teacher Education and Special Education, 9*(4), 173–179.

Laurie, T. E., Buchwach, L., Silverman, R., & Zigmond, N. (1978). Teaching secondary learning disabled students in the mainstream. *Learning Disability Quarterly, 1*(4), 62–72.

Lewis, R. B., & Doorlag, D. H. (1987). *Teaching special students in the mainstream* (2nd ed.). Columbus, OH: Merrill.

Long, J. D., & William, R. L. (1973). The comparative effectiveness of group and individually contingent free time with inner-city junior high school students. *Journal of Applied Behavior Analysis, 6,* 465–474.

Lott, G. W. (1983). The effect of inquiry teaching and advance organizers upon student outcomes in science education. *Journal of Research in Science Teaching, 20*(5), 437–451.

Lovitt, T. C. (1991). *Preventing school dropouts: Tactics for at-risk, remedial, and mildly handicapped adolescents.* Austin, TX: PRO-ED.

Lovitt, T., Rudsit, J., Jenkins, J., Pious, C., & Benedetti, D. (1985). Two methods of adapting science materials for learning disabled and regular seventh graders. *Learning Disability Quarterly, 8,* 275–285.

Lovitt, T., Rudsit, J., Jenkins, J., Pious, C., & Benedetti, D. (1986). Adapting science materials for regular and learning disabled seventh graders. *Remedial and Special Education, 7*(1), 31–39.

Maria, K., & McGinitie, W. H. (1982). Reading comprehension disabilities, knowledge structures, and non-accommodating text processing strategies. *Annals of Dyslexia, 32,* 33–59.

Massad, V. I., & Etzel, B. C. (1972). Acquisition of phonetic sounds by preschool children: Effects of response and reinforcement frequency. In G. Semb (Ed.), *Behavior analysis and education* (pp. 88–111). Lawrence, KS: Department of Human Development.

Mastropieri, M. A., & Scruggs, T. E. (1987). *Effective instruction for special education.* Austin, TX: PRO-ED.

Mastropieri, M. A., & Scruggs, T. E. (1989). Constructing more meaningful relationships: Mnemonic instruction for special populations. *Educational Psychology Review, 1,* 83–111.

Mastropieri, M. A., & Scruggs, T. E. (1991). *Teaching students ways to remember: Strategies for learning mnemonically.* Cambridge, MA: Brookline.

McCoy, K. M., & Prehm, H. J. (1987). *Teaching mainstreamed students: Methods and techniques.* Denver: Love.

McEvoy, M. A., & Brady, M. P. (1988). Contingent access to play materials as an academic motivator for autistic and behavior disordered children. *Education and Treatment of Children, 11*(1), 5–18.

Morrison, A., & McIntyre, D. (1969). *Teachers and teaching.* Baltimore: Penguin.

Morsink, C. V. (1984). *Teaching special needs students in regular classrooms.* Boston: Little, Brown.

Muller, A. J., Hasazi, S. E., Pierce, M. M., & Hasazi, J. E. (1975). Modification of disruptive behavior in a large group of elementary school students. In E. Ramp & G. Semb (Eds.), *Behavior analysis: Areas of research and application* (pp. 269–276). Englewood Cliffs, NJ: Prentice-Hall.

Nickerson, R. S., Perkins, D. N., & Smith, E. E. (1985). *The teaching of thinking.* Hillsdale, NJ: Erlbaum.

Novak, J. D., & Gowin, D. B. (1984). *Learning how to learn.* New York: Cambridge University Press.

O'Flahaven, J. F., & Tierney, R. J. (1991). Reading, writing, and critical thinking. In L. Idol & B. F. Jones (Eds.), *Educational values and cognitive instruction: Implications for reform* (pp. 41–64). Hillsdale, NJ: Erlbaum.

O'Leary, K., & O'Leary, S. (1977). *Classroom management: The successful use of behavior modification* (2nd ed.). New York: Pergamon.

Paris, S. G., & Winograd, P. (1990). How metacognition can promote academic learning and instruction. In B. F. Jones & L. Idol (Eds.), *Dimensions of thinking and cognitive instruction* (pp. 15–52). Hillsdale, NJ: Erlbaum.

Pearson, P. D., & Raphael, T. E. (1990). In B. F. Jones & L. Idol (Eds.), *Dimensions of thinking and cognitive instruction* (pp. 209–240). Hillsdale, NJ: Erlbaum.

Reid, D. K. (1988). *Teaching the learning disabled: A cognitive developmental approach.* Boston: Allyn & Bacon.

Resnick, L. B. (1987). *Education and learning to think.* Washington, DC: National Academy Press.

Rieth, H., Polsgrove, L., & Semmel, M. (1981). Instructional variables that make a difference: Attention to task and beyond. *Exceptional Children Quarterly, 2,* 61–71.

Robertson, S. J., DeReus, D. M., & Drabman, R. S. (1976). Peer and college-student tutoring as reinforcement in a token economy. *Journal of Applied Behavior Analysis, 9*(2), 169–177.

Roth, K. J. (1990). Developing meaningful conceptual understanding in science. In B. F. Jones & L. Idol, *Dimensions of thinking and cognitive instruction* (pp. 139–175). Hillsdale, NJ: Erlbaum.

Salend, S. (1990). *Effective mainstreaming.* New York: Macmillan.

Schoenfeld, A. (1985). *Mathematical problem solving.* New York: Academic Press.

Schutte, R. C., & Hopkins, B. L. (1970). The effects of teacher attention on following instruction in a kindergarten class. *Journal of Applied Behavior Analysis, 3*(2), 117–122.

Scruggs, T. E., & Mastropieri, M. A. (1992). Effective mainstreaming strategies for mildly handicapped students. *The Elementary School Journal, 92*(3), 389–409.

Scruggs, T. E., & Mastropieri, M. A. (1993). Current approaches to science education: Implications for mainstream instruction of students with disabilities. *Remedial and Special Education, 14*(1), 15–24.

Scruggs, T. E., Mastropieri, M. A., Levin, J. R., McLoone, B., & Morrison, C. (1987). Mnemonic facilitation of text-embedded science facts with LD students. *Journal of Educational Psychology, 79,* 27–34.

Secada, W. G. (1991). Student diversity and mathematics education reform. In L. Idol & B. F. Jones (Eds.), *Educational values and cognitive instruction: Implications for reform* (pp. 297–332). Hillsdale, NJ: Erlbaum.

Silbert, J., Carnine, D., & Stein, M. (1981). *Direct instruction mathematics.* Columbus, OH: Merrill.

Silver, E. A., & Marshall, S. (1990). Mathematical and scientific problem solving: Findings, issues, and instructional implications. In B. F. Jones & L. Idol. *Dimensions of thinking and cognitive instruction* (pp. 265–290). Hillsdale, NJ: Erlbaum.

Skiba, R. J., & Deno, S. L. (1991). Terminology and behavior reduction: The case against "punishment." *Exceptional Children, 57*(4), 298–312.

Smith, D. D. (1981). *Teaching the learning disabled.* Englewood Cliffs, NJ: Prentice-Hall.

Solomon, R., & Wahler, R. (1973). Peer reinforcement control of classroom problem behavior. *Journal of Applied Behavior Analysis, 6,* 49–56.

Sprick, R. S. (1979). *A comparison of recall scores for visual-spatial, visual-serial, and auditory presentations of intermediate grade content.* Unpublished doctoral dissertation, University of Oregon, Eugene.

Stanberry, M., & Harris, J. (1974). Reduction of tardy behavior in junior-high school pupils. In R. V. Hall, *Managing behavior: Behavior modification: Applications in school and home* (p. 28). Lawrence, KS: H & H.

Strain, P. S., & Kerr, M. M. (1979). Treatment issues in the remediation of preschool children's social isolation. *Education and Treatment of Children, 2,* 197–208.

Sulzer, B., Mayer, A., & Cody, J. (1968). Assisting teachers with managing classroom behavioral problems. *Elementary School Guidance and Counseling, 3,* 40–48.

Sulzer-Azaroff, B., & Mayer, R. (1977). *Applying behavior analysis procedure with children and youth.* New York: Holt, Rinehart & Winston.

Tribble, A., & Hall, R. V. (1971). Effects of peer approval on completion of arithmetic assignments. In F. W. Clark, D. R. Evans, & L. A. Hamerlynck (Eds.), *Implementing behavioral programs for schools and clinics: Third Banff International Conference.* New York: Brunner/ Mazel.

Turnbull, A. P., & Schulz, J. B. (1979). *Mainstreaming handicapped students: A guide for classroom teachers.* Boston: Allyn & Bacon.

Tweney, R. D., & Walker, B. J. (1990). Science education and the cognitive psychology of science. In B. F. Jones & L. Idol, *Dimensions of thinking and cognitive instruction* (pp. 291–346). Hillsdale, NJ: Erlbaum.

Volrath, F., & Clark, M. (1974). Effects of reinforcement procedures on talking frequency in a slow-reading group. In R. V. Hall, *Managing behavior: Behavior modification: Applications in school and home* (p. 14). Lawrence, KS: H & H.

Weinstein, C. E., & Mayer, R. E. (1986). *Students' cognitive processes while learning from teaching* (Vols. 1 & 2). Instructional Psychology Research Group (NIE Final Report, Grant No. NIE-G-79-0098). Burnaby, British Columbia: Simon Fraser University.

West, J. F., Idol, L., & Cannon, G. (1989). *Collaboration in the schools: An inservice and preservice curriculum for teachers, support staff, and administrators.* Austin, TX: PRO-ED.

White-Blackman, G., Semb, S., & Semb, G. (1977). The effects of a good-behavior contract on the classroom behaviors of sixth-grade students. *Journal of Applied Behavior Analysis, 10*(2), 312.

Wolf, M. M., Giles, D. K., & Hall, R. V. (1968). Experiments in a remedial classroom. *Behavioral Research and Therapy, 6,* 51–64.

APPENDIX 7.A

GUIDELINES FOR USING AN INSTRUCTIONAL FORMAT SHEET

This format is used whenever a teacher plans an instructional program in any subject for which instruction is provided. It is used for direct instruction and for independent work. It is used for individual and group instruction. It is always accompanied by the multiband chart. It contains the following components.

Task

Briefly describe the subject areas for which instruction is provided. Some examples are:

- Oral reading
- Reading comprehension
- Spelling
- Oral language
- Two-place addition
- Cursive handwriting

Instructional Intervention

Write a behavioral statement that describes the specific instruction that is used. Another instructor should be able to replicate your procedure by imitating the behavior(s) described. This baseline measurement is labeled with the letter A within a circle, $\textcircled{A}$. An example is: $\textcircled{A}$ Daily, John will read orally with the instructor from the *Economy* basal reader. A minimum of one story will be read per day. If time permits, more stories will be read. A 100-word time sample will be measured daily.

As the student(s) progresses or fails to progress, the teacher makes changes in the initial instructional intervention. Only one new intervention is implemented at a time. A minimum of 5 instructional days per intervention change is normally used. Each new intervention is labeled with a succeeding alphabet letter. If a total of five interventions is used over the academic year, then they would be labeled $\textcircled{B}$, $\textcircled{C}$, $\textcircled{D}$, $\textcircled{E}$, and $\textcircled{F}$. An example of an intervention is: $\textcircled{B}$ The student will practice the phonetic sounds associated with the *Blue Dilly Dilly* book of the *Economy* series. These sounds are listed on teacher-made sound sheets.

Then, of course, the criterion, consequences, error correction procedure, time, and measure are listed on the format sheet as indicated. If it should happen that some columns on the format sheet change but others do not, list only the changes. For example, the criterion for rate might change, but the remaining columns (intervention, consequences, etc.) remain constant and are not written.

Criterion

The exact minimum standards of measured performance are stated here. An example is:

- 95% correct for accuracy
- 80% correct for comprehension
- 40 cwpm (correct words per minute) for rate

Consequences

Failure to meet the stated criterion (or criteria) results in a particular consequence. This consequence is described with clear, measurable terms. An example is: If the reader fails to meet the stated criteria on the timed sample, the story will be reread on the following instructional day. This will continue until the criteria are met.

Error Correction Procedure

When the student responds incorrectly, the teacher uses an exact and replicable procedure for correcting errors. An example is the error correction procedure in Figure 7.4. The procedure is written out completely so that another instructor could replicate the procedure.

Time

The time spent for instruction and performance measurement is stated here. An example is:

- 5 minutes for sound drill
- 15 minutes for oral story telling
- 5 minutes for comprehension questions for the story
- 5 minutes for the timed sample

Measure

The dependent measures that are used to measure pupil performance are listed here. Some examples are:

- Number of stories completed
- Percent correct for comprehension
- Percent correct for word accuracy
- Correct words per minute

APPENDIX 7.B

DEFINITIONS OF VARIOUS TYPES OF CONSEQUENCES

Back-up reinforcer. An object or event received in exchange for a specific number of tokens, points, and so forth.

Conditioned reinforcer. A stimulus that has acquired reinforcing function through pairing with an unconditioned or natural reinforcer. Includes most social, activity, and generalized reinforcers. (Also called a *secondary reinforcer.*)

Negative reinforcement. The contingent removal of an aversive stimulus immediately after a response. Negative reinforcement increases the future rate or the probability of occurrence of the response (or both).

Positive reinforcement. The contingent presentation of a "desired" stimulus, immediately after a response, that increases the future rate or the probability of occurrences of the response (or both).

Premack principle. A principle that states that any high-probability activity may serve as a positive reinforcer for any low-probability activity. (Also called *activity reinforcement.*)

Primary reinforcer. A stimulus (such as food) that may be said to have biological importance to an individual. Such stimuli are innately motivating. (Also called a *natural, unlearned,* or *unconditioned reinforcer.*)

Punisher. A consequent stimulus that decreases the future rate or the probability of occurrence of a behavior (or both).

Reinforcer. A consequent stimulus that increases or maintains the future rate or the probability of occurrence of a behavior (or both).

Reinforcer sampling. Allowing learners to come in contact with potential reinforcers. Reinforcer sampling allows teachers to determine what reinforcers are likely to be effective with individual learners.

Response cost. A procedure for the reduction of inappropriate behavior through withdrawal of specific amounts of reinforcer contingent on the behavior's occurrence.

Schedules of reinforcement. The patterns of "timing" for delivery of reinforcers.

Seclusionary time-out. A type of time-out procedure whereby the learner is removed from the instructional setting as a means of denying access to reinforcement.

Secondary reinforcer. A stimulus that is initially neutral and acquires reinforcing qualities through pairing with a primary reinforcer. (Also called a *conditioned reinforcer.*)

Social reinforcers. A category of secondary reinforcer that includes expressions, proximity, contact, privileges, words, and phrases.

Time-out. A procedure for the reduction of inappropriate behavior whereby the learner is denied access, for a fixed period of time, to the opportunity to receive reinforcement.

Note. From *Applied Behavior Analysis for Teachers,* 2nd ed., P. A. Alberto and A. C. Troutman, 1986, Columbus, OH: Merrill. Copyright 1986 by Charles E. Merrill Publishing Company. Reprinted by permission.

CHAPTER 8

Evaluation and Follow-Up: Principles and Techniques

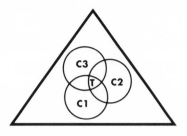

A HALLMARK OF EFFECTIVE COLLABORATIVE consultation teams is their willingness and ability to evaluate their work. In this chapter we describe evaluation principles and specific techniques to assess the impact of collaborative consultation services at various levels. Procedures for eliciting feedback from those who participate on collaborative consultation teams (e.g., classroom teachers, counselors, special educators, administrators, parents, and learners) are explained in the context of establishing evaluation processes that are responsive to all constituents. Follow-up evaluation decisions must be made for learners, collaborators, and school systems and include (a) continuing the collaborative consultation services, (b) redesigning, (c) exiting (gradually withdrawing, transferring responsibility, or terminating) from services, and (d) formulating new goals or target issues.

RESPONSIVE EVALUATION

Evaluation of the Collaborative Consultation Model as a system for delivering services as well as an interactive process should capitalize on the best features of evaluation required of special education programs. Some of those features include attention to (a) micro-level concerns, such as learner progress, satisfaction, needs and goals; (b) mezzo-level issues, such as classroom methods, curriculum, physical setting, and staff development; and (c) macro-level challenges, such as entry and exit requirements, philosophy, and involvement of parents and other agencies (George, George, & Grosenick, 1990).

In our experience, the most useful evaluation techniques are those that are responsive to the persons who receive or benefit from the collaborative consultation services being offered. Guba and Lincoln (1981) described responsive evaluation as a process that could include aspects of other evaluation models as long as the concerns and issues pertinent to the program are being evaluated. Thus, responsive evaluation should deal with program aspects that respond to the collected information in a way that will ensure both program and individual growth. Guba and Lincoln noted that failure to evaluate and use findings in this way has almost assumed the proportions of a national scandal. They posited that failure to use responsive evaluation simply illustrates the poverty of traditional evaluation systems that fail to identify initially the concerns and issues of the actual audiences. Such systems can produce information that is statistically significant but not necessarily worthwhile as a basis for encouraging program growth and development.

When making judgments about the value of a program, collaborators must ensure that criteria and standards for the Collaborative Consultation Model are accurate, effective, economical, and satisfying. The judgments themselves can be either quantitative or qualitative, or a combination of the two. In this connection, Bloom (1981) suggested that evaluation is a two-edged sword that can either enhance or destroy learning and development; it can have either a positive or a negative effect on teachers, curricula, and school systems.

To achieve effective and responsive evaluation, all collaborators (including parents) and learners should identify the parts of learning and curricula that are most important to evaluate. The evaluation processes should be reliable and objective, thereby minimizing the role that chance and error might play in determining the adequacy of learner performance and program effectiveness. In the context of the Collaborative Consultation Model, objective and reliable evaluation methodologies should be used for the assessment of (a) learner performance; (b) the perceptions of important persons involved in the program (i.e., teachers, specialists, parents, administrators, aides, other learners); (c) collaborators' mutual acquisition and practice of the relevant underlying knowledge base and interpersonal, communicative, problem-solving skills; (d) systems level changes; and (e) efficacy of each part of the program (i.e., before, during, and after program implementation).

The collaborative consultation team designs a responsive evaluation system by (a) establishing criteria and standards for evaluating program effectiveness, (b) creating measurement systems that will be used positively to enhance program growth, (c) having the people involved in the program identify the parts to be evaluated, and (d) designing a system that meets the evaluation standards for reliability and objectivity.

These components of a responsive evaluation system reflect adherence to a belief that, under the appropriate conditions, everyone can learn and progress. Specifically, the essence of mastery learning is that

> most [learners] (perhaps more than 90 percent) can master what we have taught them, and it is the task of instruction to find the means which will enable our [learners] to master the subject under consideration. Our basic task is to determine what we mean by mastery of the subject and to search for the methods and materials which will enable the largest proportion of our [learners] to attain such mastery. (Bloom, 1981, p. 153)

Traditionally, it should be noted, educators have been led to expect that about one third of their class would fail, one third would perform adequately, and the final third could be expected to learn a good deal. In rejecting this traditional view, Bloom noted that it reflects a system that creates a self-fulfilling prophecy such that the final sorting of [learners] through the grading process becomes approximately equivalent to the original expectations. This set of expectations, which fixes the academic goals of teachers and [learners], is the most wasteful and destructive aspect of the present educational system. It reduces the aspirations of both teachers and students; it reduces motivation for learning in students; and it systematically destroys the ego and self-concept of a sizable group of [learners] who are legally required to attend school for ten to twelve years under conditions which are frustrating and humiliating year after year. The cost of this system in reducing opportunities for further learning and in alienating youth from both school and society is so great that no society can tolerate it for long. (Bloom, 1981, p. 289)

The evaluation principles described below support both a mastery approach and the collaborative consultation process. Not only should we expect 90% of the learners in a classroom to master concepts; through careful programming and collaborative consultation processes, mastery can also be achieved by the learners who are difficult to teach and likely to be within the remaining 10%.

Dimensions of Collaborative Consultation Evaluation

Many variables have been identified as important contributors to success in consultation interactions. In a comprehensive interdisciplinary review of school consultation literature, West (1988) used three categories as organizers for variables that impacted on consultation success: *input variables* (consultee and consultant characteristics, nature of problems studied, and reasons for initiating consultation); *process variables* (consultation techniques, styles, and models); and *outcome variables* (measurable changes in knowledge, skill, attitudes of teachers or consultees and learners or clients, and organizational or system changes). Although methodological and definitional problems reduce the generalizability of many of the findings, evidence shows that school personnel have a preference for collaborative approaches. Addressing such variables can be helpful as collaborative consultation teams develop their evaluation systems.

Emerging Issues in Collaborative Consultation Evaluation

Collaborators who are mindful of alternatives to the traditional typically quantitative methods of evaluation, as well as to the types of questions that are addressed, tend to generate more comprehensive and sensitive evaluation systems. For example, Villa, Thousand, Paolucci-Whitcomb, and Nevin (1990) called for new paradigms to study questions of interest to those who evaluate the Collaborative Consultation Model and the effectiveness of teams who use collaborative consultation processes. As shown in Table 8.1, questions related to establishing the collaborative ethic and the interactive processes

---

TABLE 8.1. Questions of Interest in Evaluation of Collaborative Consultation Processes

---

1. Which training content (and formats) have teams found to be most effective to establish the collaborative consultation skills among school staff?

2. Under what organizational conditions (e.g., peer coaching, site-based management, school leadership training teams) are collaborative consultation skills generalized from theory to practice?

3. To what degree can and do faculty acquire their collaborative skills through direct (e.g., inservice training) or indirect (e.g., teaching learners to use collaborative skills) processes?

4. How much time is required for a school staff to embrace a collaborative ethic?

5. To what degree does the formal structure of schools change as a result of suggestions generated by teams who use collaborative consultation processes for problem solving?

6. Do members of collaborative consultation teams engage in more reflective thinking (i.e., talking about the impact of their beliefs and attitudes on learner outcomes) than teachers who problem-solve in isolation?

7. Are the outcomes (e.g., new conceptualizations and novel solutions) for adults who engage in the collaborative process similar to those documented for learners as reported by Johnson and Johnson (1989)?

Note. Excerpted from "In Search of New Paradigms of Collaborative Consultation" by R. Villa, J. Thousand, P. Paolucci-Whitcomb, and A. Nevin, 1990, *Journal of Educational and Psychological Consultation, 1*(4), p. 289. Reprinted with permission from Lawrence Erlbaum Associates, Inc.

---

among the members of the collaborative consultation team are of particular interest. Pryzwansky and Noblit (1990) described the advantages of using qualitative case study approaches to understand and improve consultation practices.

Other emerging issues include developing processes that are sensitive to the needs of culturally diverse populations. The presence of increasing numbers of learners with limited English proficiency has led many schools to search for culturally unbiased assessment, instructional, and evaluation materials. The movement toward cultural pluralism stimulates added responsibilities so as to ensure respect and equal participation from diverse ethnic groups. Ensuring that competencies such as those recommended by Harris (1991) are practiced within a collaborative consultation team can lead to important distinctions so as to generate an evaluation system that is sensitive and responsive to culturally and linguistically diverse communities.

EVALUATION PRINCIPLES

The following principles may be applied specifically to the Evaluation stage of the collaborative consultation process. These form the basis for the various evaluation techniques described in the following sections.

1. *The evaluation system should provide information on the overall program.* This means that, in advance of data collection, the total program should be defined by its various parts. Those involved in the program should have input in determining what constitutes the total program; then the various parts of the program should be systematically evaluated. The overall evaluation of a Collaborative Consultation Model should be based on information from collaborators regarding both the impact of the program on the learners and the collaborative consultation process itself. It should also reflect parental perception of the program's impact. Clearly, evaluative conclusions based on these various information sources rather than a single source will be more comprehensive.

2. *The learner evaluation system should be designed to match the goals and objectives of the IEP.* Even though this requirement seems straightforward, it contains an important implication. It means that the IEP should reflect not only what is contained in the learner's direct service, special education program, but it should also reflect the contents of the consultation program in the learner's general classroom. The measurement process used to evaluate the learner's progress should then be indicated in the IEP.

3. *The evaluation system should include criterion levels of performance as a means of defining mastery learning.* In effect, guides for making decisions should be determined in advance of collecting information. This is especially true for the collection of learner progress data, in which criterion levels are established to define lesson mastery during the assessment and intervention stages of the learner's program.

4. *The evaluation system should include assessment of changes in the collaborators.* The impact of the Collaborative Consultation Model on all collaborators can address changes in their respective underlying knowledge bases, interpersonal skills, and intrapersonal attitudes. Examples of documenting changes in collaborators can be found in Cross and Villa (1992); Givens-Ogle, Christ, and Idol (1991); Patriarca and Lamb (1990); and Vlasak, Goldenberg, and Idol (1992).

5. *The evaluation system should include assessment of organizational or systems-level changes.* Assessment of impact at the organizational or systems level

is of particular importance for documenting changes at the building level, school system level, and community level. Policy changes are the most comprehensive and require the most diverse representation. An example of this level of change was given by Peck et al. (1989) as they worked with several rural communities to implement an ecological process model that resulted in community-generated policies for designing early childhood programs that integrated preschool-age learners with special education needs. Examples of administrative and organizational changes at the building and school system levels are described by Idol and West (1991), Kaskinen-Chapman (1992), and Lutkemeier (1991).

6. *All collaborators should be directly involved in the evaluation process.* It is essential to the spirit of Collaborative Consultation that all collaborators be responsible for evaluation of both the learners and the collaborative consultation process. Our experience has been that, when one person assumes total responsibility for evaluation, difficulties can arise. In such cases, because others were not actively involved in the data-collection process, they may not perceive that the learner is improving and may actually terminate the program. Thus, at the very least, collaborators should refer to learner progress data as frequently as possible.

7. *The data collection system should be simple and easy to administer.* If collaborators design a data collection system that is elaborate and time-consuming, it is not likely that the system will be implemented for any significant length of time. For this reason, the teaching schedules and responsibilities of collaborators must be carefully considered when designing tools and schedules for evaluation. The resulting system must be one that each collaborator can use efficiently while continuing to assume responsibility for all of the learners in the classroom, not just for learners with special needs. This consideration extends to the entire professional day; in particular, the evaluation system for the collaborative consultation process itself must be one that does not require too much time. An important rule might be to establish a percentage of total time that will be spent on any one aspect of evaluation and then be careful not to exceed the allotted time (see examples in Blankenship & Lilly, 1981; Idol & West, 1993).

8. *The evaluation data should be frequently monitored.* Both the data-collection system and the data the system produces should be checked frequently and carefully. In overall program evaluation, this is not likely to pose a problem, because the data are usually collected at periodic points in time and analyzed at the time of collection. However, for particular aspects of the program that are monitored on a continuous basis

(e.g., the monitoring of daily learner progress), problems may arise if the data are not checked as they are collected. These problems may involve misperceptions regarding program effectiveness, failure to make instructional decisions based on performance data, or lack of communication among the collaborators regarding progress of the targeted learners.

9. *Implementation of a responsive evaluation system means sharing and using the results.* The primary purpose of program evaluation is to ensure that the program improves. For this to happen, the evaluation data must be shared with others involved in the collaborative consultation program. The involved individuals will find different types of information useful, depending on the aspect of the program with which they are concerned. For instance, some collaborators may be most interested in detailed learner progress data, evaluation of the collaborative consultation process, or total program impact of the Collaborative Consultation Model. A parent may be more interested in learner progress and the quality of consultation, as well as the impact of the Collaborative Consultation Model. An administrator may be interested specifically in summary data reflecting total program impact of learners' progress as well as teacher and staff morale. Teachers may value the impact of using collaborative consultation processes on their abilities to make a difference in the curriculum or schedules they follow.

For each collaborator, some type of evaluation feedback may be positively reinforcing, thus impacting on future involvement. Thus, learners, collaborators, classroom aides, parents, and other educators may all find various aspects of the learner progress data to be especially reinforcing. Collaborators may be particularly motivated by positive summary data for total programs across all learners. In short, the results of a responsive evaluation can and should be used to reinforce significant others and serve as a means of further enhancing participants' achievement of goals.

Together, the nine evaluation principles form the underlying base for implementation of responsive evaluation of the Collaborative Consultation Model.

EVALUATION PROCESSES

In this section, we describe evaluation techniques that have been developed in consulting teacher programs at the University of Vermont, the University of Illinois at Urbana-Champaign, and various implementation sites across North America. For discussion purposes, the techniques may be classified as general or situation-specific.

General Evaluation Techniques

The general techniques for evaluation described in this section are applicable to the following areas:

- Evaluating by use of a discrepancy analysis
- Establishing a committee of responsible parties
- Identifying dimensions of a program to be evaluated

Discrepancy Analysis. An adaptation of the Discrepancy Evaluation Model (DEM) (Provus, 1971) has been used by collaborators to evaluate service to learners and to evaluate the training for teachers in providing special education services (Paolucci-Whitcomb, Bright, Carlson, & Meyers, 1987; Paolucci-Whitcomb & Nevin, 1985; Tuckman, 1979). Specifically, this adaptation is useful for determining the effectiveness, efficiency, and affectiveness of program service and training. Effectiveness is determined by asking if the program objectives were achieved. Efficiency is measured by ascertaining whether the objectives were achieved within a designated amount of time. Affectiveness is measured by finding out whether the learner and/or collaborator enjoyed the program, based on self-reports.

In this adaptation of DEM, first the use of *inputs* (both personnel and monetary) is examined; then the *processes* (teaching/learning activities) are studied; and, finally, the achievement of the learner *outputs* (accomplishment of objectives) is analyzed. During the evaluation process, data on learner performance are gathered and compared with the standard (goal and objectives) that has been established. A difference between the performance and the standard is considered a discrepancy, which is identified and reported to appropriate personnel. Discrepancies are resolved through problem solving, resulting in one of three decisions: (a) to change or revise control of the performance, (b) to redesign unrealistic or inadequate standards, or (c) to terminate a portion of the original goals or objectives. Termination would occur only if serious discrepancies could not be resolved (e.g., a lack of monetary resources needed to conduct training or provide service). In this model, a continuous cycle of evaluation is used. As illustrated in Figure 8.1, the program is constantly subject to revision based on the resolution of discrepancies between input, process, and output.

In this version of DEM, the collaborators (e.g., teachers, parents, learners) interactively identify and agree on the specific evaluation components for the learner. Each evaluation procedure includes data in response to the following nine questions:

1. What will be evaluated (what is the target performance, including a rationale for selection)?

FIGURE 8.1. Evaluation cycle of the discrepancy evaluation model.

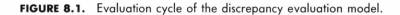

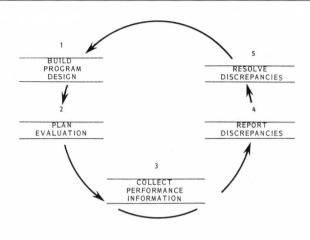

2. Who will actually conduct the evaluation (external, internal, or a combination of both, including a rationale for selection)?

3. Which instruments will be used and what questions will be asked (including a rationale for selection)?

4. When will the evaluation information be collected (including a rationale for the frequency)?

5. How will the data be collected (including a rationale for the processes)?

6. How will the results be analyzed and disseminated (including a rationale)?

7. Which criteria will be used to determine effectiveness, efficiency, and affect (including a rationale for selection)?

8. What was learned as a function of the processes and results?

9. Which changes will or will not be made (based on the results and including a rationale)?

Guba and Lincoln (1981) defined evaluation as a process of

determining to what extent the educational objectives are actually being realized. . . . However, since educational objectives are essentially changes in human beings, that is, the objectives aimed at are to produce certain desirable changes in the behavior patterns of the students, then evaluation is the process for determining the degree to which these changes in behavior are actually taking place (p. 4).

In the context of this definition, the DEM can be seen to be a particularly useful tool for analyzing the effectiveness of collaborative consultation programs for learners with special needs.

A Committee of Responsible Parties. Once a model for evaluation has been selected, it is essential to determine who will be responsible for carrying out the various evaluation duties. Joyce, Hersh, and McKibbin (1983), and Paolucci-Whitcomb et al. (1987), have suggested that the responsibility for improving the quality of schools and education belongs to an interactive team of "responsible parties." Such teams can consist of teachers, parents, administrators, learners, and community representatives working together. In evaluating Collaborative Consultation, such a team of responsible parties acts as the focal point for the collection of evaluation information for instruction of learners with special needs, for changes in collaborators, and for overall program impact.

Program Dimensions. A collaborative consultation program is likely to have several dimensions that should be evaluated. Specific examination of each of these dimensions will help to ensure successful implementation of the full comprehensive program. Each of the seven possible dimensions (Baer, Wolf, & Risley, 1968) is a target area for evaluation. The seven dimensions are:

1. *Applied.* The behavior to be changed should be important to both the individual and the individual's larger society (family, classmates, neighbors, and the like).

2. *Behavioral.* The target behavior should be observable and measurable in reliable terms. Reliable, in this case, refers to two independent observers who collect the same information using identical measurement procedures. Reliability of measurement helps to ensure that changes in behavior are real and free of observer bias.

3. *Technological.* The teaching/learning (training or intervention) procedures should be clearly described so that a person with similar training can adapt or apply them. This requires description of the antecedent stimulus, the target response, and the consequences.

4. *Conceptual.* The intervention procedures should be based on effective research and/or model programs to help further the development of an adequate information base.

5. *Generality.* The changes in the learner's academic or social behavior should be such that they can be demonstrated over time, settings, people, and related behaviors.

6. *Effective.* Improvements should be large enough to be considered valuable; for example, the change should have reached the objective level for a specified period of time.

7. *Analytic.* An evaluation design should be established to enable collaborators to determine if the intervention procedure was responsible for the behavior changes.

Evaluation systems that are designed to encompass all of these seven dimensions can give collaborators important information regarding program effectiveness.

Summary. It is recommended that three general techniques be applied to the evaluation process: Use a discrepancy evaluation analysis to assess program effectiveness; select a committee of responsible parties to evaluate the program (these persons should work as a team to identify and evaluate various program components); and include the applied, behavioral, technological, conceptual, generality, and analytic dimensions when evaluating the collaborative consultation program.

Specific Evaluation Techniques

Once an evaluation system has been designed, applying the above general techniques to each aspect of the program, a variety of situation-specific techniques may be employed for detailed program evaluation. These techniques may be categorized in the following areas:

- Learner evaluation and feedback
- Feedback from collaborators
- Feedback from parents
- Overall evaluation of the Collaborative Consultation Model
- Evaluation of impact on collaborators (changes in adults)
- Evaluation of impact on systems

Learner Evaluation and Feedback. It is useful to develop some type of background information form for each learner who receives collaborative consultation services. For example, the form shown in Figure 8.2 can be used to record and analyze background information on a learner and the teachers

FIGURE 8.2. A summary sheet for recording and analyzing background information on the learner and teachers.

BACKGROUND FORM
LEARNERS (SUBJECTS AND SETTING)

General information

	Learner(s)	Teacher 1	Teacher 2
A. Age			
B. Grade and/or subject(s)			
C. Type of class			
D. No. in class			
E. Previous Sp.Ed. experience			
F. Additional important information			
G. No. in school			
H. Grades and/or subjects			
I. Size of district			

BEHAVIORS

Define behavior(s) to improve

Learner(s)	Teacher 1	Teacher 2

How do you record behavior(s)?

Learner(s)	Teacher 1	Teacher 2

TEACHING/LEARNING PROCEDURES

Learner	Teaching Material(s)	Learner Responses	Consequences for Correct and Incorrect Responses

Teacher 1

Teacher 2

Explain your rationale for the material and responses (i.e., relate to specific literature and indicators from the natural environment, etc.).

FIGURE 8.2. Continued.

DESIGN
A. What was planned? _____
B. What was implemented? _____

RESULTS (oral and graphic please)
A. Baseline (ranged from _____ to _____ with an average of _____)
B. Intervention (ranged from _____ to _____ with an average of _____)

DISCUSSION
A. Strengths of procedure(s) _____
B. Weaknesses of procedure(s) _____

involved. In the form, target responses and both antecedent and consequential stimuli can be identified. This particular form can also be helpful in planning intervention strategies.

Collaborators are often interested in what learners have to say about the teaching/learning procedures they use. Figure 8.3 is designed to elicit feedback from learners about what they like and how they like to learn.

Collaborator Feedback. A background information sheet may be used to record initial information regarding consultation problems. The form shown in Figure 8.4 is an example of this type of evaluation device. Note that it provides a framework for clarifying possible facilitators and barriers to solving a consultation problem.

The form displayed in Figure 8.5 can be used to gather information about effectiveness after one or more conferences. This feedback can be used to adjust personal behaviors so that they are most helpful to the collaborative process. Also, with this feedback, changes in conference meetings can be made to improve effectiveness, efficiency, or affect.

The collaborative consultation log in Figure 8.6 was designed to help collaborators gather information regarding the progress being made with each other. This information can be compared with that in Figures 8.3 and 8.4 to determine congruencies and discrepancies about perceptions. The log provides information on the three areas considered to be essential to the evaluation of the collaborative consultation process: *effectiveness* (Are the problem-solving stages being followed?), *efficiency* (How much time is being utilized?), and *affect* (How do collaborators feel about the collaborative processes?).

FIGURE 8.3. Sample learner feedback form.

Learner's Name (optional) _____ Class _____ Date _____

	Not at all		So-so		To a great extent
I like the subject(s) we study in this class.	1	2	3	4	5
I like the variety of people in my class.	1	2	3	4	5
I like the way we study and do our work together.	1	2	3	4	5
I have fun with people in my class.	1	2	3	4	5
I'm accepted by my classmates.	1	2	3	4	5
I can ask for help when I need it.	1	2	3	4	5
I ask different people when I have questions.	1	2	3	4	5

Some things that I would like to change in this class: _____

What I like best about my learning in this class: _____

What I still don't understand in this class: _____

What I want you to know about me is: _____

Parent Feedback. An evaluation questionnaire for parents, like that in Figure 8.7, can be helpful in obtaining written evaluation feedback from the parents of learners receiving special education services. The resulting data can be used not only for assessing program impact as perceived by individual parents, but also for comparative assessment of parental responses to determine the degree of satisfaction in the total parent population concerning collaborative consultation services.

Overall Evaluation of the Collaborative Consultation Model. In addition to implementing specific techniques to evaluate the ongoing collaborative consultation process, it is recommended that some type of summary evaluation be conducted. Collaborator's overall perception of services may

FIGURE 8.4.   Background information form for recording initial information regarding collaborators' problems.

FORM FOR IDENTIFYING BARRIERS AND FACILITATORS

Collaborator _____ Date _____

1. *Who* is on your collaborative consultation team?
   a. administrator(s) _____
   b. teacher(s) _____
   c. specialist(s) _____
   d. parent(s) _____
   e. learner(s) _____
2. *How* were collaborators selected?
3. *Why* were collaborators selected?
4. *When* will collaborators meet?
   time of day _____
   day of week _____
5. *What* are the *two* most critical problems that collaborators want to work on?

6. Describe the facilitators and barriers for Problems A and B.

               Facilitators   Barriers

Problem A
_____   X   _____
_____   X   _____
_____   X   _____
_____   X   _____

Problem B
_____   X   _____
_____   X   _____
_____   X   _____
_____   X   _____

---

also be evaluated. The evaluation questionnaire in Figure 8.8 provides a broader view of perceptions. This form may be used to summarize the effects of collaborative training and services as a whole.

Collaborators may need to evaluate a learner's adjustment to the classroom. The School Adjustment Scale shown in Figure 8.9 was developed as a pre/post measure of attitude about a learner in a mainstream classroom who was referred for special education services. Dramatic positive changes in the attitude of the classroom teacher toward the learner were noted after the

FIGURE 8.5. An evaluation feedback form for recording information from a collaborative consultation session.

CONFERENCE EVALUATION FORM

Name _____ Date _____

Effectiveness

1. What was the expected outcome(s)? _____

2. Did you achieve the expected outcome(s)? _____ Why? _____

3. Did the meeting enable you to complete the outcome? _____ Why? _____

4. How could the meeting have been more helpful or effective? _____

Efficiency

1. How much time did you spend on the meeting? _____
2. Does more or less time need to be scheduled for this type of meeting in the future? _____ Why? _____

Affectiveness

1. How do you feel about the meeting? Positive _____ Neutral _____ Negative _____ Why do you think you feel the way you do? _____

2. What change(s) could be made to make the meeting more enjoyable? _____

---

consulting teacher had collaborated to provide special services to the learner (Hawkes & Paolucci-Whitcomb, 1980).

Information collected from the evaluation instruments described above can provide a summary of collaborative consultation services for administrators. Data on the schools, the teachers, and the learners served can be summarized in such a way that an administrator can see at a glance the progress that has been made since the last report. These data provide the administrators (principals, superintendents, and coordinators of special education) with information that enables them to reinforce positive progress and suggest changes in areas that have been problematic.

Evaluation of Impact on Collaborators (Changes in Adults). Collaborators are often interested in monitoring and evaluating the effectiveness of

FIGURE 8.6. Log for recording collaborators' self-perceptions of the collaborative consultation process.

COLLABORATIVE CONSULTATION LOG

Collaborator _____

Who did you meet?	Date: _____ Start time / Finish time	Purpose of Conference		How did you feel about the conference?			Additional comments
		Expected outcome (problem-solving stage, etc.)	Actual outcome (What was actually accomplished?)	Positive	Neutral	Negative	

FIGURE 8.7.   Questionnaire for obtaining feedback on parental satisfaction with the Collaborative Consultation Model.

PARENT FEEDBACK FORM

Dear Parents:

As you know, _____ is receiving special education services through an IEP (Individualized Education Program) that is being designed and revised by a collaborative consultation team including you. To help us improve our service, please complete the following questions and return this form by _____ .
     (date)

1. Have you noticed any improvement in your child since we started?
   Yes _____ No _____

2. Please check any areas below that you think your child has improved in.

   a. My child is more interested in _____ . Yes _____   No _____
   b. My child seems more self-confident.   Yes _____   No _____
   c. My child enjoys school more.   Yes _____   No _____
   d. My child's school work has improved.   Yes _____   No _____

3. Have we given you enough information about your child's progress?
   Yes _____ No _____

4. Are you satisfied with the special education services that your child has received through the collaborative consultation program?
   Yes _____ No _____

5. Please comment on anything that you have especially liked or not liked about the services that your child has received.
   _____
   _____
   _____
   _____

6. Do you think we have provided enough time for your child's special need?
   Yes _____ No _____

Thank you for taking the time to complete and return this information. We appreciate your help.
                                        Sincerely,

Note. This form was originally developed by David Giguere, consulting teacher intern, University of Vermont.

FIGURE 8.8. Questionnaire for evaluating collaborators' perceptions of impact.

COLLABORATOR FEEDBACK FORM

Collaborators:

Please take a few minutes and respond to the statements and questions below for a learner(s) receiving special education services through a collaboration consultation program.

UN—Unsatisfactory   AV—Average   E—Excellent

	UN	AV	E
1. Has (have) the learner(s) met the IEP objectives?	1	2	3
2. Have you had adequate support to enable you to implement the portion of the learner's IEP that you carried out? Have you attempted to get help?	1	2	3
3. Have you seen evidence in the classroom of improvement in skills that have been taught by other staff?	1	2	3
4. Have learners shown an improvement in positive attitude toward school?	1	2	3
5. Have you learned any new procedures from the collaborative consultation team?	1	2	3
6. Have you used any materials supplied by the team?	1	2	3
7. Do you feel better prepared to meet the needs of the learners with special needs? Why or why not?	1	2	3
8. Have you been satisfied with the collaborative consultation services provided this year? Why or why not?	1	2	3
9. How do you view the role of the collaborator(s) you have worked with this year? Circle appropriate role(s):	1	2	3

       colleague   trainer   supervisor   partner
       tutor   professional peer   resource person

10. Which of the roles listed above do you prefer? Why?

    _____

    _____

12. What improvements need to be made to provide better collaborative consultation service to you and your learners? _____

    _____

    _____

Please return to _____ by _____ .
Who was on your collaborative consultation team this year? _____

Thanks for your time and effort.

Note. This form was originally designed by David Giguere, consulting teacher intern, University of Vermont.

FIGURE 8.9. Informal school adjustment scale for assessing collaborator's perceptions of a learner's classroom adjustment.

SCHOOL ADJUSTMENT SCALE

Learner: _____ Date: _____
Collaborator: _____

Please rate the learner using your own personal impressions/opinions of him or her as you know and observe him or her in the classroom setting using the following areas. Circle the number that most closely describes the learner.

1. Learner's general attitude toward school.

   1——2——3——4——5——6——7——8——9——10

   Extremely · · · · · · · · · · · · · · Doesn't care · · · · · · · · · · · · · · Very positive
   negative

2. Learner's degree of social maturity for her or his age.

   1——2——3——4——5——6——7——8——9——10

   Immature · · · · · · · · · · · · · · · · · Average · · · · · · · · · · · · · · · · · Very mature

3. Learner's self-image.

   1——2——3——4——5——6——7——8——9——10

   Negative · Very positive

4. Relationship with peers.

   1——2——3——4——5——6——7——8——9——10

   Usually · · · · · · · · · · · · · · · · Has 1 or 2 · · · · · · · · · · · · · · Usually positive
   negative · · · · · · · · · · · · · · · friendships

5. Learner's ability to work independently.

   1——2——3——4——5——6——7——8——9——10

   Unable · · · · · · · · · · · · · · · · · · · Needs · · · · · · · · · · · · · · · · · · Works very
   to work · · · · · · · · · · · · · a good deal of · · · · · · · · · · well independently
   independently · · · · · · · · direction in work

6. Learner's degree of demand for teacher attention.

   1——2——3——4——5——6——7——8——9——10

   Makes excessive · · · · · · · · Appropriately · · · · · · · · · · · · · Makes little
   demands · · · · · · · · · · · · · · · seeks teacher · · · · · · · · · · · or no demand
   · attention

7. Learner's general ability to handle stress in school setting.

   1——2——3——4——5——6——7——8——9——10

   Handles · · · · · · · · · · · · · · · · Shows no · Handles
   stress · · · · · · · · · · · · · · · · · · reaction · · · · · · · · · · · · · stress very well,
   poorly · makes adjustments easily

8. Learner's degree of positive response to teacher attention in the form of praise, encouragement, etc.

   1——2——3——4——5——6——7——8——9——10

   Unresponsive · Very responsive

FIGURE 8.9. Continued.

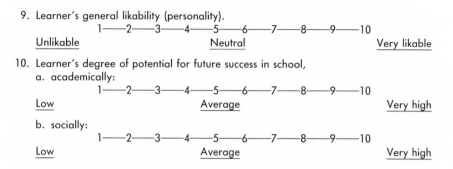

9. Learner's general likability (personality).

1——2——3——4——5——6——7——8——9——10

Unlikable   Neutral   Very likable

10. Learner's degree of potential for future success in school,
    a. academically:

1——2——3——4——5——6——7——8——9——10

Low   Average   Very high

   b. socially:

1——2——3——4——5——6——7——8——9——10

Low   Average   Very high

Note. This scale was originally designed by Kristin M. Hawkes, consulting teacher intern, University of Vermont.

their interactive processes. They can select one or more of the generic principles of Collaborative Consultation (i.e., the communicative, interactive, and problem-solving skills elaborated in Chapter 2) to monitor. As collaborators acquire the necessary degree of proficiency, new skills can be added. Collaborators may find it helpful to adapt the monitoring procedures used by Johnson and Johnson (1989) for heterogeneous cooperative learning groups. One collaborator can be appointed to be the process observer (a role that rotates to another collaborator the next meeting) who tallies frequencies on a simple grid with the skills listed on the left and collaborators' names across the top. Periodically during the meetings, collaborators consult with the process observer to discover how they are doing on practicing the selected skills.

As the collaborative consultation processes are iterated, collaborators may notice changes in their respective knowledge bases due to technical assistance provided as a result of the collaboration. Individuals may be interested in formally documenting such changes. Examples of recommended knowledge bases are reflected in the various chapters in this book. Figure 8.10 provides an example of some knowledge bases collaborators are typically interested in improving. Remember that these represent the knowledge bases the authors have found to be important in the effective instruction of learners with special needs; however, each individual collaborative consultation team will bring their own unique areas of expertise to the process. In these cases, Figure 8.10 can simply serve as a prototype in monitoring individual acquisition of the relevant knowledge base.

Collaborators may periodically ask each other to rate the degree to which the principles of Collaborative Consultation (see Chapter 2) are being implemented. Simple rating scales can be developed to monitor changes as a func-

FIGURE 8.10. Evaluation system for monitoring collaborator acquisition and practice of essential components of relevant knowledge bases.

Collaborator _____ Date _____

I have acquired competence in:

	Low		Some		High
Elements of effective instruction	1	2	3	4	5
Effective instructional decision making	1	2	3	4	5
Student portfolio assessment	1	2	3	4	5
Curriculum-based student assessment	1	2	3	4	5
Observation of instructional environments	1	2	3	4	5
Strategic and cognitive instruction	1	2	3	4	5
Curriculum adaptation	1	2	3	4	5
Instructional adaptation	1	2	3	4	5
Educational materials evaluation and selection	1	2	3	4	5
Effective classroom management and student discipline	1	2	3	4	5
Management of the teaching and learning environment	1	2	3	4	5
Student progress evaluation	1	2	3	4	5

Note. Adapted from *Effective instruction of difficult-to-teach students* (p. iii) by L. Idol and J. F. West, 1993, Austin, TX: PRO-ED.

tion of the collaborative consultation processes. Figure 8.11 provides an example of an evaluation system for monitoring individual accountability for demonstrating these principles. If this system is used, it is very important for collaborators to support and reinforce positively one another for the progress that is made.

Collaborators may encourage one another to practice and improve intrapersonal attitudes. This should be done on an individualized and personal basis. Figure 8.12 is presented only as a suggested prototype for monitoring individual acquisition of personally identified intrapersonal attitudes. Refer to Chapter 2 for the authors' recommended intrapersonal attitudes that have facilitated their collaborative processes. Individuals may identify different yet equally valid attitudes from their own personal experiences. Individuals can request support from other group members for individual efforts to practice these attitudes. As described in Chapter 2, it is equally important in the development of intrapersonal attitudes for group members to support and reinforce one another for progress made. See Figure 8.13 for an example of the intrapersonal attitudes identified by individuals practicing Collaborative Consultation in various settings. A final caveat must be stated: Monitoring or publicly sharing collaborators' progress on acquiring competence in any of these areas

FIGURE 8.11. Evaluation system for monitoring collaborator acquisition and practice of generic principles of Collaborative Consultation.

Collaborator _____ Date _____

	Never		So-so		Often
I feel team ownership of the identified problem.	1	2	3	4	5
I recognize and respect individual differences.	1	2	3	4	5
I use situational leadership.	1	2	3	4	5
I use cooperative conflict-resolution processes.	1	2	3	4	5
I use appropriate interviewing skills.	1	2	3	4	5
I actively listen to others.	1	2	3	4	5
I communicate using common nonjargon and positive nonverbal language.	1	2	3	4	5

FIGURE 8.12. Evaluation system for monitoring collaborator acquisition and practice of intrapersonal attitudes.

Collaborator _____ Date _____

The intrapersonal attitudes that I practiced today are:

	Not at all		So-so		To a great extent
Face fear.	1	2	3	4	5
Share humor.	1	2	3	4	5
Behave with integrity.	1	2	3	4	5
Live with joy.	1	2	3	4	5
Take risks.	1	2	3	4	5
Use self-determination.	1	2	3	4	5
Think longitudinally.	1	2	3	4	5
Create new norms.	1	2	3	4	5
Respond proactively.	1	2	3	4	5
Adapt upward.	1	2	3	4	5
Use self-differentiation.	1	2	3	4	5

should be voluntary and confidential. Data should be treated as privileged information and should be released to the school system only if all collaborators agree and have made appropriate efforts to protect individual anonymity.

Evaluation of Impact at the Systems Level. As collaborators engage in responsive evaluation, it is important to determine both proactively and

FIGURE 8.13. Changes in intrapersonal attitudes.

Collaborative consultation processes were implemented by graduate students enrolled in master's of education degree programs at the University of Hawaii during the spring semester, 1988. Ten case studies showed the generalizability of the Collaborative Consultation Model in a variety of settings (e.g., a vocational rehabilitation agency, public schools, an institutional day program for adults with severe handicaps). As part of their evaluation, participants cited personal changes that occurred concurrent with their implementation of the collaborative consultation process (Nevin, 1988).

[I learned that] Collaborative Consultation requires not only knowledge and skills but the human element of cooperation and understanding. [S.H.]

I felt a bit fraudulent . . . because I did not feel I had a great body of knowledge or techniques that would help. . . . As our sessions continued, I felt more confident that I had more to offer than I originally thought. . . . I had difficulty establishing parity and really working as a team. I became impatient with the slow methodical manner of process. I found I had a strong tendency to do things myself rather than working as a team. . . . I think I have become more tolerant and less judging of others. [C.M.]

The most significant frustration was the time element. Although we may see the need for intervention strategies, they may be slow to acquire. However, there was a value obtained in this fact, too. It became apparent that research, follow-through, and patience were the factors that contributed to achievement of results. The significant change in me came with the review [evaluation] of this project . . . only then did I put together the accomplishments that had occurred. [D.W.]

The most valuable benefit of learning and practicing [Collaborative Consultation] was the personal maturity I noticed in myself. I realize that CC is simply a guideline for better and clearer communication, and the more I practice these techniques, the more instinctual and habitual they become. Another benefit is an increase in the number of deep relationships I have developed with my colleagues. Finally, I realize that one of my weaknesses is playing the role of the "enabler." I tend to assume personal responsibility for every situation [now I can support team ownership]. [E.L.]

I have a better insight and understanding of [the] potential when people set mutual goals and act on them. [I.P.]

responsively the types of system-level influences that might change as a result of the collaborative process being implemented. It is important to recognize that some of these influences will have much broader impact on the schooling system at large (e.g., changes toward more collaborative leadership practices) than will the outcomes of a single and individual process (e.g., changes at the classroom level).

Figure 8.14 lists examples of systems-level variables that the authors have found to be influenced as a result of implementing collaborative consultation activities. Many of these variables have been validated in the research literature on school consultation as summarized in West (1985) and West et al. (1989). Other examples of data-based evaluations of the effects of Collaborative Consultation are reported by Cross and Villa (1992), Givens-Ogle

FIGURE 8.14. Evaluation of the impact of the Collaborative Consultation Model at the systems level.

Impact on Learners	Yes	No
Decreased number of referrals to special education	☐	☐
Changes in academic achievement of learners	☐	☐
Changes in learner behavioral (social, attitudinal, and study skills) achievement	☐	☐
Increased learner involvement, participation, and satisfaction	☐	☐
Increased number of learners at risk for school failure who succeeded	☐	☐
Impact on Adults		
Changes in leadership styles of key decision makers	☐	☐
Changes in staff attitudes and tolerance for individual learner differences	☐	☐
Changes in staff attitudes and tolerance for adults with differences	☐	☐
Changes in staff expertise in effective problem solving	☐	☐
Changes in staff expertise and underlying knowledge bases	☐	☐
Impact on Policy		
Changes in assignment of instructional staff to other roles	☐	☐
Staff schedules that include time for collaborative activities	☐	☐
Impact on Community		
Increased parent involvement, participation, and satisfaction	☐	☐
Increased interagency collaboration	☐	☐

et al. (1991), and Kaskinen-Chapman (1992). The authors encourage collaborators to identify systems-level variables that are relevant to their situations and school systems, thus relying on Figure 8.14 as a prototype for guidance. Another approach to evaluating the impact of collaborative consultation processes at the systems level is shown in Figure 8.15, which assesses changes in norms for faculty and staff performance. The development of a collaborative ethic within a school building or a district may be traced by asking faculty to complete the self-assessment at various times during the implementation of collaborative consultation activities.

FIGURE 8.15. Collaborative work environment self-assessment.

Name _____ Position _____ School/Unit _____

Instructions: The norms for staff behavior listed below are those frequently found in collaborative work environments in schools. Please read each statement carefully. Then rate the degree to which each statement reflects the current work environment in your school, with 1 = our staff always behave this way; 2 = our staff behave this way most of the time; 3 = our staff behave this way sometimes; 4 = our staff behave this way rarely; or 5 = our staff never behave this way.

_____ 1. The staff share a common language about instructional techniques.

_____ 2. The staff often observe each other in their classrooms and give feedback on instruction.

_____ 3. The staff frequently discuss instructional techniques and methods in the workroom/lounge.

_____ 4. The staff work together to master new instructional methods or strategies.

_____ 5. The staff plan and design educational materials together.

_____ 6. The staff pool their expertise and share their resources with each other.

_____ 7. The staff learn from and with each other.

_____ 8. Time is specifically devoted at staff meetings to demonstrate and discuss innovative educational techniques, materials, or strategies.

_____ 9. Discussions in the staff lounge/workroom center mostly on instructional practices rather than on social concerns or complaints about learners.

_____ 10. Time is specifically provided for professional staff to plan and problem-solve together.

Note. Adapted from *Collaborative School: So What! So What!,* paper by P. Roy and P. O'Brien, November 1989, presented at the Annual Conference of the National Staff Development Council, Anaheim, CA.

EVALUATION DECISIONS

Collaborators need to use evaluation information to decide to celebrate, to redesign, or to discontinue the interventions. When discussing the evaluation data, collaborators may remind each other of the narrow line between exercising judgment and being judgmental. When collaborators work effectively together, they become more likely to be objective and less likely to lay blame if the interventions are not achieving the desired outcomes. The use of inclusive models for problem solving and the reliance on responsive evaluation processes lead collaborators to continually adjust goals and objectives, redesign assessment systems, and search for new arrangements of the learning environment so as to facilitate student progress.

Collaborators need to *use* the evaluation information to make several evaluation decisions together regarding redesign of the interventions or exit from the interventions. These decisions will impact on several possible actions of the collaborative consultation team, such as (a) expanding the membership of the team to procure technical assistance and other expertise or (b) changing the level of the problem to be solved. The Collaborative Consultation Model relies on iterative, recursive, and reflective processes wherein collaborators continually adjust their goals or rearrange their environments and interactions to facilitate goal achievement. The following discussion highlights evaluation decisions at the micro, mezzo, and macro levels.

Micro-Level Evaluation Decisions

At the micro level of learners and classrooms, evaluation decisions to redesign, continue, or exit from interventions must comply with procedural safeguards and parental consent that are the hallmark of P.L. 94-142. When the available evaluation data show improved learner performance during and after the implementation of the services, the procedure is usually deemed effective. However, many procedures can be effective in terms of improving learner performance but are costly in terms of time, attention from classroom teachers or tutors, and so on. Procedures can be redesigned to ameliorate these negative attributes without losing learner achievement (see West et al., 1989, Module 47).

For example, effective interventions can be gradually withdrawn while carefully monitoring to assure the learner maintains the desired performance. Generalization of the desired performance to other settings and situations may also be facilitated through the redesign of the special program. If necessary, steps can be taken to transfer a newly designed program to other implementers (peers, volunteers, aides, parents, etc.).

When the evaluation information does not show improvement, compared with preintervention learner performance, the program is often deemed to be ineffective. Collaborators can decide either to redesign the program or to provide more intensive support for the implementer. In such circumstances, or when providing more-intensive support for the implementer(s), it is important that the collaborators communicate that the program produced by the collaborative consultation *team*, not the primary implementer, is the focus. In essence, the program is the responsibility of the entire team, not just those responsible for actual delivery of the program.

The attention of all collaborators must be focused on the expected *and* unexpected changes in the learner's performance, as well as any impact on the learner's classmates. Thus, it is important to respond to what the evaluation data indicate about the effectiveness or ineffectiveness of the program. Often, collaborators will want to continue a procedure for just a few more days, or weeks, even though the data show no changes in the learner's performance. This resistance to feedback can be attributed to personal investment in making the existing procedures work—an investment that is often directly related to the amount of time it took to learn the procedure.

Collaborators should also be sensitive to other sources of feedback concerning the effectiveness of a program. The data may yield outcomes (both negative *and* positive) that were unexpected or unintended, and this can lead to changes in data collection or even changes in the scope of the team's impact. The important idea is to examine what the evaluation information is showing— and to respond appropriately.

Mezzo- and Macro-Level Evaluation Decisions

When micro-level interventions for learners or classrooms fail to succeed, many collaborative consultation teams realize they need to work toward changes that require involvement of colleagues at the building, district, state, or national level. Evidence of success of a particular intervention procedure or curriculum can influence curriculum choices for other grade levels, decisions to assign learners homogeneously or heterogeneously, assignments of paraprofessionals and specialized personnel to classrooms or resource rooms, and so on. Similarly, evidence of failure of a particular intervention may signal the need for building and district staff development efforts so as to broaden the skills and knowledge of all faculty and staff (see, e.g., Idol & West, 1989, and West et al., 1989, for model staff development programs that facilitate collaboration).

On the other hand, mezzo- and macro-level actions are no guarantee that changes will be made at the micro level. It is well known that mandating or legislating change does not assure programmatic implementation (e.g., Mills & Hull, 1992; Semmel, Lieber, & Peck, 1986; Weatherley & Lipsky, 1977). For example, in the context of designing, implementing, and evaluating programs for integrating preschool learners with special needs in their least restrictive environments, Peck et al. (1989) developed a transactional process for program development, including goal setting and evaluation, that encouraged and addressed divergent interests of a variety of constituents. Pedagogical needs (e.g., curricula, instructional design, classroom environment) were considered as one dimension of the "social ecology" (p. 283), along with other needs (e.g., the personal and logistical needs of the parents and learners as well as the teachers and administrators, or the sociopolitical needs of the community). The transactional process was guided by a basic assumption of respect (e.g., a belief that the "behavior of parents and professionals represents intelligent and active attempts to cope with problems and situations" [p. 283]) and an assumption of ownership (e.g., that "social educational policies can only be effective when the people who are in direct 'hands-on' contact with children choose to implement them" [p. 283]). In this model, it is clear that goals and objectives are negotiated through a give-and take process (thus, the term *transactional*).

Peck and colleagues collaborated with a variety of agencies to show how the model works. Richarz, Peck, and Peterson (1986) reported how Project RAMP (Rural Area Model Preschools), conducted at Washington State University, resulted in increased availability of integrated preschool options for children with disabilities. Their results show that macro-level changes can be successfully negotiated through this transactional process.

In summary, the Collaborative Consultation Model is similarly transactional and offers a systematic method by which to mutually derive goals and procedures that empower implementers, parents, and policymakers to achieve beneficial changes for all learners. Collaborators must ensure frequent opportunities to reflect on evaluation information and discuss implications. Frequent contacts enable collaborators to identify troublesome aspects of interventions in a timely fashion to enable them to make meaningful decisions about continuing, exiting, or redesigning the intervention or changing the focus of the team's work.

Finally, the Collaborative Consultation Model requires persistence. Persistent efforts to make interventions effective will result in improved performance of the learner(s) with special needs or at risk for school failure as well as their classmates. The attitude of "toughing it out" is summarized in the familiar adage: If at first you don't succeed, try, try, again. In fact, collaborators might learn to point to their ineffective attempts as evidence of their flexibility and willingness to change.

SUMMARY

Collaborative Consultation involves the interaction of at least two persons who share the responsibility of solving a problem. Part of that responsibility involves the evaluation of the progress they are making toward changes regarding the problem. The evaluation design should be responsive to the needs of the persons involved in the collaborative consultation program and should reflect all components of the program. In addition to the principles of consultation that are important for collaboration and should be present in any stage of consultation, there are eight principles relevant to the evaluation stage. Within this strategic context, several general and situation-specific principles can be used to facilitate evaluation of the Collaborative Consultation Model. These principles can aid greatly in the development of a program that is continually growing in a positive direction.

To make an evaluation system *responsive,* collaborators must use the evaluation information they have collected. Evaluation decisions must be addressed at the learner and classroom level (micro level) as well as at the building level (mezzo level) and district, state, or national level (macro level). Follow-up decisions include (a) continuing, (b) redesigning, or (c) exiting (gradually withdrawing, transferring responsibility, or terminating) from interventions and (d) formulating new goals or target issues at the micro, mezzo, or macro levels.

In our experience, those who implement the Collaborative Consultation Model most successfully are leaders, trainers, listeners, and learners—all at the same time. They are willing to model the techniques they expect others to use with learners. These various roles continually expand each collaborator's skills and beliefs about human growth. The ability and willingness to evaluate one's own progress, as well as others', is one of the most important skills in effective Collaborative Consultation.

STUDY QUESTIONS

1. The authors describe several dimensions of evaluation of Collaborative Consultation. Describe three that are most meaningful to you. Explain why and how you would address these dimensions.

2. Elaborate on each of the evaluation principles. Explain how you might implement each principle in your setting.

3. Why is evaluating the impact of Collaborative Consultation an important follow-up task of the collaborative consultation team? Describe how your team might evaluate the acquisition of various knowledge bases, generic principles, interpersonal skills, and intrapersonal attitudes in your setting.

4. When collaborators are faced with the evidence that what they planned did not have the effects they desired, yet they want to continue as a collaborative consultation team, how might a technical assistance person benefit the team?

5. When should a collaborative consultation team end their collaboration? Why is it important to celebrate endings?

6. Describe situations in which a collaborative consultation team might decide to end working on a particular issue, and yet still be considered successful. Example: A collaborative consultation team consisting of special and general educators in a public school worked together for a year to develop effective interventions for a group of learners in a second-grade classroom who had language delays. They terminated their collaborative consultation teamwork because the entire district adopted a new curriculum and the site-based management team at the building level designed a reassignment of faculty, specialists, and paraprofessionals for reading and language arts instruction that resulted in a more flexible assignment of all learners to small, heterogeneous learning groups. In this example, a micro-level (classroom) situation was corrected by a macro-level (district curriculum task force) decision and a mezzo-level (school building) assignment of faculty.

REFERENCES

Baer, D. M., Wolf, M. M., & Risley, T. R. (1968). Some current dimensions of applied behavior analysis. *Journal of Applied Behavior Analysis, 1*, 91–97.

Blankenship, C., & Lilly, M. S. (1981). *Mainstreaming students with learning and behavior problems.* New York: Holt, Rinehart & Winston.

Bloom, B. S. (1981). *All our children are learning: A primer for parents, teachers, and other educators.* New York: McGraw-Hill.

Cross, J., & Villa, R. (1992). The Winooski School System: An evolutionary perspective of a school restructuring for diversity. In R. Villa, J. Thousand, W. Stainback & S. Stainback (Eds.), *Restructuring for caring and effective education* (pp. 219–240). Baltimore: Brookes.

George, M., George, N., & Grosenick, J. (1990). Features of program evaluation in special education. *Remedial and Special Education, 11*(5), 24–30.

Givens-Ogle, L., Christ, B., & Idol, L. (1991). Collaborative Consultation: The San Juan Unified School District Project. *Journal of Educational and Psychological Consultation, 2*(3), 267–284.

Guba, E. G., & Lincoln, Y. S. (1981). *Effective evaluation improving the usefulness of evaluation results through responsiveness and naturalistic approaches.* San Francisco: Jossey-Bass.

Harris, K. (1991). An expanded view on consultation competencies for educators serving culturally and linguistically diverse exceptional students. *Teacher Education and Special Education, 14*(1), 25–29.

Hawkes, K. M., & Paolucci-Whitcomb, P. (1980). A consultation model—Helping teachers use peer tutoring. *The Pointer, 24*(3), 47–55.

Idol, L. (1993). *Special educator's consultation handbook* (2nd ed.). Austin, TX: PRO-ED.

Idol, L., & West, J. F. (1991). Educational collaboration: A catalyst for effective schooling. *Intervention in School and Clinic, 27*(3), 70–78, 125.

Idol, L. & West, J. F. (1993). *Effective instruction of difficult-to-teach students.* Austin, TX: PRO-ED

Johnson, D., & Johnson, R. (1989). *Cooperation and competition: Theory and practice.* Edina, MN: Interaction Book Co.

Joyce, B. R., Hersh, R. H., & McKibbin, M. (1983). *The structure of school improvement.* New York: Longman.

Kaskinen-Chapman, A. (1992). Saline Area Schools and inclusive community CONCEPTS (Collaborative Organization of Networks: Community, Educators, Parents, The Workplace, and Students). In R. Villa, J. Thousand, W. Stainback, & S. Stainback (Eds.), *Restructuring for caring and effective education* (pp. 169–185). Baltimore: Brookes.

Lutkemeier, D. (1991). Attitudes and practices regarding the implementation of collaborative educational services. *The Consulting Edge,* 3(2), 1–3.

Mills, R., & Hull, M. (1992). State departments of education: Instruments of policy, instruments of change. In R. Villa, J. Thousand, W. Stainback, & S. Stainback (Eds.), *Restructuring for caring and effective education* (pp. 245–266). Baltimore: Brookes.

Nevin, A. (Ed.). (1988). *Implementing the Collaborative Consultation Model in Hawaii: Ten case studies.* Unpublished manuscript, Special Education Department, University of Hawaii, Honolulu.

Paolucci-Whitcomb, P., Bright, W., Carlson, R., & Meyers, H. (1987). Interactive evaluations: Processes for improving special education leadership training. *Remedial and Special Education,* 8(3), 52-61.

Paolucci-Whitcomb, P., & Nevin, A. (1985). Preparing consulting teachers through a collaborative approach between university faculty and field-based consulting teachers. *Teacher Education and Special Education,* 8(3), 132–143.

Patriarca, L., & Lamb, M. (1990). Preparing secondary education teachers to be collaborative decision makers and reflective practitioners: A promising model. *Teacher Education and Special Education,* 13(3-4), 200–224.

Peck, C. A., Richarz, S., Peterson, K., Hayden, L., Mineur, L., & Wandschneider, M. (1989). An ecological process model for implementing the least restrictive environment mandate in early childhood programs. In R. Gaylord-Ross (Ed.), *Integration strategies for students with handicaps* (pp. 281–298). Baltimore: Brookes.

Provus, M. (1971). *The discrepancy evaluation model.* Berkeley, CA: McCutchan.

Pryzwansky, W., & Noblit, G. (1990). Understanding and improving consultation practice: The qualitative case study approach. *Journal of Educational and Psychological Consultation,* 1(4), 293–307.

Richarz, S., Peck, C., & Peterson, K. (1986). *Developing integrated preschools in rural communities.* Proposal funded by the U.S. Department of Education, Handicapped Children's Early Education Program, to Washington State University, Pullman.

Roy, P., & O'Brien, P. (1989, November). *Collaborative school: So what! So what!* Paper presented at the Annual Conference of the National Staff Development Council, Anaheim, CA.

Semmel, M., Lieber, J., & Peck, C. A. (1986). Effects of special education environments: Beyond mainstreaming. In C. J. Meisel (Ed.), *Mainstreaming handicapped children: Outcomes, controversies, and new directions* (pp. 165–192). Hillsdale, NJ: Erlbaum.

Tuckman, B. W. (1979). *Evaluating instructional programs.* Boston: Allyn & Bacon.

Villa, R., Thousand, J., Paolucci-Whitcomb, P., & Nevin, A. (1990). In search of new paradigms for Collaborative Consultation. *Journal of Educational and Psychological Consultation,* 1(4), 279–292.

Vlasak, L., Goldenberg, D., & Idol, L. (1992). *Resource/consultation: A preliminary evaluation of the effects of a multiple district training project.* Unpublished manuscript, Institute for Learning and Development, Austin, TX.

Weatherley, R., & Lipsky, M. (1977). Street level bureaucrats and institutional instruction: Implementing special education reform. *Harvard Educational Review, 47,* 171–197.

West, J. F. (1985). Regular and special educators' preferences for school-based consultation models (Doctoral dissertation, The University of Texas at Austin, 1985). *Dissertation Abstracts International, 47*(2), 504A.

West, J. F. (1988). School consultation research: An interdisciplinary review. In J. F. West (Ed.), *School consultation: Interdisciplinary perspectives on theory, research, training, and practice* (pp. 55–75). Austin: Research and Training Project on School Consultation, Association for Educational and Psychological Consultants, P.O. Box 202020, Austin, TX 78720.

West, J. F., Idol, L., & Cannon, G. (1989). *Collaboration in the schools: An inservice and preservice curriculum for teachers, support staff, and administrators.* Austin, TX: PRO-ED.

CHAPTER 9

Field-Based Examples of the Collaborative Consultation Model

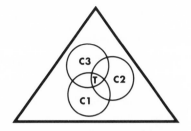

IN THIS FINAL CHAPTER, we present two case studies to illustrate implementation of the Collaborative Consultation Model. To some extent, they are also examples of how the various collaborators used a collaborative problem-solving process and developed team ownership of the problem to be solved.

The case studies are the result of projects completed by a consulting teacher intern at the University of Vermont (first case study) and a resource/consulting teacher intern at the University of Illinois (second case study). The first case study concerned a young child with severe learning needs who was enrolled in a kindergarten classroom. The second study was conducted in a secondary school home economics class with learners with mild behavior problems. For both case studies, commentary is provided as a means of clarifying when the collaborators reached various points in the problem-solving process.

The reader is also referred to several other sources that contain examples, reports, and case studies illustrating use of the Collaborative Consultation Model or application of the collaborative problem-solving process. Idol (1993) reported on 37 data-based case studies of resource/consulting and classroom teachers working together to include learners with special needs in general classrooms. Saver and Downes (1991) reported the impact of using a peer intervention team and the collaborative problem-solving process in an elementary school (mezzo level). They reported high levels of classroom teacher satisfaction and team ownership, and an appreciable decrease in special education referrals. At the macro level (an entire school district in Sacramento, California), Givens-Ogle, Christ, and Idol (1991) described some important types of changes in adults and within the system. A change in the collaborators was reported for special education resource teachers who, as they were prepared to use the Collaborative Consultation Model, became more collegial and collaborative among themselves. After staff development preparation, they continued to remain loyal to a peer support group of collaborators, who continued to improve their collaborative skills. Another example of a macro-level change was reported in Idol, Vlasak, and Goldenberg (1988), as well as in Idol (1993). In this project, another group of special education resource teachers were prepared to use the Collaborative Consultation Model, with emphasis on assisting these resource teachers to become resource/consulting teachers. The participating teachers reported significant and positive shifts in spending more time consulting with classroom teachers, as well as valuing such collaborative efforts as an important component in their job definitions.

In the first case study, the primary author, Susan Alnasrawi, had worked for several years prior to the study as a teacher's assistant in the school. She had studied both the history of special education and the role of consultation as part of her MEd studies in special education. The case is based on the document she submitted in partial fulfillment of an internship in special education, instructed and supervised by Phyllis Paolucci-Whitcomb, associate professor in the Department of Special Education, Social Work and Social Services at the University of Vermont. At the time, Susan was a consulting teacher intern in a suburban school district in Vermont. Another collaborator was Julie Snee, consulting teacher, who provided additional supervision and instruction. Other collaborators included a classroom teacher, a paraprofessional, a teacher's assistant, an intinerant teacher, and the learner's parents. Figure 9.1 depicts the relationship of the various collaborators. T represents the learner with special needs. C1 represents the people who provided some of the expertise or instruction related to the classroom curriculum or schedule, such as the classroom teacher or the paraprofessional. C2 represents the people who provided some of the expertise for specialized instruction, such as the consulting teacher intern, the consulting teacher, and the itinerant teacher. C3 represents those who were not present on a daily basis and who provided additional technical assistance related to the specialized instruction such as the intern's graduate professor or information related to the learner such as the learner's parents.

This case study was only one of several required as part of the internship. It was selected for inclusion here because it shows the importance of the qualitative data collected from the records of the various consultation interactions of the collaborators. These records (known as the consultation log) enabled the collaborators to monitor the progress made by the team at several levels: learner progress (micro level), changes in the collaborators (mezzo level), and changes in curriculum and schedules (macro level). Thirty-seven other case studies can be found in Idol (1993).

The text of Alnasrawi's original manuscript is reprinted in the left column. Comments shown on the right side of the page explain the various steps of the collaborative consultation process in which the collaborators in the case study engaged.

CASE STUDY 1: MAINSTREAMING A KINDERGARTEN LEARNER

Susan Alnasrawi
Consulting Teacher Intern, University of Vermont
(at the time of this study)

The participants in this case study were a 7-year-old girl in a kindergarten classroom	Comments. Since the consulting teacher intern (CTI) had worked in this school for

FIGURE 9.1. The Collaborative Consultation Model in action.

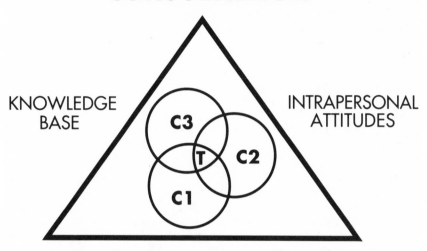

COLLABORATIVE
CONSULTATION

KNOWLEDGE
BASE

INTRAPERSONAL
ATTITUDES

C3

T C2

C1

INTERPERSONAL COMMUNICATIVE,
INTERACTIVE PROBLEM-SOLVING SKILLS

C1 = The people who provided some of the expertise or instruction related to the classroom curriculum or schedule such as the classroom teacher or the teacher's paraprofessional assistant.

C2 = The people who provided some of the expertise for specialized instruction such as the consulting teacher, the consulting teacher intern, and the itinerant teacher.

C3 = Those who were not present on a daily basis and who provided additional technical assistance related to the specialized instruction such as the intern graduate professor or information related to the learner such as the learner's parents.

T = The learner.

and her classroom teacher. The classroom teacher was a woman with 12 years of teaching experience at the elementary level and a master's degree in special education. The learner, Rita, had spent the previous 3 years in a special class at a special school. The special school served fifty-two 3- to 6-year-old children in special classes. The school accepted only learners with definite delays in the areas of gross-motor, fine-motor, language, and social and self-help

several years, she had already utilized the principles and techniques for gaining entry described in Chapter 4 so as to gain acceptance with school personnel. In this case study, readers will observe the teacher's gradual acceptance and ownership of the mainstreamed learner through excerpts from the consultation log.

skills. During the first 4 months of this study, Rita continued to attend the special school each afternoon, after completing her morning in a general kindergarten classroom.

Rita was diagnosed as having mild cerebral palsy. She experienced some fine-motor difficulties in her hands. Her primary difficulties were social behavioral problems. Among her repertoire of behaviors were (a) being very destructive of objects around her, (b) throwing temper tantrums, (c) biting others and herself, (d) head banging, and (e) a very short attention span. Rita had been under constant medical supervision by her physician and the staff at a child development clinic.

The Classroom. The classroom was a kindergarten of 15 learners in a suburban elementary school of approximately 400 students. The entire school district (K–12) had a faculty of 236. Academic work on a one-to-one basis with the consulting teacher intern (CTI), Susan Alnasrawi, took place in a corner of the classroom. In the beginning, both Susan's and Rita's desks faced away from the classroom, and there was a visual barrier between them and the rest of the class. Academic work on a one-to-one basis with the classroom teacher was completed at the teacher's desk, which was in the middle of the room.

Management System. Initially, Susan worked with Rita in various capacities throughout the kindergarten day (8:30 to 11:00 A.M.). On any given day, this involved one-to-one tutoring, facilitating participation during small- and large-group activities, and accompanying Rita to music class and the library.

Susan kept daily data on academic progress during the tutoring sessions. The scheduling of these sessions was initially unsystematic and for varying lengths of

Comments. Assessment principles and techniques similar to those described in Chapter 5 were utilized through a team approach. Personnel from the special school that Rita initially attended and from the neighborhood school in which she was being mainstreamed worked together to collect and share assessment information.

Comments. Annual goals and specific instructional objectives for the learner (micro level) that were developed for Rita's IEP, as suggested in Chapter 5, were developed and implemented.

Comments. Initially, many people and much time were involved in mainstreaming Rita. At the time she was the learner with the most severe special needs in the school

time. As time progressed, the schedule became more fixed. The teacher then became involved in more of the activities. Data were collected for approximately ½ hour daily. During that time, it was noted how often the classroom teacher and Susan made direct contact with Rita during the disruptive behaviors.

Informal daily meetings and more formal weekly meetings were held. These meetings were attended by two or more of the following people: the consulting teacher (CT), Julie Snee, the consulting teacher intern (CTI), Susan Alnasrawi, and the classroom teacher. After the meetings, notes on content (IEP progress) and teacher affect (positive and negative statements about working with Rita) were recorded in the consultation logs by both Julie (CT) and Susan (CTI).

Materials. A variety of commercial and teacher-made materials were used. Examples of teacher- and/or CTI-made materials were:

- Sightword flash cards

- Sightword work sheets

- Number flash cards

- Concept work sheets

- Body part work sheets

The commercial materials included:

- *Boehm Resource Guide for Basic Concept Teaching* by A. Boehm (New York: Psychological Corp., 1976)

- *Beginning to Read, Write and Listen* by P. Rowland (New York: Boston Educational Research Co., 1971)

- *Contemporary Mathematics Readiness* by R. McDonnell, A. Lombardi, and G. Grossman (New York: W. H. Sadler, 1970)

district. Her parents and teachers believed that she would need less and less assistance as she gained appropriate skills and knowledge in the mainstream setting. They did expect, however, that, at first, she would need a great deal of help. These expectations turned out to be true.

- *Hear, Say, See, Write!* (New York: Holt, Rinehart & Winston, 1980)

- A tape recorder with earplugs

Measurement and Reliability Procedures. Disruptive behavior data were recorded by Susan and Julie. Six categories for disruptive behavior were used:

Comments. It is important that the behaviors of concern are clearly defined and observable by at least two independent observers.

1. *Throwing*—taking an object in hand and throwing it through the air

2. *Running*—moving (at a pace faster than walking) away from a task or person

3. *Screaming*—vocalizations louder than normal classroom tone

4. *Biting*—clamping gums or teeth on any part of herself or others

5. *Kicking*—using her feet to bang forcefully into objects or people

6. *Pushing*—moving an object or a person forcefully from one place to another

Each day, one person (either Julie or Susan) observed in the kindergarten classroom from approximately 10:30 to 10:55 A.M. The tape recorder was used with an earplug. Every 10 seconds, there was a sound indicating the beginning of an observation period. Ten seconds of observation followed. In this time, the frequency of disruptive behaviors was noted. Then another sound on the tape indicated the end of the observation period and the beginning of a 5-second interval for recording purposes only. The observation data were recorded on a special sheet, and the results were transferred to a graph (see Figure 9.2).

A reliability test was conducted on the timed samples by a second observer during

Comments. The CT, the CTI, the classroom teacher, and Rita's parents helped develop Rita's goals and objectives during the Individualized Education Program (IEP) process. The classroom adaptations (see Chapter 7) were developed by school personnel and approved by Rita's parents.

FIGURE 9.2.   Graphic display of Rita's disruptive behavior, based on observational data.

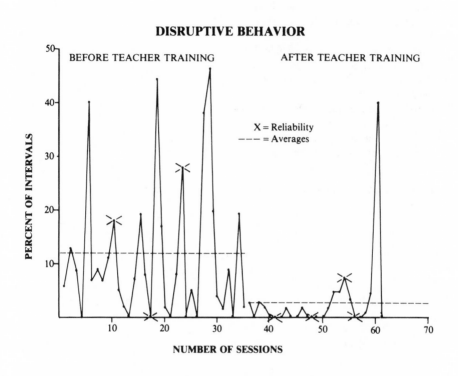

DISRUPTIVE BEHAVIOR

BEFORE TEACHER TRAINING   AFTER TEACHER TRAINING

X = Reliability
——— = Averages

PERCENT OF INTERVALS

NUMBER OF SESSIONS

random intervals. Reliability was computed as follows:

$$\left(\frac{\text{number of agreements}}{\begin{array}{c}\text{number of agreements}\\ +\ \text{number of}\\ \text{disagreements}\end{array}}\right)100\ =\ \begin{array}{c}\text{percentage}\\ \text{of}\\ \text{agreement}\end{array}$$

The teacher behaviors that were measured were: (a) the amount of time spent in contact with Rita and (b) the classroom teacher's attitude toward Rita and the consultation process.

Data on teacher contact time and CTI contact time were kept by Julie and Susan. Contact was defined as direct physical or verbal contact with Rita, for example, touching, praising, giving directions, disciplining, and so on. This did not include verbalizations intended for the class as a whole. These data were collected with the same procedure that was used to collect data on disruptive behaviors. The data on contacts were transferred to separate graphs. One graph contained data on CTI-learner contact (see Figure 9.3); the other graph contained data on teacher-learner contact (see Figure 9.4).

FIGURE 9.3. Graphic display of CTI-learner contact, based on observational data.

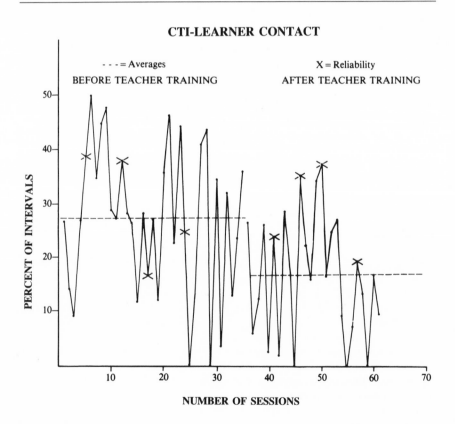

CTI-LEARNER CONTACT

FIGURE 9.4. Graphic display of teacher-learner contact, based on observational data.

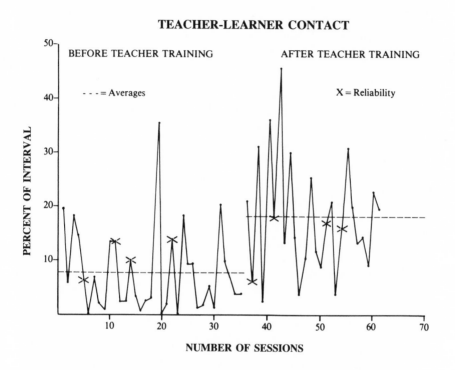

TEACHER-LEARNER CONTACT

Data regarding teacher attitude and consultation progress were recorded in an informal log. The log consisted of notes taken by Susan during or after meetings with the classroom teacher. Each entry contained information on the content (discussions about IEP progress, teaching/learning techniques, materials) and teacher affect (statements about Rita, the mainstreaming process, meaningful experiences, and so on). The log notes were later condensed into the description of the consultation process.

The Consultation Process

Both formal and informal meetings were held throughout the year. Meetings of a formal nature were scheduled weekly. These meetings were attended by Julie, Susan, and the classroom teacher. Informal meetings were held on a daily basis and were also usually attended by the classroom teacher, Susan, and Julie.

October 6 to January 4 (Sessions 1 to 35). In this period, the focus during informal meetings was primarily on the learner's disruptive behaviors. Everyone seemed to need to exchange information on a daily basis.

The classroom teacher expressed concern about roles in reference to the itinerant teacher and to Julie. She wanted to know who was responsible for the development and implementation of Rita's program. Who was responsible if the goals on the IEP were not met? How much of Susan's time would she be able to count on?

During this period, there was also urgent concern about the time Susan would spend in the classroom. There were frequent comments on this point, such as: "I need to be sure there's someone in here all the time!" "I have 14 other children to worry about; I can't be expected to spend all my time with Rita." "If she's in one of my small academic groups, I want someone there at all times." Despite the above concerns, the classroom teacher's attitude toward having Rita in her room was always positive. She expressed a willingness to try anything to facilitate successful mainstreaming. She also maintained a warm and loving attitude toward Rita at all times.

During the early stages, both Susan and Julie had some strong feelings about the lack of structure in the classroom. The organization seemed very "loose." When pressed

Comments. The summaries of qualitative information (collected from the consultation log) provide a rich understanding of the effectiveness, efficiency, and affectiveness of the consultation process.

Comments. Without prior training and experience, classroom teachers have legitimate concerns about their ability to mainstream learners with special needs effectively. In this case, the classroom teacher had an MEd in special education, but she had never worked with a child who had the severe problems that Rita exhibited. The teacher maintained a positive attitude about having Rita in her class, but she required technical assistance and emotional support from the CT and the CTI.

for schedule information, the teacher always seemed to have somewhat of a plan for the day in her head. There was, however, no immediate written reply from the classroom teacher on this point.

It appeared important that Susan not have to second-guess the classroom teacher as to what was coming next. There was a real need for Rita to have a consistent, predictable schedule. At this stage, Susan was with Rita at all times.

Formal meetings in the very early stages centered around IEP formulation. There were discussions concerning the skills that Rita needed and those that it seemed reasonable to expect of her.

Informal meetings continued on a daily basis with emergency meetings for crises. Susan and Julie made another attempt to get the teacher to identify specifics of her daily and weekly plans, and this time they requested something in writing. They pointed out that Rita seemed to have her most difficult periods during times of transition. Susan noted she found herself aggravating the situation by having to shuffle Rita from one activity to another with very little or no warning, simply because she herself was unaware of what came next. The classroom teacher seemed to have observed the difficult transitions herself and appeared more receptive to the idea of a formalized schedule. The teacher verbalized a general format that Susan recorded and then used as a reference (see Figure 9.5).

Further consultation later in October focused on the need for a more specific schedule, emphasizing the hope that such a schedule might improve Rita's behavior. The teacher responded by designing a laminated schedule, which then became the source of information on a daily basis (see Figure 9.6).

At this stage, Rita became more and more attached to and dependent on Susan, whom she called "Mrs. A." She was often

Comments. At this point, it became clear that strategies needed to be developed to decrease the contact time and reinforcers

FIGURE 9.5.   Format of initial schedule for Rita.

INITIAL SCHEDULE

Monday	Tuesday	Wednesday	Thursday	Friday
Work time	Work time	Work time	Work time	Work time
Guidance	Music	Group time	Library	Guidance
				Gym
Snack	Snack	Snack	Snack	Snack
Gym		Music		Work time
Group activities	Group activities	Math	Group activities	Group activities

FIGURE 9.6.   Format of revised schedule for Rita.

REVISED SCHEDULE

Monday	Tuesday	Wednesday	Thursday	Friday
Guidance	Math	Guidance	Math	
		Work time		Work time
Language arts	Music	Circle time	Circle time	Story
	Work time	Language arts	Work time	Circle time
Math		Project	Library	Gym
Snack	Snack	Snack	Snack	Snack
Gym	Language arts	Music	Language arts	Language arts
Circle time	Story	Math	Story	Math
Story	Body movement		Project	
Project	Project			Project

heard to ask, "Where Mrs. A?" "When Mrs. A. coming?" "Don't go away, Mrs. A!" "Mrs. A. come too!" On many occasions, the classroom teacher made Susan's presence contingent on good behavior. For example, the teacher would say, "Oh, if you can't stop screaming, Mrs. A. will have to leave!" In fact, Rita was beginning to refuse to interact with the teacher, shouting for the classroom teacher to go away and for Mrs. A. to come.

Both Julie and Susan felt that this was becoming an unhealthy situation. The process of normalization necessary for successful mainstreaming was not being made. Instead of joining larger groups led by the teacher and interacting with the most natural authority figure—the classroom teacher—Rita was becoming totally dependent on Susan. It seemed that, though the schedule was far more concrete than in the first month of school, it did not specify clearly with whom Rita was to perform the activities on the agenda. It was therefore still Susan who was most often in charge of Rita's day.

The classroom teacher also appeared to be feeling jealous about the relationship between Rita and Susan. On various occasions, she made the following remarks: "Gosh, she never listens to me like she listens to you!" "You should have heard her yelling for you when you left the room; she never does that with me."

between Rita and the CTI and increase the contact time and reinforcers between the teacher and Rita.

On one occasion, the classroom teacher made a special point of stopping Julie in the hall to let her know that Rita had finally called for her, not for Mrs. A: "When Mrs. A. made her pick up, she yelled, 'I want Mrs. B. (classroom teacher)!' That was the first time she did that!" The teacher was unmistakably pleased at Rita's response to her. She later also mentioned this incident to colleagues.

Comments. These data indicate that the teacher was beginning to take ownership for service and was becoming reinforced by the progress of the learner with special needs.

Rita's behavior throughout this period remained of great concern. She was disruptive and difficult to manage. The teacher noted: "That can't go on. She's disrupting my whole day!" "I can't seem to get through to her." "I wonder if this is the best placement for her."

Comments. This was a critical time for Julie. Julie had to maintain support services so that the classroom teacher wouldn't give up and recommend that Rita be excluded from her class.

January 5 to March 31 (Sessions 36 to 61). There now existed the need for Rita to interact more with the teacher on a one-to-one basis and with teacher-led groups. This required the establishment of a better rapport between the teacher and Rita and more specific planning. At this time, a decision was made to eliminate Rita's afternoon session at the special school. This move shifted the entire responsibility for Rita's IEP to those who were involved in her classroom. At this point, the classroom teacher had had sufficient time to acquaint herself with the other learners in the class, to assess their needs, and to begin their programs.

The combination of all these factors stimulated Julie and Susan to present on January 5 (Session 36) a rough draft of a more specific activity chart. At the same time, they expressed their feelings about the need for more and better teacher-learner interaction and less reliance on Susan. To the great pleasure of both Julie and Susan, the timing seemed to be right. The classroom teacher was not only interested but spoke of designing an even more detailed schedule. She requested a copy of Susan's draft and arrived the next day with a detailed schedule with room for comments. She had run some copies off on oak tag paper (for Rita to take home) and some on regular paper (for the school to keep) (see Figure 9.7).

Both Julie and Susan considered this a major breakthrough and acknowledged the classroom teacher's increasing responsibility for Rita with positive feedback for her time

Comments. The changes in the schedule represented a variety of positive events. The teacher wanted ownership of Rita's program. She was willing to alter her open, flexible planning to be more specific, and she was willing to provide more of the instruction for Rita.

FIGURE 9.7. Format of final schedule for Rita.

Date	
Thursday	
_____ Comments _____	
Arrival (Mrs. A)	
Exercises (Mrs. A)	
Math Worktime (Mrs. B)	
Worktime (Mrs. A)	
Worktime (Mrs. B)	
Playtime (total group)	
Circle time (group and Mrs. B)	
Library (with Mrs. A present)	
Snack (total group)	
Speech (one-to-one Mrs. Q)	
Story (group and Mrs. B)	
Body movement (group and Mrs. B)	
Project (group and Mrs. B)	
Departure (total group)	

Note: Mrs. A = Consulting Teacher Intern
Mrs. B = Classroom Teacher
Mrs. Q = Speech Teacher

and effort. The formulation of this schedule made the daily routine more predictable. The final schedule specified with whom Rita was to work at any given time, and the teacher had set aside a greatly increased amount of time for interaction with Rita.

Rita's behavior throughout this period was greatly improved. The teacher was on various occasions heard to say: "You know, I think she's going to make it!" "She's attending better and progressing. What a change from the beginning of the year." "She's a pleasure to work with."

The teacher became more involved in academic programming for Rita. She started her in a math workbook and began other readiness projects. She also began to come to meetings with concrete suggestions for Rita's academic work.

Toward the end of this time, the teacher took it upon herself to approach a colleague who had been chosen to be Rita's first-grade teacher and set up with her a schedule whereby Rita would gradually be integrated into the first-grade classroom for a short period of time each day. This was intended to facilitate the transition to the next year.

Additional Measures. The entire basic staffing team agreed on the need to focus on Rita's disruptive behaviors (throwing, running, screaming, biting, kicking, and pushing). However, an important purpose of the individualized educational process is to increase the probability of important skill acquisition. Therefore, additional data on major areas of Rita's IEP annual goals (pre-academic, fine motor, gross motor, social adaptive) were gathered.

Data on skill acquisition were recorded by Susan during daily one-to-one tutoring sessions (see Figure 9.8). A plus (+) indicated a correct first response, and a minus (-) indicated an incorrect first response. Three consecutive pluses indicated mastery. To facilitate retention, the mastered skills were retested at random intervals. At a later time in the study, the teacher also worked with Rita, recording on a separate sheet the data regarding skills covered. These data were then transferred to a cumulative graph (see Figure 9.9).

Another concern was to keep relatively constant the number of skills addressed,

Comments. Hasazi (1976) found that classroom teachers gained confidence as their skills increased while working with exceptional learners: "When we express confidence in teachers, and provide them with the appropriate consultative support and an effective educational technology, we have found them to be accepting and enthusiastic" (p. 58).

FIGURE 9.8. Daily tab sheet on Rita's skill acquisition, maintained by CTI.

SKILL	1	2	3	4	5	6	7	8	9	10	11	12	13	14	15	16	17	18	19....
Sight Words																			
cookie	+	−	−	+	+	−	+	+	+	(mastered)				+	+	+			
cut	−	−	−	−	−	+	+	−	+	−	+	+	−	+	+	+	(mastered)		
milk	−	−	−	−	+	−	+	−	−	+	+	+	(mastered)			+	+	+	
pencil										−	−	+	−	−	+	+	+	(mastered)	
draw										−	−	−	+	+	−	+	+	+	(mastered)
paste													−	−	−	+			
shoe													−	−	−	−			
Counting Objects																			
one	+	+	−	+	−	+	+	+	(mastered)										
two	+	+	+	(mastered)															
three	−	−	−	−	+	−	−	+	+	−	−	+	−	+	+	+	(mastered)		
four	−	−	−	−	−	−	−	+	+	−	−	+	−	−	−	+	+	+	(mastered)
five	−	−	−	−	−	−	−	−	−	+	+	−	−	−	+	+	−	+	+
Identifying Numbers																			
zero	−	−	+	−	+	+	−	+	+	+	(mastered)			+	−	+	+	+	
one	−	+	−	−	+	−	+	+	−	+	−	+	+	+	(mastered)		+	+	+
two	−	−	−	+	−	−	+	+	−	+	+	+	(mastered)			+	+	+	
three							−	−	−	−	−	+	−	+	+	−	+	+	+ (mastered)
four										−	−	−	−	+	+	+	(mastered)		
five										−	−	−	−	−	+	−	+	+	+ (mastered)
Recognize Shapes																			
rectangle	−	−	−	+	+	−	+	+	+	(mastered)					−	+	+	+	
triangle	−	−	−	−	+	+	−	+	−	+		+	(mastered)				+	+	
circle	−	+	+	+	(mastered)							+	+	+					
square	−	−	+	−	−	−	+	+	−	−	+	−	+	+	+	(mastered)			

despite the shift from exclusive interaction between Susan and Rita to increased interaction between Rita and the classroom teacher. Therefore, Rita's skill-acquisition data were presented for each month as the average number of skills taught on a daily basis (see Figure 9.10).

Reliability checks were conducted at random intervals during both teacher- and CTI-directed teaching/learning sessions. At such times, the teacher or Susan recorded data on the number of skills taught. The

FIGURE 9.9.   Graphic display of Rita's cumulative skills acquisition.

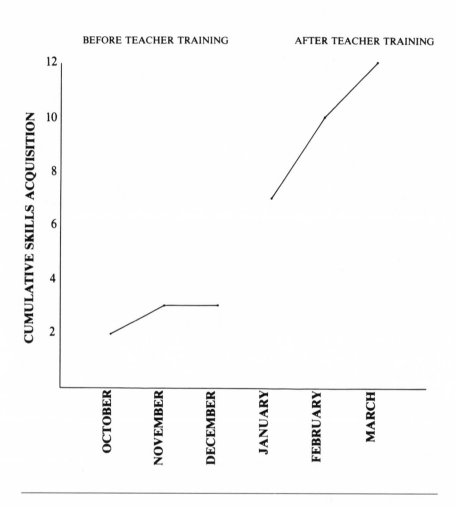

percentage of reliability was computed as follows:

$$\left(\frac{\text{number of agreements}}{\begin{array}{c}\text{number of agreements}\\ + \text{ number of}\\ \text{disagreements}\end{array}}\right) 100 = \begin{array}{c}\text{percentage}\\ \text{of}\\ \text{agreement}\end{array}$$

FIGURE 9.10. Graphic display of daily average number of skills taught to Rita.

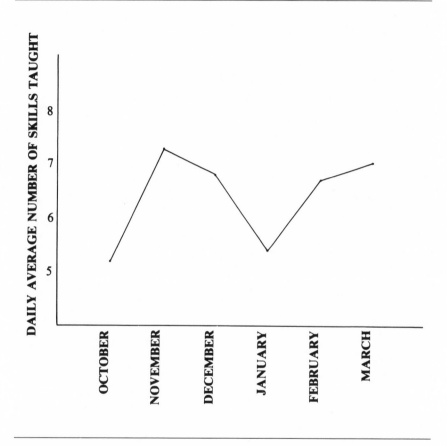

Discussion

The results seem to demonstrate the viability of Collaborative Consultation as a means of encouraging a classroom teacher to gain confidence and competence in working with a learner with special needs.

Although the consultation process evolved over many months, it was not until Session 36 that the efforts to promote better classroom organization and more teacher-learner contact finally culminated in a

Comments. Susan used many of the forms described in Chapter 8 to help her develop systematic processes for monitoring progress, adjusting services, and disseminating information to Rita's teacher and parents.

teacher-initiated time schedule. At that time, there also occurred a number of other changes in the behaviors being measured. The changes are summarized in Table 9.1.

The collaborative team responsible for Rita's education believed that the following were important changes in Rita's behavior: (a) a decrease in daily average disruptive behaviors from 11.6 to 3.2; (b) a decrease in one-to-one instructional intervals with Susan from 55.1 to 33.7; (c) an increase in teacher-

TABLE 9.1. Summary of Quantitative Changes in Rita's Behavior and Performance

Parameter	Baseline Values (%)		Intervention Values (%)	
	Range	Average	Range	Average
Intervals of disruptive behavior:	0 to 46	11.6	0 to 40	3.2
Reliability:	89 to 100	93	89 to 100	97
Intervals of CTI-learner contact:	0 to 100	55.1	0 to 74	33.7
Reliability:	82 to 99	93	92 to 100	95
Intervals of learner-teacher contact:	0 to 71	15.5	6 to 91	36.3
Reliability:	86 to 100	93	82 to 97	92
Number of IEP skills taught (daily average): Reliability:		100		100

Sample of Qualitative Changes

Beginning of year: "I need to be sure there's someone in here all the time! I have 14 other children; I can't be expected to spend all of my time with Rita!" "I can't seem to get through to her; I wonder if this is the best placement for her."

Middle of the year: "You know, I think she's going to make it. She's attending better and progressing. What a change from the beginning of the year."

End of year: "I want to meet with you and Rita's teacher for next year. I've learned some techniques that will help Rita get a better start."

learner contact intervals from 15.5 to 36.3; and (d) the achievement of 12 instructional objectives in Rita's IEP.

Rita was transferred from full-time attendance in a special class to full-time attendance in her own community school. It took many people and much time (one academic year) to facilitate that transition to the mainstream. While evidence of the teacher's acquisition of confidence and competence in meeting the needs of a learner with special needs was often obscure and subtle, the quotes noted during the collaborative consultation process reveal a clear picture of her changing attitude and willingness to become an advocate and effective instructor for this learner.

Over the years, in the course of mainstreaming learners with special needs, the need for systematic study of the most effective means for facilitating the mainstreaming process has increased. In that context, this case study was undertaken to create a more normalized environment for one learner with special needs using the Collaborative Consultation Model. While maintaining a relaxed, nondirective atmosphere as suggested by Tharp and Wetzel (1969), the consultation process emphasized collaboration among all team members. An appropriate structure for the program was also emphasized, as recommended by Smith and Neisworth (1975) and Reynolds and Birch (1977).

Although the results cannot be used to prove definitive functional relationships, they do show changes concurrent with the stages of the collaborative consultation process and a better structured classroom schedule with three major changes: (a) an increase in teacher-learner contact, (b) a decrease in CTI-learner contact, and (c) improved learner behavior.

Wolfensberger's (1972) classic concept of normalization indicated that it is important, not only to normalize the environment surrounding a person who is different, but also to have the person perceived as "normal." In this classroom, the increase in contact between the classroom teacher and Rita was a factor in normalizing Rita's environment, since such contact was the normal routine for the other learners in the class. Concurrently, the decrease in CTI-learner contact furthered normalization, since such contact was not the normal routine for the other learners. As a result of these two changes, not only was Rita's environment more normalized, she was also perceived increasingly as nondeviant by others who saw her working and playing among her peers and interacting with the classroom teacher. The third change, the decrease in the incidence of disruptive behavior, was also an important factor, in that there appeared to be a strong correlation between that decrease and the shifting of Rita's contacts from Susan to the teacher.

The decreased incidence of disruptive behavior and increased teacher-learner contact also appeared to be important factors in the change in the teacher's attitude. This is shown in the various teacher comments cited in the consultation log and from the actions taken by the teacher at the end of the year to ensure a successful beginning for Rita in the coming year.

The major value of this case study lies in its depiction of the collaborative consultation process as a crucial factor in the normalization and mainstreaming of one learner with special needs.

Comments. As the classroom teacher became more skilled and confident, the collaborators used the collaborative consultation principles and techniques to redesign so as to decrease CTI contact in the classroom.

CASE STUDY 2: IMPROVING CLASSROOM CLIMATE IN AN INCLUSIVE SECONDARY CLASSROOM

Julie Haizman Mills, Consulting Teacher
Donna Kwirant, Home Economics Teacher

The home economics teacher, Donna Kwirant, approached the consulting teacher, Julie Mills, asking for suggestions on how to improve her classroom climate by chang-

Comments: In the first stage of problem solving, Gaining Acceptance, the classroom teacher approached the consulting teacher requesting her assistance with disruptive

ing the disruptive classroom behavior in her Advanced Foods class. This was a class consisting of 12 learners, including five learners either currently enrolled in special education or who had been formerly enrolled in special education classes.

The class had been exhibiting very inappropriate classroom behavior during the first 9 weeks; there had been many fights in the class, and although the parents of several learners had been telephoned several times, no apparent improvement was seen in the learners' self-control nor in the classroom management.

The two collaborators talked together about the types of problems that were occurring, which included talking out of turn, insulting each other (the learners referred to this as *smashing*), inattentive behavior, and loud laughing.

Julie asked if she could observe the class for a period and then meet again with Donna to discuss possible methods of changing behaviors. They agreed to this, and Julie observed the following day.

As Julie observed, she listed those behaviors that seemed to be most disruptive (including those mentioned by the teacher). She recorded which learners were exhibiting each behavior through simple frequency counting (see Figure 9.11).

After school that same day, Donna began the conversation by saying she felt a new seating chart was needed to separate several learners. Julie pointed out that the most disruptive learners were all seated together, toward the back of the class, and that moving them apart and forward to the front of the classroom might be helpful.

Julie shared the frequency chart with Donna (Figure 9.11). They determined that three learners seemed to be causing most of the problems. The biggest problems seemed to be (a) learners coming to class without

classroom behaviors. The classroom teacher's willingness to approach the consulting teacher indicates that these two teachers had previously established a professional rapport and that they had developed an informal system for requesting assistance and working together to solve classroom-related problems.

Comments: In the second stage of problem solving (Assessment), the collaborating teachers defined the types of problem behaviors that were occurring.

Comments: The collaborators agreed to having the consulting teacher observe in the classroom (still a part of the Assessment stage).

Comments: The consulting teacher observed in the classroom, making a list of observed behaviors (a continuation of the Assessment stage). She then counted the behaviors each learner exhibited.

Comments: The collaborators met again to further clarify the problem (Assessment stage). In the same meeting, the collaborators moved to explore possible solutions to the identified problems.

Comments: Although only one person collected the classroom observational data, at this point the data became owned by the collaborating team. The collaborators reached consensus on the problem.

FIGURE 9.11. Initial list of observable behaviors.

Students:	Laughing/Yelling	Smashing	Talking to others	Tardy	Out of seat	No books	Sleeping	Throwing	TOTAL
David				1		1			2
Demetrius				1		1			2
Glenda	1		3		3				7
Renee			3		2			1	5
Maria									0
Sandra	5	2	22						30
Leslie	5		6	1					12
Todd			3			1			4
Kristen									0
Michelle			2						2
Alicia									Absent
Susan									Absent

Note. In determining the class rules after looking at these initial data, the collaborators combined laughing/yelling and smashing as a single category of behavior. Sleeping and throwing were eliminated, as there was little or no occurrence.

books (and the subsequent confusion), (b) learners turning around in their seats, talking and laughing with each other, and verbal smashing (making derogatory comments about one another), as well as (c) not paying attention to the teacher.

Although the collaborators agreed that a new seating chart might eliminate some of the disruptive behaviors, Donna wanted a point system to use, rewarding those learners who were behaving appropriately and punishing those who were disruptive.

Comments: The collaborators began to weigh the pros and cons of various solutions to the problem.

The collaborators agreed to use a point scale of 1 through 10, where the learners would enter the room with an A grade (10 points) for classroom behavior and then keep their A unless they broke class rules (losing 1 point for each infringement). Donna defined the class rules most important to her as (a) being on time to class, (b) having books and materials, (c) being quieter by not laughing and making loud noises, (d) talking to other learners only about classwork and not about other topics, and (e) staying in assigned seats. These desired behaviors would become the rules that could enable learners to maintain their points.

Comments: The collaborators reached consensus on an intervention.

Comments: The classroom teacher was instrumental in defining rules that were appropriate for her classroom and that reflected standards of behaviors she expected from her class. The collaborators agreed on the rules, stating them as specific behaviors and as clearly and positively as possible.

Julie and Donna decided to wait until the following Monday to begin the behavior management program so Julie could gather observation data for 2 more days. This ensured that these were the behaviors that were of most concern. Donna said she would make a poster of the class rules and a grade chart, both to be posted on the wall, so learners could see the rules and their grades each day.

On Friday, after the third day of baseline, Donna and Julie talked again. The behavior in the classroom had been unacceptable, and Donna was at the point of really beginning to dislike all of the learners in the class. (Julie felt this was beginning

Comments: The collaborators agreed to continue to gather more baseline information to ensure that their data were stable and accurate.

Comments: Reciprocity was demonstrated here with both teachers being willing to be responsible for certain tasks; for example, the consulting teacher collecting data and the classroom teacher preparing necessary materials.

to be reflected in the way she communicated with the learners.) Because she had been relating to the learners in such a negative way, the collaborators talked about how this grading system could be presented in a positive manner to the class.

Julie suggested that Donna talk with the learners, telling them that she really didn't enjoy the class atmosphere at all and that it was bothering her to have such a poor relationship with the class. Donna would then present the scale, emphasizing that she was giving every learner an A each day (which could help them all feel good), and that it was their responsibility to keep that A through the class period. Julie's rationale included several thoughts. With this method even the learners with lower academic achievement, as well as the learners who were most disruptive, could start out with an A. Since these were mostly sophomores and juniors, the A-reinforcement was very meaningful to them, given their concerns about grade-point averages.

Comments: At this point, the consulting teacher seized the opportunity to reflect again on the positive nature of the planned intervention program and the likelihood that it would help to alleviate the negative feelings the classroom teacher had toward disruptive behaviors.

It was hoped this point system would provide an incentive to the learners that could also help Donna improve her classroom management skills. It could also be particularly helpful during the last 15 minutes of this period (which was a particularly noisy time), as learners could be reminded of the good grade they had earned up to that point and encouraged to maintain it.

Donna agreed to the rationale and also felt she should go over the rules with her class (even though the rules were normally expected classroom behaviors). She felt it was important to point out the grade chart on the wall, explaining the A, B, C, D, and F cutoff levels (A = 10; B = 9, 8; C = 7, 6; D = 5; F = 4–0).

Comments: Here the collaborators reached agreement on the consulting teacher's rationale, and the classroom teacher demonstrated true ownership of the problem by specifying exactly how the behavior management program could be initiated.

Donna devoted 15 minutes of class on the following Monday to explain the rule system and grading scale to the class. The class was agreeable to the system, but asked

Comments: With a genuine extension of the collaborative spirit, the classroom teacher and the learners decided what some of the finer points of program implementa-

how they would know they had lost a point. Together, Donna and the learners decided if the teacher needed to take a point away, she would quietly tell the person he or she had post a point and write her or his name on the blackboard with a *1* by it. Additional points would result in more marks (1s) by the name. The learners seemed to understand and accept the grading scale and were well behaved the rest of that class period.

Julie continued to observe in the class, taking data on the learners' behavior for the following 3.5 weeks (see Figure 9.12). Julie then observed the class two times per week to assure the improved classroom behaviors remained at an acceptable level.

tion needed to be. In essence, this was an early movement to a redesign decision in the *Evaluation* stage. The responsibility was transferred to a different group of collaborators, who, in this case, were the ones primarily responsible for implementation and participation (i.e., Donna and the learners themselves).

Comments: The consulting teacher continued to offer nonparticipatory support by collecting the behavioral data (*Evaluation* stage) but not by intervening in the program itself. She was careful to slowly withdraw her own presence by reducing the number of classroom visits; this was also an integral part of collecting intermittent maintenance data.

Results

Figure 9.12 illustrates that all inappropriate behaviors showed a marked decrease ranging from 75% to 100%. The classroom climate improved considerably, and all learners appeared to be more polite and task oriented, contributing to improved overall classroom climate.

Discussion

As Donna began using the point system, several problems occurred. The learners began telling her to put another person's name on the board and arguing about their loss of points. Donna reminded the entire class of the rules and also told them *she* would decide whether a point would be deducted and that arguing or "tattling" would be considered the same as smashing or yelling. This seemed to resolve the problems.

The classroom management program was especially effective in helping the learners demonstrate self-discipline and for supporting Donna in managing the class, especially during the last 10 minutes of the

Comments: Here, the classroom teacher returned to the Evaluation stage, using the data to redesign the intervention. She did it without collaborating with the consulting teacher and solved the problem successfully. This was a demonstration of improvement in her own classroom management skills, as well as her strength in clarifying to the learners her own responsibility for being the final authority in the classroom. She did this concurrently while relying on the fairness and clarity of the classroom management program.

FIGURE 9.12. Frequency of disruptive behaviors during a 50-minute period.

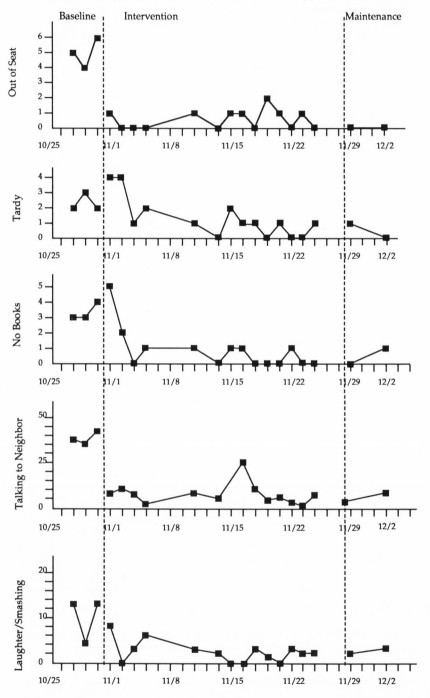

period. The learners would quiet down when reminded of how many points they still had and the grade they had earned thus far (see Table 9.2).

SUMMARY

In both of these case studies, some important types of changes occurred. First, classroom teachers became willing to include and take responsibility for learners with special needs. In both case studies, it is evident that the sometimes difficult challenge of encouraging classroom teachers to take ownership was accomplished. Second, this lofty goal was accomplished by collaborators working together to solve problems, not by one person trying to solve the problem, nor by one person trying to tell another person how to solve that problem. Third, in both case studies, the collaborators met often and when needed, although sometimes for very brief periods of time. Fourth, the collaborators used some type of system for measuring the problem, as well as for evaluating impact of the interventions. Fifth, the interventions that were used were planned in a collaborative manner, with all parties providing input into how to solve the problem. Sixth, all involved collaborators reached consensus on how best to solve the problem. Seventh, when the intervention was implemented, all collaborators took responsibility for ensuring implementation and evaluation of their plan. They used the stages of collaborative problem solving that are illustrated in this book and they turned seemingly insurmountable problems into successful outcomes by working as a team.

TABLE 9.2. The Average Frequency Count of the Number of Disruptive Behaviors in a 50-Minute Class Period

Behavior	Baseline	Intervention		Maintenance	
		Mean	% Decrease	Mean	% Decrease
Out of seat	5	.57	88.6%	0.0	100%
Tardy to class	2	1.28	36.0%	.5	75.0%
No books and materials	3	.66	78.0%	.5	83.3%
Talk to others	38.3	5.27	82.5%	5.5	85.6%
Laughter/smashing	9.6	1.66	82.7%	2.0	79.1%

REFERENCES

Givens-Ogle, L., Christ, B. A., & Idol, L. (1991). Collaborative Consultation: The San Juan Unified School District Project. *Journal of Educational and Psychological Consultation,* 2(3), 267–284.

Hasazi, S. (1976). The consultant teacher. In J. B. Jordan (Ed.), *Teacher, please don't close the door* (pp. 50–59). Reston, VA: Council for Exceptional Children.

Idol, L. (1993). *Special educator's consultation handbook* (2nd ed.). Austin, TX: PRO-ED.

Idol, L., Vlasak, L., & Goldenberg, D. (1988). *Resource consultation: Ongoing staff development and evaluation.* Austin, TX: Institute for Learning and Development.

Reynolds, M. C., & Birch, J. W. (1977). *Teaching exceptional children in all America's schools.* Reston, VA: Council for Exceptional Children.

Saver, K., & Downes, B. (1991). *PIT Crew: A model for teacher collaboration in an elementary school. The Consulting Edge.* Austin, TX: Association for Educational and Psychological Consultants.

Smith, R. M., & Neisworth, J. T. (1975). *The exceptional child: A functional approach.* New York: McGraw-Hill.

Tharp, R. G., & Wetzel, R. J. (1969). *Behavior modification in the natural environment.* New York: Academic Press.

Wolfensberger, W. (1972). *Normalization: The principle of normalization in human services.* Toronto, Canada: National Institute on Mental Retardation.

Epilogue

FUTURISTS HAVE PREDICTED THAT COLLABORATION and cooperation skills will be required for almost every human endeavor. School systems all over the world face several challenges in meeting the needs of learners with (a) increased diversity of individualized learning styles, (b) broader cultural and ethnic differences, (c) wider ranges of economic and social status, and (d) expectations for joining a technologically advanced international business community. What this means for learners, teachers, administrators, and the communities that they serve is that the classroom is no longer a private place. Learners are interacting with those who are intellectually, socially, and ethnically different from their customary milieu. Teachers are expected to participate with those who have different perspectives, such as specialists, other educators, parents, and community and business advocates. Administrators are accountable to local, state, national, and international demands for excellence. Thus, everyone must acquire and practice the interactive problem-solving and collaborative skills to participate as functioning members of effective teams.

The difficult truth is that a collaborative ethic does not prevail in American public schools, as currently configured. Indeed, as noted educator Seymour Sarason stated in 1990:

> No one warmly seeks, let alone embraces, significant intellectual and personal change. . . . Schools have been intractable to change and the attainment of goals set by reformers. A major failure has been the inability of reformers to confront this intractability. . . . What is called reform is based on an acceptance of the system as it has been and is. Change will not occur unless there is an alteration of power relationships among those in the system and within the classroom. Altering these power relationships is necessary, but it is not a sufficient condition for obtaining desired changes. This is especially true for proposals that seek to give a greater role in decision making to teachers. There are two basic issues. The first is the assumption that schools exist primarily for the growth and development of children. That assumption is invalid because teachers cannot create and sustain the conditions for the productive development of children if those conditions do not exist for teachers. The second issue is that there is now an almost unbridgeable gulf that students perceive between the world of the school and the world outside of it. Schools are uninteresting places in which the interests and questions of children have no relevance to what they are required to learn in the classroom. Teachers continue to teach subject matter, not children. Any reform effort that does not confront these two issues and the changes they suggest is doomed. (pp. xiii–xiv)

School reform is, however, being undertaken at local, state, and national levels to address these issues by creating communities of collaborators. There is evidence of the effectiveness of collaborative models for management of schools (see, e.g., the research synthesis by David, 1989), as well as collaborative models for staff development such as peer coaching in both general educator circles (see Glatthorn, 1987) and special education circles (e.g., Ludlow, Faieta, & Wienke, 1989). Idol and West (1991) recommended educational collaboration as a catalyst for effective schooling and offered specific strategies for building effective collaboration in schools. There are, however, several challenges that must be addressed if we are to conscientiously recommend the implementation of the Collaborative Consultation Model and the related process described in this book. We've observed the following types of challenges as related to implementation of the Collaborative Consultation Model: personnel preparation, policy, practice, and paradigms.

PERSONNEL PREPARATION ISSUES

There is a lack of agreement related to theoretical constructs, definitions, and measurement systems for preparing educational professionals to practice Collaborative Consultation. A compelling need exists for further development of assessment instruments for measuring collaborators' acquisition of relevant underlying knowledge bases, interpersonal communicative, interactive and problem-solving skills, and intrapersonal attitudes. An imperative need is the search for better processes that lead to adaptations of existing assessment and teaching practices and development of new practices. Although several model undergraduate and graduate programs are in use that ensure that public school personnel practice effective collaboration, we need more timely dissemination, adaptation, and replication processes.

POLICY ISSUES

Policy issues fall into three levels: local, state, and national. At the local level, decision makers must consider creative means to arrange released time for participating in collaborative consultation activities, as well as ensuring the presence of additional staff. Idol and West (1991) suggested that school staff must develop time-release options suitable for their situations (e.g., hiring a permanent floating substitute teacher assigned to a single school who can take over an individual classroom at a predetermined time to allow a classroom teacher to participate in collaborative planning and problem-solving sessions). At the state level, there is a need to coordinate and streamline the myriad staff development activities so that general and special educators can participate together instead of separately. At the local, state, and national levels, there is a need for formal recognition of collaborative activities and formal methods of effecting changes in systems-level barriers to implementing collaborative activities.

PRACTICE ISSUES

A major issue facing professionals is the conflict that arises when multiple responsibilities interfere or conflict with each other. Collaborators often find themselves confused about their respective roles and unsure about moving into other people's arenas. Idol and Baran (1992) elaborated on this challenge in the context of describing how the roles of three traditional professionals (elementary school counselors, special educators, and classroom teachers) can result in role conflicts and power struggles. By applying the collaborative consultation processes, the roles and responsibilities of the three professionals can become complementary rather than adversarial.

A second issue of concern to professionals is the maintenance of professional integrity in the delivery of their services. Professionals with special certifications and licenses have been certified and thus carry with them additional responsibilities for maintaining professional integrity. When these professionals release their role-specific knowledge and skill during collaborative consultation processes, they may notice that other members of the team acquire and demonstrate their skills. It may be important to document this transfer of professional expertise to ensure the learner receives the services intended. Recently, researchers have raised this issue in another context. Fuchs and Fuchs (1992) and Gresham (1989) urged researchers to analyze the impact of their collaborative consultation efforts by including specific data on treatment integrity. These researchers have suggested that data should be collected to document the implementation of the interventions (i.e., treatment integrity) in addition to documenting achievement and other gains of the learners served because of collaborative consultation practices.

PARADIGM ISSUES

People with diverse areas of expertise who work together in collaborative consultation relationships often find that they speak different languages and operate from divergent world views. Kuhn (1970) described situations where people with one particular view (a paradigm) of the world reached a point when their experience (e.g., unexplained or unexplainable events) showed that their old view no longer fit and yet a new view had not emerged. "Such changes, together with the controversies that almost always accompany them, are the defining characteristics of scientific revolutions" (Kuhn, 1970, p.6). Implementing the Collaborative Consultation Model may result in a revolution in the way people perceive problems, generate solutions, and so on.

It is clear that establishing an ethic for collaborative practices within an essentially bureaucratic, hierarchical organization sets the context for a search for new paradigms. It is also clear that the field is exploring new models. For example, Ferguson and Ryan-Vincek (1992) summarized a series of challenges to the "scientific technical rationality which has guided theoretical development throughout education" (p. 8). They described the emergence "of a small but growing body of literature [of] alternative ways to think about and change practice" (p. 8) leading to a "new appreciation that skillful practice involves not so much mechanical rules as heuristic ones" (p. 15). Another example was provided by Harris, Nevin, and Peck (1992), who set the context for another level of Collaborative Consultation, which relies on co-creating or constructing the processes, beliefs, and shared values that must surface so as to address the deep conceptual shifts necessary to make the changes from a bureaucratic to a collaborative ethic.

The process of engaging in collaborative consultation teams can facilitate the invention of a new paradigm (see arguments advanced by Villa, Thousand, Paolucci-Whitcomb, & Nevin, 1990). Because Collaborative Consultation relies on the continuous adaptations developed by those who practice it, is important to make room for multiple views regarding theory and practice. And new paradigms need to address certain domains of inquiry to ensure a shift in educators' perceptions (their paradigms) as well as their practices toward a collaborative ethic. To illustrate, Table E.1 (excerpted from Villa et al., 1990) contrasts emerging views about Collaborative Consultation with prevailing or traditional views that seem incompatible with achieving a collaborative ethic.

Our experiences tend to support Sarason's observation that "no one warmly seeks, let alone embraces, significant intellectual and personal change." It is also our experience that the processes of collaborative consultation can temper the emotional and intellectual upheavals that structural and paradigmatic change require. Collaborative consultation processes may provide the vehicle for nurturing the growth of teachers as they seek to close the "unbridgeable gulf that students perceive between the world of the school and the world outside of it" (Sarason, 1990, p. xiv). It is in the spirit of facilitating beneficial change that we offer the following practical advice in using the collaborative processes described in our book.

SOME PRACTICAL ADVICE

- *Join or start a collaborative consultation support team.* Make sure it's heterogeneous—the more diverse the better! Structure it so that each person has a chance to (a) give and receive feedback on his or her collaborative consultation experiences and (b) practice collaborative consultation skills. Set it up so it is "normal" for new collaborative consultation experiences to be invented when a planned experience doesn't seem to be working out the way it was intended. Learn to ask for "Help!" one thousand different ways, even when you think you don't need help. In other words, you don't have to be in a crisis situation to ask for feedback.

TABLE E.1. Six Domains of Inquiry to Facilitate New Paradigms of Collaborative Consultation

Domain	Traditional View	Emerging View
What are the purposes of Collaborative Consultation?	To respond to learner needs.	To respond to teacher and systems needs (e.g., exchange of knowledge and skills, reorganization of instructional arrangements for interdisciplinary team teaching), as well as learner needs.
Is Collaborative Consultation for all educators and all children?	Only some learners are eligible. Some people don't have to participate.	Any learner is eligible. All are expected to participate.
Who benefits, who is trained, and who is empowered?	Learners with certain disabilities. The classroom teacher receives training and can be empowered.	Any learner with any disability. All participants are trained. All are empowered.
What are organizational and staff development assumptions?	Because the general education system is not set up to meet the needs of all learners, the system needs a continuum of placements/services.	General and special education in combination with the community can accommodate all learners. What is needed is the continuous invention of new nonstandard instruction and curricula to prepare learners to enter the ever-changing and unknown 21st century.
What is needed for accountability?	Different groups of school personnel (e.g., principals, department chairs, special education coordinators) supervise to ensure accountability.	Collaborators document how they hold one another accountable for learner outcomes, the processes they use to achieve outcomes, and the relationship between their beliefs and actions.

TABLE E.1. Continued

Domain	Traditional View	Emerging View
Which research methodologies and questions are needed?	University-based teacher educators and researcher-experts decide which theories, skills, and measures are "best."	What is needed is a research, evaluation, and training agenda collaboratively developed by university and school personnel.

Note. Excerpted from "In Search of New Paradigms" by R. Villa, J. Thousand, P. Paolucci-Whitcomb, and A. Nevin, 1990, *Journal of Educational and Psychological Consultation, 1*(4), pp. 285–289.

- *Be reflective.* Keep a diary/log/journal of collaborative consultation experiences for at least 6 months—and read it. Notice (be honest) what's working and what's not working. Be reflective, rather than judgmental. *Do not* grade yourself (e.g., 7 out of 8 collaborative consultation skills implemented = A). Instead, celebrate every time you participate in a collaborative consultation experience. Celebrate every outcome (intended or unintended). Treat perceived failures as opportunities to invent new experiences. Make sure that redesign becomes a way of life.

- *Be willing to celebrate unexpected, unintended outcomes.* Educators who have used Collaborative Consultation report subtle as well as obvious changes in their learners, their schools, and their working relationships with others. And, most important, they have been willing to celebrate changes within themselves.

REFERENCES

David, J. (1989). Synthesis of research on school-based management. *Educational Leadership, 46*(8), 45–53.

Ferguson, D., & Ryan-Vincek, S. (1992, April). *Problems with teaming in special education: From technical solutions to reflective practice.* Paper presented at American Educational Research Association, San Francisco.

Fuchs, D., & Fuchs, L. (1992). Where is the research on consultation effectiveness? *Journal of Educational and Psychological Consultation, 3*(2), 151–174.

Glatthorn, A. (1987). Cooperative professional development: Peer-centered options for teacher growth. *Educational Leadership, 45,* 31–35.

Gresham, F. (1989). Assessment of treatment integrity in school consultation and prereferral intervention. *School Psychology Review, 18,* 37–50.

Harris, K., Nevin, A., & Peck, C. (1992). *A constructivist approach to Collaborative Consultation: An emerging paradigm* (Working Paper #1). Phoenix: Arizona State University West, Education Unit.

Idol, L., & Baran, S. (1992). Elementary school counselors and special educators consulting together: Perilous pitfalls or opportunities to collaborate? *Elementary School Guidance & Counseling, 26,* 202–213.

Idol, L., & West, J. F. (1991). Educational collaboration: A catalyst for effective schooling. *Intervention in School and Clinic, 27*(2), 70–78, 125.

Kuhn, T. (1970). *The structure of scientific revolutions.* Chicago: University of Chicago Press.

Ludlow, B., Faieta, J., & Wienke, W. (1989). Training teachers to supervise their peers. *Teacher Education and Special Education, 12,* 27–32.

Sarason, S. (1990). *The predictable failure of educational reform: Can we change course before it's too late?* San Francisco: Jossey-Bass.

Villa, R., Thousand, J., Paolucci-Whitcomb, P., & Nevin, A. (1990). In search of new paradigms. *Journal of Educational and Psychological Consultation, 1*(4), 279–292.

Appendix: Resources

NETWORKS

Association for Educational and Psychological Consultants (AEPC)
Dr. Lorna Idol, Executive Director, P.O. Box 202020, Austin, TX 78720-2020, (512) 338-4757

National Cooperative Learning Center
202 Pattee Hall, University of Minnesota, Minneapolis, MN 55455, (612) 624-7031

American Educational Research Association
Special Interest Group for Cooperative Learning Theory, Research & Practice; Dr. Karl Smith, Department of Civil and Mineral Engineering; 122 C & M Engineering Building; University of Minnesota, 500 Pillsbury Dr. S. E., Minneapolis, MN 55455

NEWSLETTERS

The Consulting Edge (Bi-annual AEPC Newsletter)
P.O. Box 202020, Austin, TX 78720-2020

The Cooperative Link
Judy Bartlett, Editor, 202 Pattee Hall, University of Minnesota, Minneapolis, MN 55455

JOURNALS

Journal of Educational and Psychological Consultation (Official AEPC journal)
Lawrence Erlbaum Associates, Publishers, Howard Margolis, Editor, 1067 Pendleton Court, Voorhees, NJ 08043

Index

About the Authors

Lorna Idol, PhD, is an internationally recognized speaker, author, and researcher in the area of school consultation, school-based teams, and reading/learning disabilities. Dr. Idol is co-director of the Institute for Learning and Development located in Austin, Texas. She is also the editor-in-chief of the scholarly journal, *Remedial and Special Education*, and founder and executive director of the Association for Educational and Psychological Consultants. She is a former university professor, special education teacher, and classroom teacher. While associate professor of special education at the University of Illinois, she developed and implemented the original research and training modules related to the Resource/Consulting Teacher Model.

Ann Nevin, PhD, is professor of curriculum and instruction at Arizona State University West in Phoenix. As a professional scholar, she is committed to discovering what teachers can do to effectively accelerate the academic and social progress of their learners. Dr. Nevin is a former professor of education at the University of Vermont, where she collaborated in the development and implementation of the original research and training modules for the Vermont Consulting Teacher Program.

Phyllis Paolucci-Whitcomb, EdD, is an associate professor in the Department of Social Work at the University of Vermont, Burlington. She spearheaded the Interactive Leadership Program, a model leadership preparation program for collaboration between general and special education administrators. Dr. Paolucci-Whitcomb also collaborated in the development and implementation of the original research and training modules for the Vermont Consulting Teacher Program.